SEEING GOD
IN MANY MIRRORS

Wisdom Editions

Minneapolis

First Edition June 2025
*Seeing God in Many Mirrors: How an endless stream of
revelation and reason renews religion and unites humanity.*
Copyright © 2025 by Gary Lindberg. All rights reserved.

No parts of this book may be used or reproduced by any means, graphic, electronic, or mechanical, including photocopying, recording, taping or by any information storage retrieval system, without the written permission of the publisher except in the case of brief quotations embodied in critical articles and reviews.

10 9 8 7 6 5 4 3 2 1

ISBN: 978-1-962834-51-3

Cover and book design by Gary Lindberg

SEEING GOD
IN MANY MIRRORS

How an endless stream of revelation and
reason renews religion and unites humanity

GARY LINDBERG

Minneapolis

These Manifestations of God ... all abide in the same tabernacle, soar in the same heaven, are seated upon the same throne, utter the same speech, and proclaim the same Faith... they are all the Luminous Luminaries who have successively shed light upon the worlds of the visible and the invisible.

– Bahá'u'lláh, *Kitáb-i-Íqán* (The Book of Certitude)

Table of Contents

Chapter 1: The Spiritual Quest 1

PART ONE – HOW RELIGIONS CHANGE 11

Chapter 2: One Unfolding Religion 13
Chapter 3: The Syncretism Theory 25
Chapter 4: Dangers of Syncretism and Evolving Relligious Thought . . 37
Chapter 5: The Source of Religious Thought 43
Chapter 6: An Inflection Point 63
Chapter 7: Aliens or Divine Educators? .105
Chapter 8: Understanding the Prophets 113
Chapter 9: The Essential Oneness of the Manifestations of God 131
Chapter 10: Knowing an Unknowable God 141
Chapter 11: Mirrors That Reflect God 161
Chapter 12: Our Latest Wisdom Tradition 171

PART TWO – ACKNOWLEDGING GOD'S EDUCATORS 181

Chapter 13: What's In a Name? 183
Chapter 14: Chain of Custody 223
Chapter 15: Prophecies in the Abrahamic Tradition. 231
Chapter 16: Zoroastrian Prophecies. 239
Chapter 17: Judaic Prophecies 247
Chapter 18: Christian Prophecies 263
Chapter 19: Islamic Prophecies 281
Chapter 20: Bahai Prophecies 289
Chapter 21: Shared Spiritual Principles 307
Chapter 22: The Oneness of Religion 337

APPENDICES – ARYAN RELIGIOUS TEXTS...............343

Appendix A: Hindu Texts....................................345
Appendix B: Zoroastrian Texts 355
Appendix C: Buddhist Texts 359

APPENDICES – ABRAHAMIC RELIGIOUS TEXTS.................. 363

Appendix D: Abrahamic and Judaic Texts......................365
Appendix E: Christian Texts 373
Appendix F: Islamic Texts 381
Appendix G: Baháʼí Texts 389

Research and Study Sources................................... 405
About the Author 407
Index 408

To my sister, Bonnie, who lives with matchless grace.

Also by Gary Lindberg

FICTION

The Shekinah Legacy

Sons of Zadok

The Unspoken

The Mount

Deeper and Deeper

Ollie's Cloud

John Ross

NONFICTION

Letters from Elvis

Brando On Elvis

The Roots of Elvis

The Soul of Humanity

Humanity Coming of Age

The Power of Positive Hamdwriting

An Improbable Series of Risky Events

Chapter 1: The Spiritual Quest

Throughout history, the foremost drivers of humanity's spiritual development have been the world's great religions. In the words of our most recent wisdom tradition, for most of Earth's people, the scriptures of those religions have served as "the City of God,"[1] a metaphor describing a source of knowledge so compelling it endows sincere seekers of truth with "a new eye, a new ear, a hew heart, and a new mind."[2]

This vast collection of sacred literature, to which all religious cultures have contributed, documents the transcendence experienced by generations of seekers. For thousands of years, the lives of those who have responded to the whisperings of the Divine have inspired breathtaking accomplishments in the arts and sciences. No other known force has been able to encourage such qualities of heroism, self-sacrifice and self-discipline. The moral principles of this compendium of wisdom have repeatedly been transformed into universal codes of law that regulate and elevate human relationships. From this perspective, then, the major religions emerge as primary forces motivating and guiding the civilizing process of humankind.

---

1 Bahá'u'lláh, *The Kitáb-i-Íqán*, paragraph 216.
2 Bahá'u'lláh, *The Kitáb-i-Íqán*, paragraph 216.

Unfortunately, a quarrelsome and divisive humanity struggles with deeply understanding the underlying principles of past revealed wisdom and tends to focus mostly on the superficial elements. A prism, which refracts sunlight into a spectrum of diverse colors though it is one light, is an apt analogy for humanity's misunderstanding that the various Bearers of God's light (Moses, Jesus, Muhammad, et cetera) are disconnected and competing prophets.

Many of us are acquainted with the various known Prophet-Founders of religion, though we tend to disregard and ignore all but the One we were taught to honor. The quotation above asserts, however, that all of these are true Manifestations of God, and they are all the same Reality, though they have different names and outward appearances. An individual's spiritual quest must begin by appreciating the wisdom revealed progressively by each of Them and recognizing All as Divine Educators because they are many "mirrors" Who give us the most direct path to knowing Him.

> "The light of the sun becomes apparent in each object according to the capacity of that object… in the mirror which is polished, pure and sanctified you may behold the Sun in all its fullness, glory and power…"[3]

Reawakening the World's Repressed Spiritual Quest

In recent years, the immensely rich heritage of scriptures has been largely overlooked as an agent for reawakening the world's repressed spiritual quest. Infinitely distracted by sensory overload and overwhelmed by materialism, societies have lost focus on finding fulfillment in the more subtle but effective ways taught by these previous wisdom traditions. Peripherally, some attempts are being made by places of worship to reformulate the old teachings for greater mass appeal, occasionally providing entertainment to keep

---

3   'Abdu'l-Bahá, *The Promulgation of Universal Peace*, pp. 134–135.

the churches filled, but these efforts seldom accomplish anything but to diffuse a sincere search for meaning and render incoherent messages.

In the meantime, the scriptures have not changed. The moral principles embedded in them have lost none of their validity or coherence.

> No one who sincerely poses questions to Heaven, if he persists, will fail to detect an answering voice in the Psalms or in the Upanishads. Anyone with some intimation of the Reality that transcends this material one will be touched to the heart by the words in which Jesus or Buddha speaks so intimately of it. The Qur'án's apocalyptic visions continue to provide compelling assurance to its readers that the realization of justice is central to the Divine purpose. Nor, in their essential features, do the lives of heroes and saints seem any less meaningful than they did when those lives were lived centuries ago.[4]

Although the revealed truths of the great wisdom traditions remain true and valid, the personal experience of a person in the twenty-first century is radically different from that of a person living when that guidance was originally delivered. For example, democratic decision-making has dramatically changed how an individual relates to authority. Today, women confidently assert their right to full equality with men. Science and technology have changed how society and individuals function and communicate. Universal education and workplace transformations have improved social mobility and opened up countless new career paths. Unimagined a few decades ago, issues related to stem cell research, nuclear energy, sexual identity, ecological stress, increasing disparity in the

---

4   A 2005 commentary entitled One Common Faith prepared in 2005 under the supervision of the Universal House of Justice, available at https://www.bahai.org/documents/bwc/one-common-faith

distribution of wealth, mass migrations of disadvantaged people, and frightening political polarization have confronted every person with new daily choices for themselves and society.

Globally, people raised in one religion often find themselves abruptly forced into relationships with others who have beliefs and rituals that seem irreconcilable with their own. This can lead to defensiveness, resentment, even conflict. At best, these unrequested confrontations can prompt each side to examine values the two sides have in common, which can build relationships and develop mutual understanding. At worst, however, the clash of beliefs can inhibit connection and understanding. Sometimes, it can also raise inconvenient questions, such as, "If people who believe different things and worship in different ways nevertheless live moral lives and deserve respect, how is my own faith superior to theirs?" And: "If all the religions share similar basic values, don't my own rigid, sectarian beliefs risk reinforcing unwanted barriers between them and me?"

Today, fewer people than ever honestly hold fast to the notion that any of the established religions can rightly provide the ultimate guidebook for contemporary life even if competing religions or sects would come together for that purpose. There is a strong basis for such cynicism. The world's independent religions born before the nineteenth century are caught in an inescapable trap created for themselves by their authoritative scriptures and histories. Because these religions cannot refashion their belief systems without losing their scripture-based legitimacy, they likewise cannot adequately answer the new questions posed by social evolution, intellectual development, and technological breakthroughs.

What Is Religion?

A common definition of "religion" states that it is a belief system adopted by a number of sects or denominations. This functional description proposes that a religion is the sum of its parts no matter how disparate they are. This definition often raises protests and a second proposed definition: that by religion is intended one or another of the independent wisdom traditions that have inspired entire civilizations. This second opinion often provokes a different response: "Under this definition, where exactly to you find Judaism, Buddhism, Christianity, Islam, or the others? Surely, these cannot be identified with the many irrevocably opposed sects that purport to speak with the same name."

A third common definition is that religion is really an attitude toward life, a sense of having a relationship with some kind of spiritual reality separate from material existence. This, of course, turns religion into an attribute of the individual, an impulse that cannot be organized, or an experience that is universally available. Religion thus described, unfortunately, lacks the authority of self-discipline and the unifying effect that gives religion meaning.

Yet another definition is that religion denotes the lifestyle of certain people who have adopted strict courses of daily ritual and self-denial that set them apart from society.

From this tangle of inconsistent opinions, our latest wisdom tradition cuts through the confusion and reformulates many truths that explicitly or intrinsically lay at the heart of all divine revelation. It asserts that the instrumentality through which the Creator of all things interacts with His ever-evolving creation is the appearance of prophetic Figures—Divine Educators—Who are "made manifest unto all men, that they may impart into the world the mysteries of the unchangeable Being, and tell of the subtleties of His imperishable Essence."[5] These prophetic Figures are the Founders of the world's great wisdom traditions.

For any individual or religion to judge among these Prophets and exalt one above the other would be to falsely propose that God is subject to the vagaries of human preference.

---

5   Bahá'u'lláh, *The Kitáb-i-Íqán*, paragraph 106.

> It is clear and evident to thee that all the Prophets are the Temples of the Cause of God, Who have appeared clothed in divers attire. If thou wilt observe with discriminating eyes, thou wilt behold Them all abiding in the same tabernacle, soaring in the same heaven, seated upon the same throne, uttering the same speech, and proclaiming the same Faith.[6]

To imagine that the nature of these unique Figures can be encompassed within theories borrowed from physical experience is equally presumptuous. What is meant by "knowledge of God" is actually knowledge of the Manifestations Who reveal His will and attributes. Religion, thus conceived, awakens the soul to capabilities that would otherwise be unimaginable. To the extent that an individual learns to benefit from the influence of the revelation of God for his age, his nature becomes progressively imbued with the attributes of the divine world.

That is why this book focuses on the revealed messages of the Founders of our great wisdom traditions. They are the Manifestations of God, our Divine Educators. The only available path to understand God and have a relationship with Him is to understand these Manifestations and their messages. The work of each Manifestation of God has an autonomy and an authority that transcends assessment. The work of each is also a chapter in the limitless unfolding of a single book that increasingly defines Reality.

Because the purpose of the successive revelations of God is the awakening of humankind to its capacities and responsibilities, the process is not simply repetitive but progressive, and it is fully appreciated only when perceived as continually expanding knowledge and guidance.

A recurring proof of the existence of God is that over time He has repeatedly manifested Himself. The epic tale of humanity's religious

---

6   Bahá'u'lláh, *Gleanings from the Writings of Bahá'u'lláh*, section 22.

history represents the fulfilment of a "Covenant," an enduring promise by which the Creator of all things assures humanity of the unfailing guidance essential to its spiritual and moral development.

The remainder of this book will examine the nature of the Divine Educators, the process of progressive revelation, and the expansion and evolution of Teachings from one major wisdom tradition to another.

Conventions Used in This Book

Capitalization

Throughout this book, the authors have chosen to capitalize words that refer to the Divine or the Revelation of the Divine, including pronouns. This practice honors the generally accepted conventions followed in many of the sacred Scriptures of the world's great wisdom traditions. Nevertheless, there are capitalization inconsistencies in quoted King James versions of various biblical passages. We have chosen to always use the capitalization originally used in Scriptural passages even when they are fossilized compared to modern usage.

Use of Masculine Gender

Spirits or souls are not of this material world so gender is meaningless when referring to them, and yet we lack suitable pronouns for entities that have no gender. In many languages, the use of the masculine gender, unless intended specifically to denote masculinity, is considered generic or lacking specific gender. For instance, in English we speak of the race of man, or mankind, in both instances meaning every member of the human race—men, women and children. There would be no reason to interpret "O Son of Being", or "O Son of Man" as addressed only to males. It is the same with pronouns.

> **The truth is that all mankind are the creatures and servants of one God, and in His estimate all are human.**

> "Man" is a generic term applying to all humanity. The biblical statement "Let us make man in our image, after our likeness" does not mean that woman was not created. The image and likeness of God apply to her as well. In Persian and Arabic there are two distinct words translated into English as man: one meaning man and woman collectively, the other distinguishing man as male from woman the female. The first word and its pronoun are generic, collective; the other is restricted to the male. This is the same in Hebrew.[7]

The problem of commonly used gender-specific nouns (chairman, postman, mankind) has two potential solutions. One is to change the usage of nouns; the other is to permit the consciousness of sexual equality to modify the meaning of nouns that were once standard usage. Undoubtedly, both courses will be followed in the evolution of the language. The word "doctor," for example, is now clearly of common gender in English, although originally masculine. In specifically addressing this issue, the Bahá'í Faith issued the following statement:

> Our feeling is that, in general, it is preferable to permit the change of consciousness to change the meaning that people attribute to the words, rather than to press the use of forms of words that seem contrived and, to many people, ridiculous—a reaction that does not help the advancement of the cause of the equality of the sexes.[8]

The authors agree with this assessment and have chosen to ask readers of this to interpret masculine pronouns and nouns in quoted

---

7   'Abdu'l-Bahá, The Promulgation of Universal Peace: Talks Delivered by 'Abdu'l-Bahá during His Visit to the United States and Canada in 1912, rev. ed. (Wilmette: Bahá'í Publishing Trust, 1995), pp. 174 and 374.

8   November 1989, from a memorandum from the Universal House of Justice to a Bahá'í Office of Public Information.

passages to explicitly apply to both males and females. In the fresh material written by the authors, however, an attempt has been made to avoid the issue by making inclusive word choices or including both gender-based pronouns. These language issues are not trivial, as language is our chief tool for communication with each other and bringing about the unity of humankind.

Diacritics

A diacritic is a mark near or through a written character or combination of characters indicating a phonetic value different from that given the unmarked or otherwise marked element. We often think of diacritics as accent marks or symbols above or below letters (examples: Ḍ ẓ Á í G͟h k͟h). Bahá'í Writings use a standard system of conventions used for writing a language to Romanize Persian and Arabic script. The system used in Bahá'í literature was set in 1923, and although it was based on a commonly used standard of the time, it has its own embellishments that make it unique. The authors have chosen to use Bahá'í diacritics when documenting names or words originating in the Persian or Arabic languages.

Use of Scriptural Passages and Spiritual Principles

Throughout this book, the authors refer to writings from the world's great wisdom traditions, often considered as world religions. The intent of the authors is for these passages to be considered on their own merits as traditional wisdom, not because they may have been of divine origin. There is no intent to promote one of these religions over another; in fact, we believe an individual should study them all. The fact that there are a greater number of quotations from the Bahá'í Faith is due to the fact that while older wisdom traditions spoke rationally, they were speaking to less knowledgeable societies that lacked modern scientific knowledge, and thus the older wisdom traditions seldom if ever commented on the modern issues this book addresses. Commentary on religious scriptures in this book express the author's personal views.

Lack of Religious Authorities

You may notice that I have chosen to seldom quote religious or theological authorities to comment on interpretations of their scriptures or doctrines. This is because each of the major wisdom traditions—with the exception of the Bahá'í Faith, which has no clergy—have numerous sects with often competing beliefs. There is simply no authority who can speak for all of Christianity, for example, or all of Hinduism or Islam. It is not within the constraints of this book to present all the conflicting doctrines of all the sects of all the great religions. The focus must be on the fundamental truths of each religion as presented by its Prophet-Founder—or as close to those original teachings as we can get, since in many cases a religion's scriptures were written down long after its Founder had passed away.

PART ONE

How Religions Change

Chapter 2:
One Unfolding Religion

For those who have ever wondered why there are so many "religions," and how they got started, and why they appear to disagree on so many things, we can resolve your perplexity with one statement that begins:

There is only one true religion of God...

It may seem that I have fanned the flames of religious bigotry with this statement. There are a multitude of religions in the world, and many of them have hundreds or thousands of sects. Each of these sects—some fitting the definition of a "cult"—disagree with some or many foundational doctrines of the earliest version of their religion even while recognizing the same Prophet-Founder.

Many wars have been fought between these religions. The Crusades were an ongoing battle between Christianity and an upstart new faith called Islam. Today, Islamic leaders in countries like Iran and Egypt persecute and execute members of the breakaway Bahá'í Faith for the crime of heresy.

Bloody wars have also been waged between sects of the same religion. Shortly after the death of Islam's Founder, Muhammad, a bitter dispute arose about who should be His rightful successor. This led to a bitter dispute and the cleaving of Islam into the Sunni and Shia sects that have been warring ever since. After Martin Luther nailed his "Ninety-Five Theses" to the door of the Castle Church in Germany to protest key doctrines and practices of the Catholic Church, the breakaway "Protestants" centuries later resorted to violence in Ireland where Christians fought and killed other Christians of the opposing sect. In the US, though less violent, the Protestant vs. Catholic split became political when Protestant voters were told by many clerics that a vote for presidential candidate John F. Kennedy would result in Rome and the Pope being given the keys to the White House.

Many will believe that the countless religions and their sects and cults will only be encouraged in their battles for supremacy by my assertion that "there is only one true religion." In truth, however, the bitter interfaith dissension and bloodshed has almost always been caused by the belief of each side that its religion was the *one true religion of God*, and that all the other blasphemous endeavours must be suppressed in God's name. So, my assertion comports with the existing majority view. Most devoted believers of any religion or sect believe that their cherished faith is the only correct one out of thousands of unholy competitors.

Rationally, of course, if there is but one God, there can only be one true religion of God. By religion, I mean a system of beliefs, practices and values centered around the idea of a higher power, spiritual force or sacred truth. For believers to claim that their religious community is the custodian of the one true religion is to boldly assert that they have complete and 100 percent knowledge and understanding of the nature of God and the spiritual forces at work in the world. It is also to assert that there is nothing more to learn about their acknowledged Supreme Being and His guidance to humanity. That assertion would require remarkable hubris.

My opening statement was not complete, hence the ellipsis at the end. Here is the completed statement:

> There is only one true religion of God... and knowledge of it has been unfolding to humanity for millennia in measures equal to the capacity of society in each age to understand, implement and self-correct.

The full statement describes what this book is about. The latest "wisdom tradition"—I prefer that term to "religion"—tells us that all existing religions are imperfect attempts to better discern the one true religion of God. They are merely glimpses of incomplete information that have been revealed to us, and to that narrow view, each of us contributes our own prejudices, inferences and fallible understandings. Two short stories help to illuminate this concept.

Two Stories

The River

A man built a canoe and placed it in the water at the source of the mighty Mississippi river intending to paddle down to the Gulf of Mexico. At the source, the water was pure and safe to drink. It was so clear that even in the deeper stretches of the river, he could see the bottom.

As he paddled south, occasionally casting aside a food wrapper and relieving himself into the water, his canoe passed by other merging streams that carried with them silt and debris. He passed by nearby farms that leaked fertilizer and animal waste into the once-pristine water. Farther along, the man passed by small towns spilling sewage into the river, and later watched industrial plants poison the water with chemicals and toxic waste. He could no longer see the river's floor as the canoe pushed through a soupy mix of flotsam and jetsam.

At last, however, he passed by a huge water treatment facility. On the other side of the plant, he discovered that the water was no longer polluted. Though he had to navigate through turbulent whitewater where filtered water entered the river, he could see the bottom once more and even dared to drink a handful dipped out of the watercourse.

His joy at the restored health of this mighty river was short-lived, however. After a few more hours, the man realized that pollutants, some of them natural but most man-made, were again befouling the cleansed waters. He mourned the corruption of his beloved river and hoped for a second cleansing downstream. The next day, after another city he passed had purified the water, he rejoiced, but remembering the inevitable corruption to come, he steeled himself, vowing to never again contribute to the contamination. And yet, being human, he did.

As the man proceeded down the river, he became aware of new problems such as increased barge traffic, bridge collapses, and dam obstructions that affected water flow, cattle over-grazing, and many other issues. He became aware that older remedies alone could not resolve the multitude of problems that were arising along this mighty river. New expert guidance would be needed and probably revised regulations, increased vigilance and greater funding to pay for all the fixes. Old remedies and plans could not be static, he learned.

This story is more than the tale of the making of an environmentalist, though on the surface it is certainly that. On a deeper level, it is a metaphor that can help us understand the concept of progressive revelation.

Consider the flowing river as a metaphor representing the teachings of an early religion as revealed to humanity by a Source that we can call a "Divine Educator" or "Manifestation of God" (defined later). At the headwaters—the beginning of a religion's thriving era—these teachings are unadulterated and nourishing. The water is pure. But before long, the original teachings are modified by a growing class of priests under the guise of "clarification." The Divine Educator's words are reinterpreted to better serve special needs. They are misunderstood and canonized as "traditions," even corrupted on purpose to give special privileges to religious "authorities." At some point, the river, once flowing with the pure teachings of its Source, becomes a channel of fetid misinformation and useless activities barely recognizable to anyone with knowledge of the original teachings.

The man in this story can be seen to represent each of us. As we explore the river—which represents the teachings of any religion—we often find stories and doctrines that are not logical or impossible to believe. This may lead to disillusionment and a "crisis of faith" followed eventually by departure from the polluted river unless we understand that the ideas of mere mortals are obscuring or replacing the original teachings. And yet, as the man in the canoe came to understand, he was also partially to blame by bringing his own prejudices, pre-conceived ideas and misunderstandings to the once-pure message of the Source.

The water purification plant in this story represents the Divine Educator, a Manifestation of God sent to provide teachings that guide humanity into a better way of life. Just as the river grows more polluted as it flows downstream, the teachings become more corrupted by manmade interpretations, power grabs by "authorities," political machinations, financial connivances and the human impulse to popularize the message.

In such times, just as the water treatment plant purifies the water to ensure the health of wildlife and humans, another Divine Educator appears with authority to purify and even update the teachings so they are more relevant and useful to a maturing society. This renewal inevitably unleashes a "whitewater" of social and religious upheaval as long-held beliefs, many of which may be cherished but over time are called into question because they have become irrational, harmful, counterproductive or obsolete.

The Bahá'í Faith, our most recent wisdom tradition, reminds us that to deal with the emerging problems of a new age requires a fresh perspective and a continuous renewal and modernizing of many religious concepts, which is part of the job description for each new Divine Educator:

> Every age hath its own problem, and every soul its particular aspiration. The remedy the world needeth in its present-day afflictions can never be the same as that which a subsequent age may require. Be anxiously concerned with the needs of the age ye live in...[9]

This newest wisdom tradition also warns about the consequences of a waning influence of the teachings, which may be due to their increasing irrelevance to maturing societies, the lack of specific guidance for resolving new issues, and a lack of enthusiasm for laws and rites and rituals that seem out of step with modern society.

> Should the lamp of religion be obscured, chaos and confusion will ensue, and the lights of fairness and justice, of tranquillity and peace cease to shine. Unto this will bear witness every man of true understanding.[10]

Hinduism, perhaps the most ancient of our known major wisdom traditions, recognized this need for purifying and updating the teachings after they had been corrupted or ignored. The *Vishnu Purana*, one of the most important Puranas in Hinduism, describes a future figure who will bring righteousness and truth:

> When the practices taught by the Vedas [the oldest Hindu Writings] and the institutes of law shall nearly have ceased [come into disuse], and the close of the Kali age shall be nigh... He will restore righteousness upon earth; and the minds of those who live at the end of the Kali age shall be awakened, and shall be as pellucid as crystal.[11]

---

9   Bahá'u'lláh, *Gleanings from the Writings of Bahá'u'lláh*, p. 213.
10 Bahá'u'lláh, Tablets of Bahá'u'lláh revealed after the Kitáb-i-Aqdas, p. 125.
11 *Vishnu Purana*, Book 4, Chapter 24.

Corruption of the teachings, which in all religions promote virtue and justice, necessarily results in the following of false teachings and a rise in unrighteous. Krishna, the attributed author of the *Bhagavad Gita*, explains to a prince in the Kuru Kingdom:

> **Whenever there is a decline in righteousness and an increase in unrighteousness, O Arjuna, at that time I manifest myself on earth. To protect the righteous, to annihilate the wicked, and to reestablish the principles of dharma [duty, virtue, morality], I appear millennium after millennium.**[12]

Here is the second story to help you understand the concept of progressive religion as a perpetual expansion of humanity's knowledge.

The School

A young girl began school, and her curriculum included a graduated series of lessons in math that moved her from an understanding and mastery of simple arithmetic to more advanced mathematical studies. Over her first twelve years of formal education, this was her study plan:

- Grade 1: Basic arithmetic: addition and subtraction, understanding place value, basic measurement, and introduction to time and money.
- Grade 2: More complex addition and subtraction, introduction to multiplication and division, basic fractions, and measurement concepts.
- Grade 3: Multiplication and division, understanding fractions, basic geometry, and data interpretation.
- Grade 4: Advanced multiplication and division, multi-digit addition and subtraction, fractions, decimals, and basic geometry.

---

12   *Bhagavad Gita* 4:7-8

- Grade 5: Introduction to algebraic concepts, ratios, percentages, and more advanced geometry.
- Grade 6: Ratios, rates, percentages, basic algebra concepts, and introduction to statistics and probability.
- Grade 7: Pre-algebra.
- Grade 8: Algebra I, including linear equations, functions, and inequalities.
- Grade 9: Geometry.
- Grade 10: Algebra II.
- Grade 11: Pre-Calculus.
- Grade 12: Statistics and Calculus.

The girl's instructors knew that in first grade, the girl, who was not a mathematical prodigy, would not yet have the intellectual capacity to study calculus or statistics. She would need a progression of classes that would coordinate with her maturing capacity to understand increasingly advanced concepts. Each year, and with each new lesson, her learning built upon previously acquired knowledge and thinking skills. Eventually, the girl earned an advanced degree in theoretical mathematics. But what truly mystified her family is that she still has trouble balancing her checkbook.

Here is a practical example of how this works. In grade one, the young girl in the story above learned that in simple arithmetic, $2+2=4$. But over time, in a more advanced math class, she learn that $2+2$ is a symbolic representation for the properties of elements of a group. The result of that calculation depends, she learned, on what each "2" refers to and how the mathematical operation "+" is defined. Two apples plus two apples is still four apples, as the girl learned in first grade. But if she had a glass of water with a temperature of twenty degrees and poured it into another glass of water at 20 degrees, then the combined water would have a temperature of 40 degrees, right? Well—it certainly does not. But why not?

If both glasses contained the same amount of water, the final temperature would be one half the sum of the temperatures, so that would still be 20 degrees, which makes more sense. Temperatures don't add by the rule two plus two equals four because temperature is a measure of the average energy of particles and averages don't add the same way as apples.

Deeper understanding based on more information does not necessarily invalidate what was learned previously but always expands our base of knowledge in meaningful or useful ways.

In this simple story about school, the progression of math classes represents the concept of progressive revelation. Consider this example. The Divine Educator we call Krishna gave His contemporaries as much knowledge as they could comprehend about the Supreme Being and the nature of the world. He gave them guidance to navigate the basic life and relationship issues encountered in His primitive time and to better organize as a community. Without science, the general public addressed by Krishna lacked the knowledge that later societies would acquire to allow for a deeper understanding of the physical world and the diverse cultures of a globe that no one in Krishna's time could even envision.

Krishna provided ancient peoples with a primer on the value of duty, virtue, morality and justice. Judging from later writings that purport to present His teachings, Krishna spoke in terms that His society could understand by using common metaphors, familiar cultural tropes and colorful mythic references to build an understanding of simple but essential truths. Undoubtedly, Krishna knew He could not teach calculus to His class of first graders and that it would take a few millennia for the world to be ready for advanced tutorials. In this way, progressive revelation is a movement from truth to more truth to full truth.

In his book, *Bahá'u'lláh and the New Era*, author John E. Esselmont summed up the shock and awe inflicted by progressive revelation on each existing religion as newer teachings emerged:

> It may be a shock to the Jew to be told that some of the remedies for the world's sickness which Moses ordered over three thousand years ago are now out of date and unsuitable; the Christian may be equally shocked when told that Muhammad had anything necessary or valuable to add to what Jesus prescribed; and so also the Muslim, when asked to admit that the Báb or Bahá'u'lláh had authority to alter the commands of Muhammad; but according to the Bahá'í view, true devotion to God implies reverence to all His Prophets, and implicit obedience to His latest Commands, as given by the Prophet for our own age.[13]

People are often confused by what constitutes religion. Our most recent wisdom tradition explains it this way:

> Religion is not a series of beliefs, a set of customs; religion is the teachings of the Lord God, education of souls, the refinement of character, and spiritual perfection. It is light, it is guidance, and it is the bright effulgence of mercy. It is the bond of unity, the foundation of universal peace, reconciliation, and fellowship, the destroyer of enmity and strife, the unifier of the world of humanity, the bestower of true happiness, and the awakener of the souls and the minds of men towards the realization of the mighty inflow of the Word of God.[14]

Seen this way, religion is not static but dynamic, in its origin the most revolutionary and radical of all forces. The Founders of all

---

13 Esselmont, John E., *Bahá'u'lláh and the New Era*, p. 726.
14 'Abdu'l-Bahá, *Selections from the Writings of 'Abdu'l-Bahá*, 23:6.

our religions have inevitably broken with past traditions, obsolete forms and institutions, and rituals that have lost their meaning to protect the remaining substance of God's truth and adapt it to the requirements of a new age.

Our Great Wisdom Traditions

I prefer to call the major world religions "wisdom traditions" as they together embody an accumulation of the world's wisdom gathered over many millennia. These wisdom traditions geographically organize themselves into two streams of development that are generally referred to as Aryan and Abrahamic.

ARYAN

- Hinduism
- Zoroastrianism
- Buddhism

ABRAHAMIC

- Judaism
- Christianity
- Islam
- Babí Faith
- Bahá'í Faith

The last two wisdom traditions in the Abrahamic stream may be unfamiliar to readers but will be fully explained later. Each of these eight wisdom traditions was founded—or, more accurately, "renewed"—by a Divine Educator. All "people of faith," regardless of which faith they accept as true, believe that the "Prophet-Founder" of their chosen religion was a Messenger of God sent to reveal a divine message to the residents of our planet. Here is a list of the Divine Educators who delivered the messages around which a great wisdom tradition was formed.

- KRISHNA (Hinduism)
- BUDDHA – a.k.a. Siddhartha Gautama (Buddhism)
- ZOROASTER – a.k.a. Zarathustra (Zoroastrianism)
- MOSES (Judaism)
- JESUS CHRIST (Christianity)
- MUHAMMAD (Islam)
- THE BÁB (The Bábí Faith)
- BAHÁ'U'LLÁH (The Bahá'í Faith)

Chapter 3:
The Syncretism Theory

Most scholars of religion have adopted the concept of syncretism to explain the similarities of one religion to another. Syncretism refers to a blending or merging of different religious and philosophical ideas and practices. This can occur, they say, as a result of natural cultural contact, military conquests, new trade partnerships, or other natural interactions between people of different beliefs. These scholars point to obvious examples throughout history that illustrate religions adapting, absorbing and reinterpreting existing beliefs from foreign sources to invent evolved expressions of spirituality including:

- **Hellenistic influences on Judaism** during the Second Temple period, leading to the development of concepts such as resurrection and the afterlife.

- **The adoption of Persian Zoroastrian conceptions of end things** (e.g., judgment, immortality, heaven and hell, resurrection) by other religious traditions.

- **The merging of Greek philosophical concepts into early Christian theology**, particularly through figures such as Paul and later theologians such as Augustine.

Many scholars who attempt to use the scientific method to establish the evolution of religious ideas believe that introducing God into an explanation taints the outcome of their work. The secular decision to ignore or deny that divine revelation plays a role in the development of religion may seem like a paradox to some, and yet syncretism undoubtedly does occur in the evolution of all beliefs. In all communities, particularly expanding ones, thoughts do not occur in a vacuum, consequently they are subject to outside influence. Syncretism describes the natural fluidity and adaptability of religious thought and shows how religious traditions evolve and influence each other over time. Some examples:

- Rastafarianism, the Jamaican religious and political movement practiced by pop music legend Bob Marley, clearly combined Protestant Christianity, Old Testament stories (particularly that of Exodus), mysticism and pan-African political consciousness.

- The Christian holiday of Christmas, the birthday of Jesus, was celebrated in Rome on December 25 by dictate of the Emperor, Constantine. This date was also the winter solstice, the date of a popular Roman gift-giving festival called the Saturnalia, and the birthdate of the Indo-European deity Mithra, the god of light and loyalty that was growing in popularity among Roman soldiers.

- The story of Noah and the Great Flood is a much later version of numerous other creation myths including the strikingly similar Epic of Gilgamesh from Mesopotamia.

Syncretism is a logical concept for explaining these fusions.

Progressive Revelation and Syncretism Co-exist

The concept of progressive revelation is not a replacement for syncretism in explaining how religions evolve or, as one cynical religious scholar put it, "steal the good ideas from other traditions." Syncretism—the historical blending of religious ideas—can be seen not as a contradiction to divine purpose and revelation, but as part of a method by which God's guidance can unfold progressively through time. In other words, naturally occurring syncretism and progressive revelation can both be true and operational at the same time. Here is how they can coexist.

There is unity in the diversity of religious expression

Under progressive revelation, the *core spiritual truths* of all religions are the same because they all derive from the same God. But the *social teachings, rituals, and forms of expression* of each religion differ according to historical and cultural contexts. Syncretism focuses on the diversity of religious expression and explains how these external forms can evolve over time, aligning with the view that religion is both eternal in its essence and dynamic in its outward expression.

Human interactions are a medium of divine purpose

In human history, the interactions between cultures and religions serve as a vehicle for God's will. Syncretism, therefore, is a natural expression of how humanity collectively integrates and adapts divine teaching to address society's ever-evolving needs. The process of syncretism, consequently, does not dilute the authenticity of any religion influenced by or influencing another religion. Rather, syncretism powerfully illustrates how God's revealed message is refracted through diverse human experiences and contexts to enrich its meaning with relevance.

Syncretism supports adaptation to local contexts and needs

Progressive revelation acknowledges that each Manifestation of God addresses the specific and differing needs, capacities and cultural contexts of their time. As societies change, the fusion of religious ideas through syncretism reflects this adaptability, allowing new spiritual insights to resonate with existing beliefs. For example, the adoption of ethical monotheism from Zoroastrianism into Judaism and then into Christianity can be seen as a preparatory step that enriched and deepened the understanding of all those faiths. The original insight of Zoroaster, however, may have been inspired by divine revelation.

Gradual Unfolding of Knowledge

Embedded in the concept of progressive revelation is the idea that religious knowledge is not static but unfolds gradually. As humanity evolves, its understanding of spiritual truths deepens and expands, often incorporating insights from previous religious traditions. This syncretism can be seen as part of the natural evolutionary process of religious thought in which each religion builds upon the spiritual heritage of its predecessors to refine and expand human comprehension of the divine.

A continuum of divine guidance

Rather than seeing syncretism as a dilution or corruption of religious purity, progressive revelation frames it as evidence of a continuum of divine guidance. Each Divine Educator brings teachings that resonate with the familiar while introducing new, transformative elements. The blending of ideas from earlier traditions can be viewed as a divine strategy to ease transitions and foster acceptance of new revelations, maintaining continuity while advancing humanity's spiritual journey.

Because distinctive cultures view and adjust philosophical concepts based on unique perspectives, religions emerging in India, for example, acquired different characteristics than religions in, say, Palestine. For this reason, religious scholars often place religions into one of three "branches" based primarily on their outward differences and apparent sources: Aryan religions, Abrahamic religions, and indigenous or folk religions.

Aryan Religions

Mentioned earlier, the term "Aryan" is derived from the Sanskrit word "☐rya," meaning "noble" or "respectable," and historically referred to the Indo-Aryan peoples who composed the Vedas in ancient India. More broadly, Aryan religions encompass the major spiritual traditions that arose within the Indo-Aryan cultural and linguistic sphere, including Hinduism, Zoroastrianism and Buddhism.

Abrahamic Religions

Abrahamic religions are those seen to have been part of the Abrahamic line of revelation and includes Judaism, Christianity, Islam and the Bahá'í Faith. Though it originated in Persia, the Bahá'í Faith directly follows Islam in the same way that Islam follows Christianity and Christianity follows Judaism, which in turn follows the religion of Abraham. Bahá'í teachings are deeply influenced by the Qur'an and Islamic theology, but also rely on Christian and Jewish writings to support religious truths.

The Bahá'í Faith does not draw theological roots from the Vedic tradition of scriptures (Hinduism and Buddhism) in the same way it connects with the Abrahamic tradition. But Bahá'ís respect these Aryan traditions as part of progressive revelation and recognize figures like Zoroaster, Krishna, and Buddha as Manifestations of God who guided humanity in their respective locations and eras.

Indigenous and folk religions

"Indigenous or folk religions" refer to spiritual and religious practices that are deeply rooted in the traditions, cultures, and histories of specific communities, particularly those tied to a specific geographic region or ethnic group. These religions are typically distinct from the major world religions (such as Christianity, Islam, or Hinduism) and are often oral in nature, lacking a formalized scripture or centralized religious authority. These religions often believe in multiple gods and various superstitions, and are often tied to land, ancestors and nature.

The concept of progressive revelation extends to indigenous and folk religions, which are seen as valid and integral parts of humanity's spiritual evolution. Although many of the names of the founders of indigenous or folk religions may be lost to history, many

Bahá'ís believe these traditions originated from divine revelation. The early spiritual teachers in these communities may have been Manifestations of God sent to guide those peoples.

Evidence of Human Unity and Shared Spiritual Heritage

Syncretism highlights the interconnectedness of human cultures and the shared spiritual heritage of humanity. This interconnectedness is a sign of the oneness of humanity, reflecting the overarching unity of God's purpose. The similarities between religions that arise from progressive revelation to be customized through syncretic processes reinforce the fact that all religions are chapters of the same book, one religion of God, which is continuously unfolding to guide humanity toward unity and peace.

Syncretism and progressive revelation can be reconciled by understanding that both processes reflect the dynamic, evolving relationship between God and humanity. While syncretism illustrates the natural blending and adaptation of religious ideas across cultures, progressive revelation emphasizes the divine orchestration behind this evolution, guiding humanity through successive stages of spiritual development. Together, these perspectives affirm that all religious traditions are part of a single, divinely guided process aimed at uplifting humanity and uniting it in its common spiritual destiny.

Sudden, Non-evolutionary Shifts

Syncretism best discerns the gradual adaptations and permutations of belief systems that occur slowly, the way Earth's tectonic plates grindingly transform the planet's surface. Mapping glacial shifts in folklore and religious beliefs is important work but is ill-equipped to explain more sudden changes in social attitudes and norms.

In geology, volcanoes and earthquakes sometimes cause upheavals, floods resculpt the landscape, and asteroid crashes terraform the Earth's crust. Progressive revelation explains how sudden spiritual transformations can accelerate important shifts in the consciousness of societies and reforms in the behaviors of civilizations.

According to the concept of progressive revelation, the appearance of each Manifestation of God does more than reveal divine teachings—it also releases a spiritual impulse that changes societies and accelerates human progress. The spiritual energy unlocked by each Manifestation fuels advancements in morality, social structures, human rights, and other areas of life. Below are examples related to Judaism, Christianity, Islam, and the Bahá'í Faith.

Judaism

The appearance of Moses and the subsequent establishment of a covenant with God had lasting influences on law, religion, and society, not just for the Israelites but for global civilizations. His leadership transformed a scattered group into a unified nation, with a profound impact on monotheistic faiths and legal traditions throughout history as outlined below:

- **Monotheism**: Moses introduced the worship of one God (Yahweh), which revolutionized the religious landscape of the ancient world, contrasting with the polytheism of Egypt and Canaan. This belief in a single, just and omnipotent deity became the cornerstone of Judaism and later influenced Christianity and Islam.

- **The Mosaic law**: Moses provided a legal and moral code, the Ten Commandments, which shaped the ethical behavior and governance of the Israelites. These laws covered not only religious obligations but also social justice, personal conduct, and relationships between individuals. The legal system established under Moses emphasized equality, justice, and care for the vulnerable (e.g., widows, orphans and strangers).

- **National identity and freedom**: The Exodus, led by Moses, was a defining event in Jewish history. It signified the liberation of the Israelites from slavery in Egypt and the formation of a distinct national identity. This act of deliverance, along with the covenant at Mount Sinai, helped establish the Israelites as a people bound together by their shared faith, law and destiny.

- **Cultural and social unity**: Moses united a previously enslaved and disparate people under one religious and legal system, fostering cohesion among the Israelites. The journey to the Promised Land under Moses's leadership provided not just physical freedom, but also a societal framework that strengthened communal bonds.

- **Long-term influence on civilizations**: The laws and ethical teachings of Moses influenced many legal and moral systems throughout history, impacting the development of Western legal codes, justice systems, and social norms, such as those found in Christianity and Islam.

In the words of our latest wisdom tradition:

> As to Moses, the splendor of His dispensation, the magnitude and diversity of the enterprises which it inspired, and the enduring character of the civilization which it established bear ample testimony to the truth of the assertion that, of all the Revelations which have preceded the Dispensation of the Báb, the Mosaic Dispensation has exercised the most potent influence upon the subsequent evolution of mankind and its institutions.[15]

---

15   Shoghi Effendi, *The World Order of Bahá'u'lláh*, p. 101.

Christianity

The emergence of Christianity contributed to several sudden changes in society, particularly in the Roman Empire.

- **Moral transformation**: Early Christians introduced the radical idea of love and compassion for all, including enemies, challenging often brutal Roman social norms.

- **Social equality**: The Christian message of the equality of all souls before God led to greater dignity for marginalized groups such as slaves, women and the poor.

- **Martyrdom and persecution**: The willingness of early Christians to die for their beliefs contributed to their spread, earning admiration and ultimately influencing Roman society.

- **Charitable works**: Christians emphasized charity and care for the sick, leading to the establishment of early hospitals and social welfare systems.

- **Legal and ethical changes**: Christian values began to influence Roman law, leading to the eventual outlawing of practices such as infanticide and gladiatorial games.

These and other indelible effects of Christianity on society are beautifully summarized in this quotation from the Bahá'í Faith:

> Know thou that when the Son of Man (Jesus) yielded up His breath to God, the whole creation wept with a great weeping. By sacrificing Himself, however, a fresh capacity was infused into all created things. Its evidences, as witnessed in all the peoples of the earth, are now manifest before thee.[16]

---

16 Bahá'u'lláh, *Gleanings from the Writings of Bahá'u'lláh*, p. 85.

Islam

The appearance of the Prophet Muhammad in the seventh century is believed by many to have released a profound spiritual impulse, leading to significant societal transformations:

- **Equality and social justice**: Muhammad's message stressed the equality of all believers before God, challenging the deeply entrenched tribal and class systems in pre-Islamic Arabia. The Quran introduced reforms regarding women's rights (e.g., inheritance, marriage), fair treatment of slaves, and the protection of orphans and the poor.

- **Advances in human rights**: The Quran and Hadith (sayings of Muhammad) emphasized the dignity and rights of individuals, leading to significant legal reforms. The early Islamic caliphates enshrined rights to life, property, and religious freedom (particularly for "People of the Book," i.e., Jews and Christians).

- **Scientific and cultural renaissance**: The Islamic Golden Age, which began roughly a century after the advent of Islam, saw immense progress in science, mathematics, medicine and philosophy. Islamic scholars preserved and expanded upon Greek, Persian and Indian knowledge, playing a crucial role in the development of fields such as algebra, chemistry, and astronomy.

- **Legal systems and governance**: Islamic jurisprudence (Sharia law) became one of the most detailed and progressive legal systems of the time, emphasizing justice, the rights of women, economic fairness, and the equitable treatment of all people.

Our most recent wisdom tradition summarized the impact of Islam this way:

> Muhammad, the Apostle of God, appeared, and once again the world was stirred with the resounding cry of the new Message. He summoned the peoples of the world, and through Him, the divine Teachings and Laws, designed to ensure the well-being and security of mankind, were revealed.[17]

The Bahá'í Faith

A three-volume set of books entitled 1844 by Jerome L. Clark exhaustively cataloged numerous societal and intellectual advancements that began around the year 1844. This timing is significant because a Manifestation of God known as the Báb declared his station as a Manifestation of God in 1844. Another Manifestation that He prophesied would soon appear, Bahá'u'lláh, declared His mission nineteen years later. Among the advanced teachings proclaimed by the Bahá'í Faith are:

- **Equality of men and women**: Bahá'u'lláh's teachings strongly advocate for the equality of the sexes. The Bahá'í Faith's commitment to gender equality has resonated with global movements toward women's rights and empowerment, including the twentieth- and twenty-first-century feminist movements.

- **Global governance and peace**: Bahá'u'lláh emphasized the need for collective security, global governance, and the abolition of war. His call for unity of nations and peoples parallels the rise of international institutions like the United Nations and global cooperation frameworks in the modern world.

- **Universal education**: Bahá'í teachings stress the importance of universal education, a principle that aligns with global efforts to make education accessible

---

17 Bahá'u'lláh, *The Kitáb-i-Íqán* (*The Book of Certitude*), Part Two.

to all, especially in marginalized communities. Expansion of public education systems and efforts toward universal literacy reflect this influence.

- **Interfaith harmony and unity**: The Bahá'í principle of the oneness of religion and humanity has contributed to the modern discourse on interfaith dialogue, religious tolerance, and global citizenship. The Bahá'í Faith has actively promoted cooperation between religious communities and the idea that all major world religions come from the same divine source.

The set of books titled *1844* highlights many other remarkable key advancements in human rights and societal reforms beginning shortly after the appearance of The Báb and Bahá'u'lláh—too many to be considered coincidental. They include efforts to abolish slavery; labor reforms; the push for universal public education; the temperance movement; early peace movements and peace societies; health and sanitation reforms; mental health and prison reforms; increased religious revivals; and the spread of new religious movements.

> Bahá'u'lláh appeared at a time when the world of humanity was in the utmost state of disorder and corruption, and the darkness of ignorance and heedlessness was spreading. He raised the call of the oneness of humanity, proclaimed the necessity of universal peace, and laid the foundation of the unity of nations and peoples. He established the principles for the progress and development of the world, which are the cause of the eternal glory and happiness of humanity.[18]

---

18 'Abdu'l-Bahá, *Selections from the Writings of 'Abdu'l-Bahá*, p. 118.

Chapter 4:
Dangers of Syncretism and Evolving Religious Thought

The natural evolution and syncretism of religious thought, which can be enriching and stimulating, can become dangerous or overly error-prone when it compromises the integrity, purpose, or ethical foundations of the original teachings. While religious adaptation and synthesis have historically facilitated cultural exchange and spiritual growth, these processes can lead to distortions, misinterpretations, or the reinforcement of harmful practices. Here are some key conditions under which the natural evolution and syncretism of religious thought can become problematic:

Distortion of Core Ethical Principles

One of the primary dangers of religious syncretism occurs when the integration of new ideas or cultural influences distorts the core ethical and spiritual principles of a religion. This can happen when fundamental values, such as justice, compassion, and the sanctity of human life, are compromised or reinterpreted in ways that justify unethical behavior.

In some historical contexts, the merging of religious beliefs with political agendas led to the justification of war, persecution, or exploitation in the name of religion, deviating from the original intent of promoting peace and moral conduct. A good example occurred in Germany between 1932 and 1945 when German Christians, a pressure group within the German Evangelical Church, aligned with the antisemitic, racist and *Führerprinzip* principles of Nazism to provide enormous support to Hitler under the cover of its perverted Christian beliefs. Other examples are religious practices, such as caste discrimination in Hinduism, originally not prescribed in Hindu core scriptures, but which became deeply ingrained in society over time.

Loss of Authenticity and Authority

Religious syncretism can become error-prone when it leads to a loss of clear authority or authenticity within a tradition. Over time, the original teachings can become obscured or misrepresented when religious beliefs and practices merge with local customs, political interests, priestly commentary, or personal interpretations. This can make it difficult for followers to distinguish between authentic guidance and cultural or ideological additions.

A good example of this is the proliferation of sects and denominations within major religions that claim to hold exclusive truth. There are approximately 45,000 denominations and sects of Christianity today. This division, often caused by small differences in teachings, can lead to confusion and disunity among followers, detracting from the unity and coherence of the original teachings. The syncretic mixing can sometimes dilute spiritual teachings with superstitions, magical practices, or overly rigid interpretations not intended by the original founders.

Institutional Corruption and Power Struggles

As a religion evolves and absorbs some elements from surrounding cultures and other faiths, there is a risk of institutional corruption where religious leaders or institutions use syncretic changes to consolidate power, control followers, or accumulate wealth. This can lead to a change of focus from spiritual development of followers to maintaining or boosting institutional authority.

There have been numerous historical instances of religious institutions amassing wealth and political power by manipulating religious doctrine to serve their interests, leading to exploitation and abuse as well as the prioritization of institutional survival over spiritual integrity. In many cases, clerical hierarchies actively resist needed reform or cling to outdated practices to maintain control, even when those practices are no longer relevant or beneficial.

Overemphasis on Rituals and External Forms

Syncretism can sometimes lead to an overemphasis on rituals, symbols, and external forms of worship at the expense of the inner spiritual essence of a religion. This can result in a focus on outward conformity rather than personal transformation, ethical conduct, and deep spiritual understanding.

Examples include the development of complex and burdensome rituals that overshadow the core ethical and spiritual teachings, turning religion into a formality rather than a transformative force in people's lives; also, the incorporation of superstitious practices that divert attention from the core tenets of faith, leading followers to prioritize ritual correctness over moral and spiritual growth.

Resistance to Progressive Change and Reinterpretation

Religious evolution becomes dangerous when it leads to resistance against necessary reforms or reinterpretations that align with the original spirit of the teachings but adapt to new contexts. When religions become overly attached to syncretic practices that have become outdated or harmful, they may resist progressive change, leading to stagnation or conflict with modern values.

Today, such practices include insisting on gender inequality among followers, maintaining strict caste divisions or the exclusion of marginalized groups. Often, these practices have been reinforced by cultural influences rather than the original teachings of the religion. Rigid adherence to syncretic traditions that are no longer relevant or beneficial can alienate younger generations or create friction with contemporary human rights standards.

Sectarianism and Division

When syncretic elements become a source of identity rather than a means to connect with a religion's core teachings, they can foster division and sectarianism. This happens when groups prioritize their unique interpretations or practices over the unifying spiritual principles that should bind the community.

The fragmentation of religious communities into competing sects or factions, each emphasizing different syncretic interpretations or practices, can lead to conflict, intolerance, and a loss of the sense of shared purpose. Historical conflicts between religious groups often stem from differences that arose through syncretic adaptations, leading to prolonged sectarian strife.

Misinterpretation and Loss of Spiritual Depth

When syncretism leads to superficial interpretations of scriptures or the loss of deeper spiritual insights, it is no longer true to the faith's original teachings. Simplistic or literal interpretations that arise from blended traditions can obscure the profound metaphysical and moral teachings intended by the original founders.

Common examples include the reduction of complex spiritual truths into simplistic dogmas or literalisms that fail to capture the symbolic and allegorical richness of sacred texts; also, the misinterpretation of religious teachings to justify actions contrary to the original ethical intent, such as using scripture to legitimize violence, discrimination, or exclusion.

Humanity's Ongoing Journey

For syncretism and the evolution of religious thought to be useful and beneficial, it is essential to maintain a balance that respects the core spiritual principles and ethical guidance of the original teachings while allowing for adaptation to changing contexts. According to the core principles of the world's great wisdom traditions, the process of religious evolution is guided by divine purpose as each Manifestation of God brings teachings that correct past errors in human understanding or application, expand spiritual understanding, and adapt to the needs of the time.

Of course, humankind must work to apply those core principles to new issues and problems. This framework offers a way to view syncretism not as inherently dangerous but as part of a larger, divinely guided process. When correctly understood and aligned with core spiritual principles, this process contributes to humanity's ongoing journey toward unity, peace, and maturity.

When human-caused changes and adaptations to the original teachings of a religion veer out of control and religions become harmful to individuals and society, a new Divine Educator may be sent to provide a course correction and reveal truths that civilization had previously lacked the capacity to understand. The next chapter presents a deeper study of the mysterious Manifestations of God Who have been promised to guide humanity by all the world's wisdom traditions. We have been given more knowledge about them than you may expect,

Chapter 5:
The Source of Religious Thought

In 2022, over 80 percent of the global population was affiliated with one of the major world religions with the following percentages:[19] [20]

- 31.6% Christians
- 25.8% Muslims
- 15.1% Hindus
- 6.6% Buddhists
- 0.2% Jews

Each of the world's great wisdom traditions is considered by its followers to be based on a message "revealed" to humanity by a specific Divine Educator, also called a Manifestation of God, as listed in the previous chapters. While the vast majority of the world's residents believe in the idea of a Messenger sent by God to shepherd humanity, perhaps no religious concept is more contentious than

---

19   Statista, available at https://www.statista.com/statistics/374704/share-of-global-population-by-religion/

20   The number of Zoroastrians has dwindled to less than two hundred thousand today. Members of the Bábí Faith became Bahá'ís after the death of the religion's Founder, known as the Báb. The Bahá'í Faith is our most recent wisdom tradition but is less than two hundred years old, thus in its infancy.

defining the essential nature of these Messengers—Their existence, provenance, qualities and relationships.

Some wisdom traditions present these Educators as illuminated prophets to whom God spoke directly. One now teaches that its Manifestation is, in a mysterious way, God Himself. All of them provide clues to the nature of these Manifestations, but these depictions are clearly cloaked in language directed to the limited capacity of local audiences to comprehend.

Christianity began with the premise that Jesus was an illuminated prophet with teachings that could save the world's sinners from the wages of their sins. Through a quarrelsome political process at the First Council of Nicaea in AD 325, however, a gathering of bishops voted to declare that Jesus was in fact God, inventing a novel religious concept codified in the original Nicene Creed and thereafter referred to as the Trinity.[21] This creative concept attempted to explain how an infinite and omnipresent God could inhabit the flesh of a finite human Who could not occupy more than one space at a time. The outcome of this deification syncretically mirrored the evolutionary process by which the attributes of a Supreme Being in Hinduism eventually produced a pantheon of gods, each one an anthropomorphic representation of a specific divine attribute.

This book will explore how an unfolding religion of God has progressively revealed more about the essential nature of these Divine

---

21   The original Nicene Creed opens with this translated statement: "We believe in one God, the Father almighty, Maker of heaven and earth, and of all things visible and invisible. And in one Lord Jesus Christ, the Son of God, the only-begotten son, begotten of the Father before all. Light of Light, true God of true God, begotten not made, of one essence with the Father by whom all things were made; who for us men and for our salvation, came down from heaven, and was incarnate of the Holy Spirit and the Virgin Mary and became man. And He was crucified for us under Pontius Pilate, and suffered, and was buried. And the third day He rose again, according to the Scriptures; and ascended into heaven, and sits at the right hand of the Father; and He shall come again with glory to judge the living and the dead; whose Kingdom shall have no end. And in the Holy Spirit."

Messengers. But one thing has become clear through this purposefully graduated process of revelation: while each Manifestation is fully human, each One is also much more than that.

Manifestations of God Lost to History

Earlier, we introduced some of the Divine Educators we can name. Those we listed are the Manifestations of God who gave us teachings that became the fundamental scriptures of the world's great wisdom traditions, but there were many others now lost to history. We would expect our most recent wisdom tradition to have the most thorough explanation for this. In the Writings of Bahá'u'lláh, we find these words:

> How numerous the peoples and nations that have vanished, leaving no trace behind! How many are those who, in every age and cycle, have eagerly awaited the advent of the Manifestations of God in the sanctified persons of His chosen Ones.[22]

But if we go back to more ancient times, we can find the idea of a chain of teachings delivered by multiple "Avatars," which we call Manifestations or Divine Educators. Through hundreds, perhaps thousands of years of oral teachings, many different strains of Hinduism appeared with different lists and counts of these Manifestations, which range from ten, twenty-two and thirty-nine to "innumerable."

In Buddhism, we also find references to numerous prior Manifestations, referred to as Buddhas. Due to the vagaries of oral history, the numbers of Buddhas prior to the historic Buddha Siddhartha ranges from five to twenty-five to a countless number as stated in this passage:

---

22 Bahá'u'lláh, *Gleanings from the Writings of Bahá'u'lláh*.

> At that time Shákyamunibuddha's emanations in the eastern quarter, Buddhas of the lands equal in number to the sands of a hundred thousand myriad of millions of Ganges rivers, each Buddha preaching Dharma, assembled in this place, Buddhas of ten directions all gathering in order and sitting in the eight quarters.[23]

In Zoroastrianism, the idea of a chain of prophecy presents a system of ten incarnations in the *Avesta*.[24] In the older texts, there is the notion of *kavis* (priest-kings), who are seen as forerunners of Zorostrianism. A Swedish scholar of religions named Nyberg states that "even very old Avesta-texts may have had a fixed series of such pre-zoroastrian rulers and heroes."[25]

The number of these Manifestations throughout history appears to be unknown or unlimited, according to our most recent wisdom tradition, the Bahá'í Faith.

> [T]he Manifestations of His Divine Glory... have been sent down from time immemorial, and been commissioned to summon mankind to the one true God. That the names of some of them are forgotten and the records of their lives lost is to be attributed to the disturbances and changes that have overtaken the world.[26]

Even folk religions and the beliefs of indigenous peoples have been inspired by Divine Educators, as indicated by 'Abdu'l-Bahá in the Writings of the Bahá'í Faith.

---

23 Quoted in Christopher Lamb, "Buddhism," in J. Holm & J. Bowker (eds.) *Myth and History* 1994, page 14. Cf. *The Avatansaka Sútra*, which states that "Within each atom are inconceivably many Buddhas."

24 *Yasht* 14.

25 H.S. Nyberg, *Irans fornt ida religioner.* Sv. Kyrk ans Diakonis tyrelses Bokförlag. Stockholm, page 33.

26 Bahá'u'lláh, *Gleanings from the Writings of Bahá'u'lláh*, page 20.

> In ancient times the people of America were, through their northern regions, close to Asia, that is, separated from Asia by a strait. For this reason, it hath been said that crossing had occurred. There are other signs which indicate communication. As to places whose people were not informed of the appearance of Prophets, such people are excused. In the Qur'án it hath been revealed: "We will not chastise them if they had not been sent a Messenger" (Q. 17:15). Undoubtedly in those regions, the Call of God must have been raised in ancient times, but it hath been forgotten now.[27]

Among the Manifestations specifically mentioned by our newest wisdom tradition, only three are Asiatic (Aryan), but this does not mean there were not many, as explained by Bahá'í Writings.

> The only reason there is not more mention of the Asiatic Prophets is because Their names seem to be lost in the mists of ancient history. Buddha is mentioned, and Zoroaster, in our Scriptures—both non-Jewish Prophets or non-Semitic Prophets. We are taught there always have been Manifestations of God, but we do not have any record of Their names.[28]

The purpose of sending so many Manifestations, according to Bahai Writings, was to ensure that humanity would never be without divine guidance.

> [T]he manifold bounties of the Lord of all beings have, at all times, through the Manifestations of His divine Essence, encompassed the earth and all that

---

27   https://www.bahai.org/library/authoritative-texts/abdul-baha/additional-tablets-extracts-talks/169212878/1#341827961.

28   Shoghi Effendi, *Lights of Guidance: A Bahá'í Reference File*. New Delhi, India: Bahá'í Publishing Trust. p. 503.

> dwell therein. Not for a moment hath His grace been withheld, nor have the showers of His loving-kindness ceased to rain upon mankind.[29]

My understanding of the passages above is that Divine Educators provided education and guidance to humankind even in the earliest prehistoric times wherever humans existed. Perhaps the impulse for non-material spiritual concepts in early humans (such as the existence of a God or gods, and life after death) was not just a coping mechanism to defend against fears. Maybe it was not "hyperactive agency detection" as proposed by cognitive scientists, or a "projection of intentionality on natural phenomena" as suggested by today's Theory of Mind. It may not always have been a complex interaction of brain structures and chemical processes that somehow contributed to mystical experiences and religious beliefs, or an evolution from bereavement of the deceased to ancestor worship to a longing for an afterlife as some anthropologists have proposed.

There are many theories of how and why religious belief in gods and eternal life developed in humans, but perhaps the answer is much simpler. Could it be that Divine Educators—Manifestations of God—have been the civilizing agents Who instilled in humankind the basic "reality" of a spiritual realm that coexists with the material world? If one believes in God, that possibility seems more likely than the notion of primitive humans—who had no structured knowledge of the world and no rules to live by except those of survival—evolving the complex and rather abstract constructs of a spiritual world. Even fire was first "witnessed" before humans figured out ways to start it and then make use of it.

Of course, the various origin theories proposed by scientists may have some merit and may all contribute in some way to the evolution (and in some cases devolution) of religious thinking. Humans have

---

29 Bahá'u'lláh, *Kitáb-i-íqán (The Book of Certitude)*, page 14.

an enormous capacity for imagination once triggered, but all of the world's existing wisdom traditions rely on the concept of a Prophet or Enlightened One Who teaches fundamental truths to humanity, which then builds upon that received knowledge to construct and regulate its societies. Was it any different in prehistory?

It is possible, I think, that some primitive humans thousands of years ago, having been inspired by the most basic truths delivered by Divine Messengers, proceeded to creatively expand on what they were told. Through flights of imagination, perhaps induced by locally available hallucinogenic botanicals, some early humans either misunderstood their received lessons or added their own personal touches to that knowledge, evolving a pantheon of specialized gods. Over time, as with all belief systems, the truths were altered imaginatively and, in many cases, significant power was ceded to shamans and others who became the brokers of spiritual and mystical authority. This has happened with Christianity, which now has over 45,000 sects with different beliefs—and with Islam, some sects of which war viciously against each other.

Prehistoric Societies

Since the early 1990s, advances in archaeology, genetics and anthropology have greatly transformed views of our earliest human societies, and this has modified our understanding of primitive religious beliefs. Previously, it was widely thought that "civilization" began around 4000–3000 BCE with the rise of the first cities in Mesopotamia (such as Uruk) and in ancient Egypt.

Newly developed sites like Göbekli Tepe in Turkey, however, have now been dated to around 9600 BCE. This site, with its monumental architecture, suggests that complex societies with ritualistic or spiritual practices existed thousands of years before agriculture and settled urban life. This was previously thought impossible. Since that discovery, Natufian cultural sites with facilities for religious rituals and astronomical observations have been found in the Levant dating back as far as 12,500 BCE.[30]

The migration of humans from Siberia across the Bering Straits into the Americas had previously been placed by scientists near the end of the Ice Age. But new discoveries of pictographs in Mexico and the Amazon show images of religious significance from the mid-Ice Age period. This has led some paleo-anthropologists to suggest that waves of human colonization of the Americas occurred between 60,000–100,000 years ago.[31] Such a proposition would have prompted scholarly derision four decades ago.

Knowing this, and understanding that we are a species with chronic amnesia, a scriptural quotation presented earlier resonates even more profoundly: "[T]he manifold bounties of the Lord of all beings have, at all times, through the Manifestations of His divine Essence, encompassed the earth and all that dwell therein."[32] Quite a claim, indeed—Divine Educators appearing "at all times" and having "encompassed the earth." If true, the first glimmers of civilizing and religious thought may have been sparked by Divine Messengers. This would mean, of course, that since this education came from the same God to populations around the world, there should be some visible commonality of curriculum even when the learners had no contact with each other.

To find clues to the earliest Manifestations of God, we must study mythologies, which are often imaginative masks that hide or disguise important truths. We must examine and interpret ancient rock art painted in black charcoal emulsion, black manganese, red ochre and other available materials. Unfortunately, we cannot go back in time to communicate directly with the early artists, so we must rely on informed opinion and reason to make sense of these symbols and signs.

---

30 Tarbuyotolami at https://tarbuyotolami.com/en/sacred-goddess-natufian-sites/.
31 Bradshaw Foundation at https://www.bradshawfoundation.com/south_america/serra_da_capivara/index.php.
32 Bahá'u'lláh, *Kitáb-i-Íqán (The Book of Certitude)*, page 14.

The Big Bang of All Religious Belief

The concept of progressive revelation subsumes all human existence from the time that anatomically modern man first appeared on the planet. As one of numerous creation myths, the biblical story of Adam and Eve presents an engaging explanation of the origin of humans, their relationship with God, the introduction of sin and suffering, the nature of humanity, the importance of knowledge, the perils of temptation, the consequences of choices, the inevitability of physical death, and the nature of free will. That's quite an agenda for a story with a talking snake.

Our most recent wisdom tradition explains that this story is not a historical account but rather an allegory of humanity's spiritual journey and the challenges of developing virtues, which bring the individual into a closer relationship to God. In this view, Adam represents the very first Manifestation of God to humanity, a station clarified by his direct communication with God. The creation of Adam symbolizes human spiritual awakening and the beginning of human civilization under divine guidance.[33] The spiritual awakening of this first Manifestation parallels the awakening of all the known Manifestations to the magnitude of their unique stations.

Various Hindu theologians interpret Krishna's life as a progressive self-revelation, where his awareness grows or is remembered (in human terms) alongside his life events, culminating in the full expression of his identity as an Avatar (Manifestation) during the Mahabharata.[34]

Zarathustra's awareness of his prophetic mission also appears to have been gradual. In the Gathas, he speaks of seeking truth and understanding the nature of good and evil. Moses's awareness of his prophetic mission is most directly sparked during his encounter with God in the form of a burning bush on Mount Horeb.[35]

---

33 'Abdu'l-Bahá, *Some Answered Questions*, Chapter 30, "Adam and Eve."
34 *Bhagavata Purana*, 10.16.39.
35 The Bible, *Exodus*, Chapter 3.

Regarding Jesus, Christian interpretations vary on the exact nature and timing of His self-awareness, but the Gospels depict it as a mission that he fully embraces over time. Prophet Muhammad's awareness of his role as a Messenger of God, or *rasul*, unfolded in a profound and transformative experience at the age of forty when, according to tradition, he received the first revelation from God through the angel Gabriel (Jibril.) The Báb, the founder of the Bábí Faith, revealed in His letters and writings a devotion to God and mystical insights indicating a profound inner awakening that strengthened over time.

Bahá'u'lláh, the Prophet-Founder of the Bahá'í Faith, had a profound, transformative experience while imprisoned in the Black Pit (Siyáh Chál) in Tehran. He described this experience as the "Most Great Spirit" speaking to him, announcing His role as the One foretold by the Báb. In His own words, "the breezes of the All-Glorious were wafted over Me, and taught Me the knowledge of all that hath been."[36]

Bahá'u'lláh's documented epiphany closely parallels the Adam and Eve allegory that describes an awakening of Adam and the gaining of knowledge of "good and evil"—or in Bahá'u'lláh's words, "all that hath been."

The Big Bang for which I am seeking evidence is the first (or at least an early) revelation by a Divine Educator to humankind—a memorable message that, when passed along, would change the worldview of uneducated minds. Logically, the earliest anatomically modern humans would have been totally focused on one thing—survival. They would have had certain instincts, but in a dangerous environment, like animals, they would have been obsessed with obtaining nourishment and not getting eaten. All their attention would have been on the material world—what they could see, hear, feel, smell.

I cannot imagine these earliest humans having the time, motivation or capacity for philosophical contemplation about where

---

36 Bahá'u'lláh, *Epistle to the Son of the Wolf*, p. 20.

they came from, whether there was a parallel spiritual world, what behaviors were morally good and which were bad, or what would happen when they died. At any moment, a predator or a human adversary could put an end to such thinking. But once such ideas were planted into a few brains, perhaps by some external source, it is easy to imagine how such concepts could be reimagined and reconfigured repeatedly over thousands of years to create the countless strains of religions we now have.

But, in the very beginning, where did such abstract and metaphysical concepts come from? Could they have originated from the lips of another human who happened to be a Divine Educator, or who had learned intriguing things from such an Educator? In ancient times, this Big Bang would have happened more like a string of firecrackers going off as astounding new concepts ignited the imaginations of primitive minds one at a time.

Imagine, then, the response of those early humans who, for the first time, received the mind-blowing notion that they were different from the abundant animals they lived alongside because they could think bigger thoughts; that there were better ways to do things in their life; that if they did good things rather than bad things, they might be happier and even have a life after their certain death; and that there was a god, a spirit, who would protect and guide them.

We can't know what the early Divine Educators revealed to their primitive neighbors, but Their purpose, we are told, was to guide the residents of ancient Earth into a more civilized way of living, a process that would take thousands of years and is still not completed.

Imagine the impact of these basic ideas on primitive minds that had barely engaged with anything beyond mundane tasks, instinctive responses, and survivalist activities. To see beyond their bleak and dangerous world and glimpse for the first time a station above the animals and a future beyond their current circumstances—that must have inspired a few of them. And those few likely inspired a few more by telling stories of what they had learned.

Therianthropes

I can imagine that some early humans—certainly the artistic ones who had been painting their observations on cave walls and rocky outcroppings—would have added visual depictions of their new concepts to rough-hewn galleries. We know these early humans understood and used symbols, and so they must have invented new ones to document their epiphanies. Of course, they still painted the animals they saw in the natural environment.

European rock paintings are full of Ice Age animals we know existed because their bones have been found in the European fossil records. But in 2000 CE, the world's oldest cave painting was discovered, and it contained a highly unusual image.

> Traces of what could be the world's oldest-known cave paintings have been found in northern Italy. Some slabs bearing images of an animal and a half-human, half-animal figure were uncovered during excavations by an Italian team at the Fumane Cave northwest of Verona. The slabs, painted with red ochre, had apparently fallen from the cave roof and become embedded in floor sediment previously dated to between 32,000 and 36,500 years go.[37]

The half-human, half-animal figure is called a therianthrope, a mythical being that can transform between human, animal, or human-animal hybrid forms. Such figures are featured in petroglyphs, pictographs and rock carvings around the world. Therianthropes later may have inspired the shape-shifting monsters of popular fiction such as werewolves, skin-walkers, vampires, mermaids and the like. Scientists in various specialties have offered plausible explanations for why therianthropes, and in some cases mythical animals not found in the natural world, also appear in rock paintings.

---

37 *Science*, Vol. 290, 20 October 2000, p. 419

In 1969, archaeologists excavating a cave dubbed Apollo-11 in Namibia uncovered nineteen small sculptures whittled from mammoth ivory and dated around 25,500–27,000 BCE. One of these was much larger, about 29.6 cm tall, and weighed almost .75 kg. Now called the "lion-man," this sculpted figure has the arms and legs of a human, but has felid-like paws instead of hands and the head of a feline. The upright stance and posture are human-like.[38] Scholars have rejected the notion that this figure is a man wearing a lion mask.[39] It appears to be a figure captured in transformation from animal to man or vice versa. How such a concept could have occurred to early humans and its likely meaning—assuming it is not a painted "snapshot" of an unknown hybrid animal—still eludes the experts, though theories abound. This remarkable carving was made at least 32,000 years ago but could be thousands of years older.

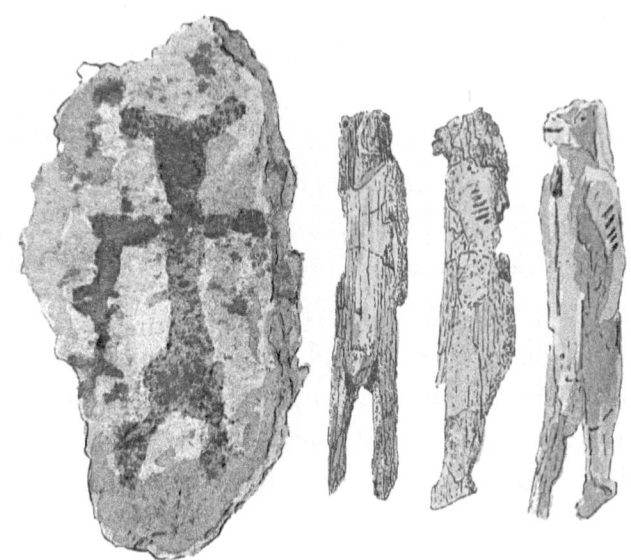

Left, the therianthrope painting discovered in Fumane Cave.
Right, three sketched views of the lion-man sculpture from the Apollo-11 cave.

---

38 Dowson and Port, "Special Objects–Special Creatures," p. 170.
39 Conrad, "Paleolithic Ivory Sculptures," p. 832.

Among the early rock art from around the world, we see a variety of therianthropic creatures—bison-men, bird-men, crocodile-men, et cetera. It seems that once the concept appeared in one place, it started appearing elsewhere. The choice of animals may have grown in importance over time as specific creatures began to acquire distinctive qualities and meanings in the minds of early humans.

How could this weird imagery take the world by storm in a time without social media? What was it about therianthropes that captured the imagination of so many cave painters? And how did such a unique concept travel almost virally around the world without direct human contact to spread it?

Scholarly Theories

The theories scholars have put forward to describe the origins of therianthropic imagery primarily explain how such images may have been exploited and adopted by other early humans throughout the world. Few theories explain the origin of the concept of therianthropes itself.

For example, the *shamanistic or visionary theory* states that therianthropes reflect shamanistic practices or the visions of shamans who used hallucinogens like ayahuasca or peyote. But this does not explain how pre-shaman humans came up with the concept of therianthropes. Some researchers see these depictions as a way to record or memorialize powerful dream experiences, obviously a possibility, but how did the same kinds of therianthropes then occur in the dreams of far-flung people with no direct contact?

The *totemic theory* states that therianthropes represent specific clans, tribes or family groups the way logos are used to brand companies and products today. But where and how did those different therianthropes originate before they were used as brands? If the blending of human and animal characteristics symbolizes a sacred connection between people and their "totem" animals, as other scholars theorize, how did the idea of sacredness originate?

The *mythology theory* tells us that therianthropes represent mythological beings or deities associated with a culture's cosmology. But what about the time *before* mythologies and religions existed? Where did the mythologies and religions come from? Some scholars say that therianthropes may represent the divine attributes embodied in specific animals. But before early humans had the idea of divinity or its association with animals—when humans were just emerging from the darkness of ignorance—where did the notion of any non-material, unnatural beings come from?

There still is no consensus among scholars about the meaning of these strange creatures and the means by which they appear in ancient rock art throughout the world.

The Fossils of God

Secular scholars and scientists have imposed on themselves a rigid limitation in forming theories about difficult subjects like these. They do not allow themselves to insert God into their theories. Because the existence of God cannot be scientifically tested or proven, they say, God cannot be used to answer the questions we are asking. God and other spiritual or supernatural entities cannot be reduced to matter and measured, weighed or counted scientifically, so God is only permitted to be used to describe the personal or societal beliefs of those who are studied. God is seen as a concept with no basis in reality rather than a transcendent reality that can have a causative effect on history or society.

If God were not banned from scholarly discussions about rock art, the following theory could be offered to explain the existence of therianthrope imagery in primitive artwork around the world. This theory derives from the concept of progressive revelation.

Assume for a moment that God sent special Messengers to guide humankind during its earliest stage of development. All messages to the various peoples around the world would have been delivered by different Messengers carrying the same basic guidance because it originated from the same Source. This guidance, however, was delivered by Messengers Who were born in various places—just as Krishna was born in India, Moses in Egypt, Jesus in a land now called Israel, and Muhammad in Saudi Arabia. These unified messages, then, which inspired the minds and rock art in Europe, also would have inspired the early humans in Africa, Australia and the Americas. Communication between these far-flung locations, which could only have occurred through direct contact—impossibile in that early era—would have been unnecessary. These core religious messages and their effects could have spread wherever Divine Educators appeared.

These simple, basic messages would have been as mind-blowing as the discovery of fire to the earliest humans. The imaginations of these beings would have been ignited by possibilities that transcend the mundane and treacherous world in which they lived. Undoubtedly, some early humans would have memorialized the new concepts symbolically on cave walls or cliff faces. These symbols, though enigmatic to scholars today, may be the fossil record of God's first lessons to humankind. If so, they require some context for interpretation, as all fossils do.

I do not claim to know what the first Divine Educator told the people of His time, but I expect it would have focused on the most fundamental truths on which all other knowledge could be built. In searching for clues to these truths, we must study the numerous creation myths that attempt to provide a similar message through allegories. Most creation myths state or infer the following fundamental concepts:

- A Supreme Being, Who cannot be seen, created the world and everything in it, including humans.

- Humans have dominion over animals because they possess higher intelligence and a soul that can distinguish what is right and wrong.

- Obedience to rules of "right" behavior generally leads to better outcomes.
- The human soul can survive physical death.

In the classic myth of Adam and Eve, God is prominently featured as the Creator of everything seen and unseen. God clearly told Adam that humans possessed a higher station than animals.

> Then God said, "Let us make man in our image, after our likeness. And let them have dominion over the fish of the sea and over the birds of the heavens and over the livestock and over all the earth and over every creeping thing that creeps on the earth."[40]

God's act of breathing life into Adam infers that God imparted a "soul" into his human creation, an act He does for no other created thing.

> Then the Lord God formed the man of dust from the ground and breathed into his nostrils the breath of life, and the man became a living creature.[41]

God establishes clear rules that must be obeyed, and when they are not, the consequences are severe. If Adam and Eve had obeyed, they could have stayed in the Garden of Eden, which implies immortality.

> And the Lord God commanded the man, saying, "You may surely eat of every tree of the garden, but of the tree of the knowledge of good and evil you shall not eat, for in the day that you eat of it you shall surely die."[42]

---

40 The Bible, *Genesis 1:26* (ESV)
41 The Bible, *Genesis 2:7* (ESV).
42 The Bible, *Genesis 2:16-17* (ESV).

The Adam and Eve story appears to have been influenced by earlier creation stories containing these same elements. A notable influence from Mesopotamia is the Epic of Gilgamesh, a long poem that predates the writing of Genesis by several centuries. The epic includes a story about a garden of the gods and a plant of immortality, thematic similarities with the Garden of Eden and the tree of knowledge of good and evil. In Sumerian mythology, we can find stories of a blissful paradise called Dilmun where sickness and pain do not exist, predators do not kill, and people do not grow old. Dilmun resembles biblical Eden. Egyptian creation myths also feature order arising from chaos and the creation of life by a god.

A sculpture depicting ancient Dilmun. Created from 3000–2000 BCE and discovered in Bahrain, it portrays Gilgamesh holding a lion and the god Enki standing where two waters meet.

Humanity's Duality

More context is provided by our most recent wisdom tradition, which states that humans have both material and spiritual dimensions, which set them apart from animals. While humans share certain qualities with animals, their intellectual and spiritual capacities give them unique potential for understanding divine mysteries and advancing spiritually.

> Man is in the highest degree of materiality, and at the beginning of spirituality—that is to say, he is the end of imperfection and the beginning of perfection. He possesses the animal virtues, but he also shares the angelic qualities.[43]

This context clarifies the basic message that while humans have "animal virtues," which connect them to the natural world—a truth easily observed by the earliest humans—they also have a spiritual capacity that allows them to develop virtues like compassion, wisdom, creativity, and selflessness. These spiritual qualities distinguish humans from other forms of life. This means that humans have a dual nature that gives them a unique potential for moral and spiritual advancement, a truth not easily observed by early humans.

Many animal virtues, which are shared by humans, can be positive. These include sensory perception to guide responses to the environment as well as survival instincts and emotions such as affection and attachment to other living beings. Humans share these virtues with animals as part of their physical existence but can also transcend them through intellectual and spiritual capacities unique to humans.

Oue most recent wisdom tradition also suggests that when humans allow their lower, negative animalistic tendencies—such as aggression, selfishness, and harmful intent—to dominate, they fall below their true human potential. These qualities are the destructive

---

43 'Abdu'l-Bahá, *Some Answered Questions*, p. 235.

part of the "animal nature" humans share with animals. Humans, however, are called to transcend these harmful traits through spiritual and moral development. The guidance for such development is provided by Divine Educators.

> If humans allow their lower, animalistic tendencies—such as aggression, selfishness, and harmful intent—to dominate, they fall below their true human potential. These qualities are part of the "animal nature" that humans share with animals, but in the Bahá'í perspective, humans are called to transcend these traits through spiritual and moral development.[44]

It is this dual *animal-human* nature that I think the first Divine Educators would have communicated to the first anatomically modern humans. This concept is a prerequisite for any understanding of the higher station and spiritual nature of humanity, which is something our distant ancestors probably could not have discerned without some prompting. And it is this breathtaking concept of a dual nature that may have been memorialized symbolically in the rock art imagery of therianthropes, which could have been allegorical depictions of the struggle between animal nature and human potential.

This basic message, combined with the other basic teachings identified in so many creation stories, surely would have been inspiring, aspirational and educational to early humans. It also would have introduced the basic concept of religion—an unseen Supreme Being who created the world and continues to guide his creation.

Is it possible that all religions originated from these basic concepts, which then evolved into multiple mutations through the natural processes of cultural adaptation, misunderstandings, sabotage, and the emergence of priestly authorities who mixed in their personal interpretations and agendas?

---

44 'Abdu'l-Bahá, *Paris Talks*, p. 73.

Chapter 6:
An Inflection Point

About 35,000 years ago, we have discovered, the earliest figurative art to have survived anywhere in the world was painted at Fumane Cave in northern Italy. The earliest extant figurative art from Africa—the paintings from Apollo-11 Cave in Namibia—date from 27,000 years ago. Other ancient paintings and engravings from this period have been found as far away as Australia. Despite the undeniable evidence of a glacially slow accumulation of human abilities over the past 100,000 years, this evolution shifted into high gear sometime after 50,000 BCE. Some kind of critical mass accrued, or some intervention occurred, which accelerated the birth of a phenomenon we call modern culture.

This inflection point seems to have begun a bit earlier in Europe, probably around 42,000 years ago. But the greatest surviving expressions of it arose during the extensive period between 35,00- and 12,000 years ago. These were the painted and engraved artworks in the caves of Italy and Franco-Cantabria, which presented a startling multitude of therianthropes that stunned and confused scholars.

I think it is no coincidence that these clearly religious allegories appear to solve the mystery of when religion began, at least so far as we can tell from evidence discovered on earth. And I think it is obvious that the appearance of Divine Educators throughout the world solves the mystery of how these unusual visual metaphors appeared among disconnected societies of early humans during this period.

It may be that the Rosetta Stone for decoding the meaning of these therianthropic cave paintings is deep within our own minds. It could be that the intellect, imagination and spiritual impulse of humans—the very qualities that separate us from animals and to which these mysterious images refer—are what finally unveil their meaning and remind us of basic truths.

The darkness of a cave is not a bad place for an early human to safely meditate on new thoughts like these. It is also a good place to secure a personal and private epiphany in visual form. But over thousands of years, I can also understand how countless other early humans could be inspired by the images but also come to see darker meanings and terrifying implications in these therianthropic creatures. It is the nature of humans to misinterpret and adapt what they encounter into new narratives. Over time, I can understand that these creatures could cease to be symbols of the struggle for balance of an individual's animal nature and human capacities, and more simply become frightening monsters. Over a longer period of time, the whole notion of therianthropes could be usurped by other artists and writers into new myths.

This seems to have happened. In Greek mythology, centaurs appeared. They were beings with the upper body of a human and the lower body of a horse, which represented both wisdom and wildness. The minotaur from Minoan mythology was a fierce creature with the body of a man and the head of a bull likely representing the complex interplay of human flaws and divine punishment. In Celtic mythology, the Púca was a shape-shifter that could appear as various animals such as horses, dogs and rabbits, often with human-like eyes. Also, in Celtic folklore, silkies were seals that could shed their skins and take human forms when ashore. Often, silkies took the appearance of attractive men or women to form doomed relationships with humans. Shape-shifting creatures, perhaps suggested by cave paintings that look like therianthropes in the process of transforming from human to animal, eventually became featured characters in folklore and works of fiction featuring vampires and werewolves.

Early Shamans

Archaeologists and anthropologists speak frequently about a shamanistic tradition that existed among early humans. Shamans were the religious leaders of their day, the "medicine men" who continue to offer their services primarily in indigenous cultures across Asia, Africa, the Americas and Oceania. They are spiritual practitioners who act as intermediaries between the human world and the realm of spirits, and they are responsible for healing, conducting rituals, communicating with spirits or ancestors, even revealing prophecy. Almost certainly they played a key role in enabling the inflection point we have seen.

Shamans are the functional ancestors of today's monks, priests, rabbis, pastors and mullahs. But where shamans directly communicate with spirits—which may include nature spirits, ancestors or deities on behalf of individuals or communities—today's clerics serve as intermediaries through more structured practices, prayers and interpretations of sacred texts. Where shamans provide healing through spiritual means such as removing spiritual "blockages," invoking spirits for help and removing curses, today's religious leaders may offer healing prayers (though some offer "faith healing,") but chiefly provide spiritual guidance and counseling.

Shamans typically enter into altered states of consciousness through meditation, drumming, fasting, or the use of hallucinogenic botanicals. Today's clerics generally do not practice altered states of consciousness, though prayer, meditation and deep worship may lead to profound spiritual experiences that are not trance-induced. And where shamans often use and serve as custodians for esoteric, orally transmitted knowledge, rites and rituals, sometimes calling on spirits or interpreting visions, today's religious leaders use sacred texts such as the Bible, the Torah or the Qur'an along with structured rituals approved by their religious communities. These texts and rituals are usually codified and lack the spirit-oriented approach used by shamans.

The questions before us are these—where did the first shamans gain their knowledge of a spiritual world? Is it possible that they encountered the first Divine Educators as other early humans did but chose to become close followers—apostles, so to speak—of the world's first religion? Is it possible they were consequently initiated into a deeper knowledge of the first religious lessons taught to humanity? Is it possible that shamans, who were serving as our first religion's ad hoc priesthood, altered some of the teachings over time by accident or on purpose? Is it possible that to gain deeper insights into the spiritual world, some shamans—perhaps most—used abundantly available hallucinogenic plants to promote altered states of consciousness and deeper connections to the Supreme Being, which in turn may have distorted understanding of the original teachings by introducing new experiences, visions and narratives?

Certainly, all of these questions can be answered affirmatively but do not provide proof. Looking at religious pre-history is like digging up broken pottery and trying to make sense of the pieces by asking the right questions and putting each artifact into context. Even though the discovered shards of pottery comprise physical evidence, the resulting conclusions about meaning are always highly subjective, though context can make the answers better informed.

Competing Theories

Most scholarly literature about shamans focuses on shamanic practices that grew out of beliefs that developed at some earlier time. It is that "earlier time"—the time at which beliefs were formed—that interests me. This is why rock art depicting therianthropes is so intriguing. Progressive revelation, a concept deriving from our surviving wisdom traditions, provides a theory in which Divine Educators were sent to humanity to guide them into civilization and spiritual development. Rock art therianthropes may be evidence of this.

But there is a competing theory of how and why therianthropic images appeared in the artwork of early humans. South African archaeologist David Lewis-Williams has studied for years primitive art from the San people of Sub-Saharan Africa. He has focused on the development of psychological models for understanding the relationship between belief systems and rock art. His research suggests that such art often represents altered states of consciousness possibly induced by the use of natural hallucinogens. Lewis-Williams argues that these altered states are reflected in common motifs and archetypes including therianthropic creatures.

In his works, such as *The Mind in the Cave* and *The Shamans of Prehistory*, Lewis-Williams connects these experiences to shamanistic practices, where shamans might have used these altered states to engage in rituals and create art that reflects their visions. Lewis-Williams also highlights the logically universal nature of certain visual experiences, suggesting that the brain's hardwiring leads to similar hallucinatory experiences across different cultures, which could then be depicted in rock art. This theory provides a bridge between the biological experiences of prehistoric people and the symbolic expressions found in their art.

In the animal world, newly hatched chicks with bits of shell still stuck to their fuzzy bodies scurry for cover when a wooden model of a hawk slides on a wire above them. When the model is exchanged for that of a duck, pigeon or heron—or when the hawk model moves backward on the wire—the chicks have no fear response. No one can tell us how that image got into the nervous system of the chick, but it is there nevertheless. Mythologist Joseph Campbell summarized the phenomenon this way:

> **The image of the inherited enemy is always sleeping in the nervous system, and along with it the well-proven reaction; flight to cover. Furthermore, even if all the hawks in the world were to vanish, their image would still sleep in the soul of the chick—never to be roused, however, unless by some accident of art [such as the wooden hawk]...[45]**

Most scientists agree, however, that general laws cannot be announced that would be generally valid from one species to another, as in the case of another bird. When the eggs of cuckoos are laid in the nest of a different species where they hatch, without any prior experience of their own species, a cuckoo fledgling will flock only with its own kind. A duckling, however, will attach as an offspring to the first creature it encounters after leaving the egg—another hen, perhaps, or a human.

Lewis-Williams's theory has been criticized for being overly reliant on specific ethnographic parallels, particularly with the San people of southern Africa, which might not universally apply to other regions or time periods. Other researchers caution against the subjective application of shamanistic interpretations to varied rock art exemplars without sufficient contextual or cultural evidence. Also, the idea that similar neurological experiences lead to similar artistic expressions globally overlooks the complex interplay of cultural, environmental, geographic, cultural and individual factors that can influence art.[46]

The notion that the brain may be hardwired to produce iconic imagery under specific circumstances, which Lewis-Williams asserts, has not been proven as a general principle for all ethnicities or other groups. But if true, such archetypes may coexist alongside more

---

45 Joseph Campbell, *Primitive Mythology: The Masks of God*, Chapter 1.
46 Cambridge Core, "Putting the Record Straight: Rock art and shamanism," available at: bit.ly/3UMt7sH.

personalized imagery and memories that defiantly lodge in our nervous systems.

Most researchers agree that dreams and hallucinated images are heavily influenced by an individual's previous real-life experiences, knowledge, and familiarity with existing imagery. The brain integrates sensory experiences and cultural context to construct the visuals seen in dreams and hallucinations. This means that what one dreams or hallucinates is often a remix of familiar elements seen or understood in waking life, although these can be recombined or distorted in novel ways. The content of dreams and hallucinations can therefore be profoundly personal and culturally specific, reflecting the mind's ability to synthesize and reinterpret the stored information.[47]

In addition, research utilizing neurological imaging and lucid dreaming techniques has emphasized the role of personal and cultural experiences in shaping the visual and thematic content of dreams. The capacity of lucid dreamers to consciously interact with the dream environment highlights the influence of learned behaviors and cognitive patterns developed during wakefulness, which can be accessed and manipulated during dreaming.[48]

The theory proposed by Lewis-Williams seems to me insufficient for determining how therianthropic images occur around the globe at the same approximate times in history. Research confirms that dreams and hallucinations are not merely random images but are intricately tied to the dreamer's life and psychological state, shaped by both personal experiences and broader cultural contexts. It seems far-fetched that universally similar imagery, such as therianthropes, would appear to shamans exclusively due to a "hardwiring" of the brain that would ignore personal memories in favor of pre-existing imagery.

---

[47] Cambridge Core, "The connection between dreaming, the brain and mental functioning: where are we now?" available at: https://bit.ly/3CtZ3Mt.

[48] 'science News, "The Mysteries of Dreams and Their Impact on Our Lives," available at: https://bit.ly/4fqZgOT.

Carl Jung's theory of the collective unconscious proposed that certain symbols or motifs he called archetypes were universal and innate to the psychological structure of humans. This theory has influenced the thinking of some scholars about the possibility of innate mental content. Lewis-Willams and a few others have suggested that the visual system of the brain can generate imagery known as entoptic phenomena, which they believe to be hardwired into the human visual system. Lewis-Williams has argued that such imagery is evident in prehistoric rock art, suggesting a neurologically universal experience that transcends individual cultural backgrounds.

Though many of Lewis-Williams's assertions are still controversial, I think it likely that neurologically-generated geometric patterns may occur during states of altered consciousness. Research in 1942 by Heinrich Klüver categorized consistent geometric patterns and shapes such as tunnels, spirals, lattices and cobwebs to be inherent to the human visual system.[49] In 1975, research by Ronald K. Siegel and Louis Jolyon West indicated that such patterns were seen by research subjects while in altered states of consciousness produced by sensory deprivation or psychedelic drugs.

I can find no evidence of such "hardwiring" of more naturalistic imagery such as therianthropes.[50] Available research appears to have been limited to interpretive studies of therianthropic rock art across cultures with conclusions based on plausible but theoretical explanation of how such similar imagery could exist in disconnected locations. There is no empirical support for this theory from science.

My chief criticism of the theory of universal, neurologically-generated images focuses on research that confirms dream and hallucinated images rely on previous real-life and personal experiences, knowledge, and familiarity with existing imagery.

---

49   Klüver, Heinrich, "Mechanics of Hallucinations" in *Studies in Personality*, 1942

50   Siefel, Rich K., and West, Louis Jolyon, *Hallucinations: Behavior, Experience and Theory*, 1975.

Recent experiments have used human subjects, many or all of whom knew about or had seen images of therianthropes in stories, myths, literature, photos, drawings, movies and other channels of communications. The concept of therianthropes and images of them had previously been implanted into the minds of these human subjects. There is no way to test this thesis on individuals who do not possess such familiarity. Even if test subjects were plucked from primitive cultures, those cultures would have contaminated it's members with local folklore containing similar concepts and images. There is no way of ensuring that only neurological factors could be proven to be the exclusive source.

Admittedly, there is neither any empirical support for the theory of progressive revelation that suggests Divine Educators introduced certain ideas to primitive humans, who then visually depicted on rocks various transformed creatures to illustrate those spiritual concepts. When we enter the murky terrain of pre-history, we must rely on existing facts and rational thinking to fill in the blanks. Searching pre-history for clues to a common source of religious and civilizing thought is like trying to follow a trail of breadcrumbs through a bakery.

The Wounded Men

In many rock images, therianthropes are seen being wounded with spears or arrows. Scholars have generally interpreted these images as shamans imagining their transformation into animals while entering an alternate state of consciousness through drumming, trance dancing or consuming natural hallucinogens. A prominent theory offered by Lewis-Williams suggests that, in many cases, the process of entering an altered state, or of being in the first stage of an altered state, was accompanied by stabbing and agonizing pains, and it is this agony that is graphically represented in self-portraits by the shamans that appear on the rocky surfaces.

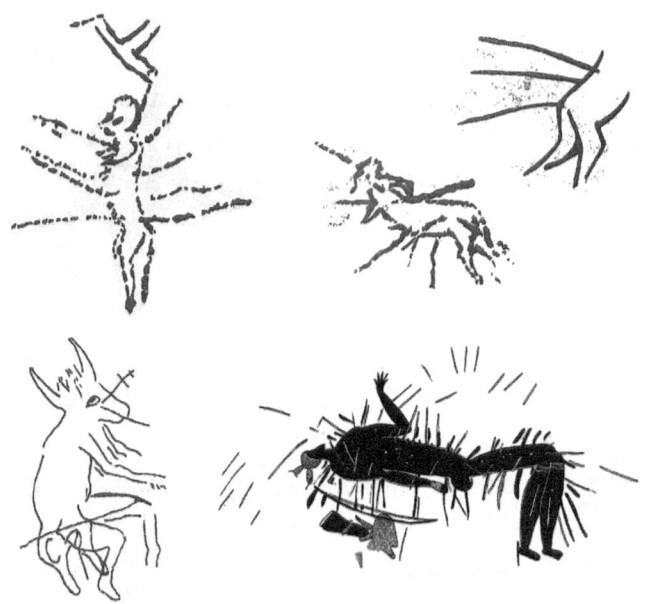

Top Left: Wounded man pierced by many spears from Pech Caves in Southern France; *Top Right*: The wounded men of Cougnac Cave in Payrignac, France; *Bottom Left*: An image of a wounded therianthrope argues against overliteral interpretations of such scenes; *Bottom Right*: San wounded man from South Africa

Such indelible images occur throughout the world, and this phenomenon has become a cornerstone of theorists who say it demonstrates the universality of iconic, neurologically-generated images in humans. Yet, when I study these images of the wounded men, it seems obvious that they are more than just straightforward visualizations of painful somatic hallucinations. The images affect me deeply, as do later depictions of impaled and violently wounded humans—St. Sebastian, or Jesus on the cross, for example. The cave painters, who may have been the experiencers, are speaking to us across thousands of years. I cannot doubt that the artists were trying to communicate some distinct meaning with these wounded figures, just as Christians attach special meaning to a crucifix— the image of Jesus painfully hung on a cross.

Left: Martyrdom of St. Sebastian.
Right: the piercing of Jesus's side.

Considering the rock images created by early humans to be neurological byproducts dilutes their obvious significance to the shamans who created them and to those who would see and likely understand them. Subjectively, I see in them not so much an expression of suffering as a sign of sacrifice—a concept perhaps delivered by the first Divine Educators to early cave artists. At this great distance in time from the original artists, we may not be able to fully decode the meaning of these images, but we can try. Relying only on scientific theories for interpreting these powerful pictures may veil us from important truths that even the earliest humans probably understood. Whether created presciently or not, these images foreshadowed the sacrifices of many Manifestations of God to come.

Is it possible that our two most prized cultural institutions, art and religion, from which have arisen many of the most noble virtues and glorious achievements of our species, were born almost simultaneously in a cave?

Living Forever

Around 32000 BCE, two boys and a middle-aged man were buried in highly ornamented style. They were wearing over thirteen thousand mammoth ivory beads, hundreds of perforated fox teeth and other adornments. Discovered in the 1960s near Sunghir, Russia, the graves also contained other items such as spears, figurines, and the hollowed-out shaft of a woman's femur, which had been packed with red ochre, a pigment often used in painting rock art. Archaeologists estimated it would have taken 2,500 hours to craft just the ivory beads.

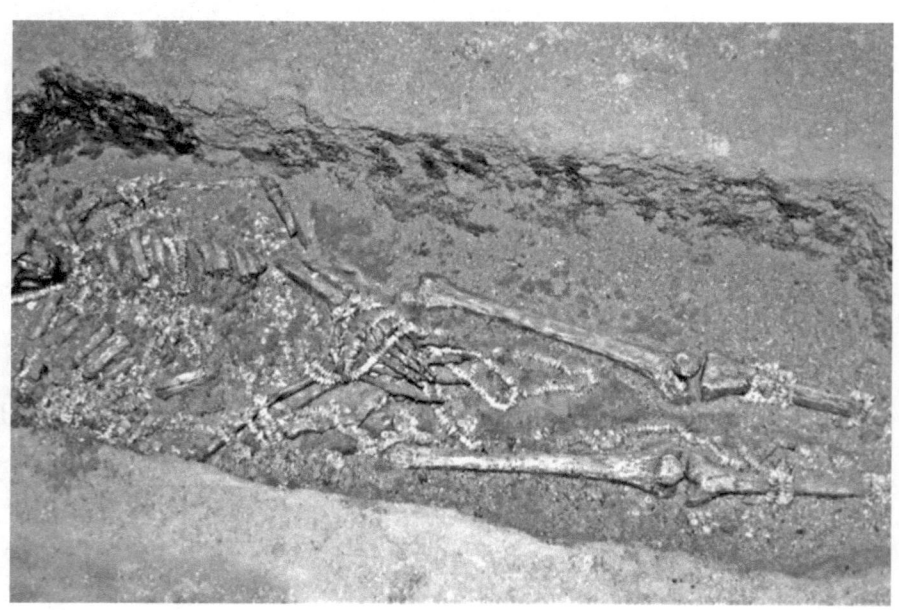

A burial at Sungir covered in beads. (Credit: José-Manuel Benito Álvarez/Wikimedia Commons)

Devoting great energy or resources to dead members of your species does not seem very worthwhile for primitive humans, so this discovery may answer the question of when humans began to invest in the dead. Obviously, they made such an investment as long ago as 32000 BCE.

Such elaborate, time-intensive burials may suggest an answer to motive as well. These anatomically modern humans probably had conceived of an afterlife and other spiritual forces at this early date, as suggested by research on Egyptian mummies and documents that tell us grave goods were thought to be a useful accompaniment to dead persons embarking on a journey to an eternal existence.

Archaeologists often use graves like these as a rough marker for the emergence of religion in human societies. Because this discovered grave sets the marker to a period not long after the first therianthrope image was found in France, it may indicate approximately when religious beliefs originated.

This raises other questions. Is it possible that early Divine Messengers taught these human ancestors the concept of life after death? Known Egyptian hieroglyphics and images explain a well-developed and complex belief in the afterlife, demonstrating that views of the afterlife continued to evolve. It is fascinating that Egyptian society, which emerged in the Predynastic era about 6000 BCE—roughly 26,000 years after the discovered grave at Sunghir—started with the establishment of simple farming communities but show little sign of revising or evolving funereal practices. Egyptian graves similar to those found in Sunghir include grave goods that reveal nonevolved belief in an afterlife.

Pharoah Narmer

Egyptian society, as we typically understand it, emerged under its first pharaoh around 3100 BCE, and the concept of an afterlife quickly evolved into a more elaborate and structured concept as revealed in numerous translated documents and hieroglyphics inscribed on walls. The pharaohs came to be understood as godly figures, often as an earthly manifestation of the god Horus. This divine status was used to legitimize the pharaoh's rule and was crucial for maintaining the social and cosmic order.

Both sides of the Narmer Pallet (public domain, https://commons.wikimedia.org/wiki/File:Narmer_Palette.jpg?uselang=en#Licensing)

One wonders if the first pharaoh, Narmer—sometimes known as Menes—could have been one of the Divine Educators lost to history that our latest wisdom tradition does not name. A study of his life, however, makes this unlikely. Manifestations of God receive direct revelation from God that provides new religious laws and teachings; Narmer is not known for this. Manifestations have all brought spiritual and moral teachings aimed at the progress and unity of humanity; Narmer's legacy, on the other hand, is centered around military conquests and administrative accomplishments. The role of a Manifestation is to foster spiritual awakening and promote qualities like unity, peace and justice; Narmer's historical role was focused on solidifying dynastic rule and territorial governance.

This clarifies the difference between the numinous Manifestations of God who serve as Divine Educators and other mortals who may have significant achievements and respect but lack indelible spiritual authority and lasting impact.

What we know about Narmer we have learned from the Narmer Palette, an archaeological artifact made of siltstone discovered around 1898 in the Main Deposit in the Temple of Horus at Nekhen, Egypt. It contains some of the earliest hieroglyphic inscriptions ever found. This artifact identifies Narmer as Egypt's first pharaoh and shows him wearing the crowns of both Upper and Lower Egypt; consequently, he was the uniter of these two kingdoms.

Following Narmer's reign, Egyptian religion evolved significantly. Compared to the previous three thousand years of Egyptian society and the 34,000-year interlude since the first therianthrope was discovered in France, the pace of change—though still lasting two thousand years, was like a tidal wave. Gods were combined or merged into each other's identities. For example, gods like Amun and Ra were combined into Amun-Ra, becoming a deity synonymous with the sun and creation—a step toward monotheism, it would seem. Then, during the New Kingdom era (1550-1079 BCE), Pharaoh Akhenaten promoted a monotheistic revolution featuring the god Aten, the supreme and only divine force, creator of the universe and source of all life.

After Akhenaten's reign, however, the religious life of Egypt backslid into traditional polytheistic beliefs, demonstrating the powerful rebound effect of outdated by rigidly held paradigms. This describes humankind's propensity for changing its mind about truth. The same thing happened when Moses, as explained in the Bible, left his tribe of monotheistic Hebrews to receive the Ten Commandments from God. When he returned to the Israelites, he was dismayed that they had already reverted to pagan idolatry in His absence.

Squaring Egyptian Rule with Biblical Ancient Hebrews

During the evolution of Egyptian society and religion, the book of Exodus in the Bible inserts the story of the ancient Hebrews who were not yet Jews because Judaism had not yet been codified in the

Hebrew Bible. These were the Israelites or Hebrews mentioned in the Bible, and they lived mainly in the region of Canaan, emerging as a distinct group sometime after 2000 BCE. This was a thousand years after Pharaoh Narmer reigned in Egypt.

The Divine Educator known as Abraham was born around 2000–1800 BCE, according to traditions. Unfortunately, there is no archaeological evidence to support any of the Bible stories about Him. He is revered as the patriarch of the Hebrews and is revered by Judaism, Christianity, Islam and the Bahá'í Faith.

The early Hebrews were mainly agrarian and polytheistic like their Canaanite neighbors. Archaeological and textual evidence shows they worshipped a pantheon of gods with El and Asherah among the main deities, and Baal and Yahweh playing significant roles. The story of the Hebrews's transformation to exclusive monotheism (recognition of only one God) is told by the biblical narratives about the covenants and laws that God delivered to Moses, a Divine Messenger named in the scriptures of our latest wisdom tradition. The book of Exodus in the Bible tells a story of the enslavement of Israelites by Egyptians and their subsequent escape under the direction of Moses. Unfortunately, there is little historical evidence directly linking the Hebrews to specific events of oppression in Egyptian texts, only in biblical sources.

Assuming that the biblical story of Moses and the Israelites is factual, who then was the evil pharaoh who ruled Egypt during the time traditionally associated with the oppression and exodus of these Hebrews? As usual, the answer is complicated by the lack of specific dates, but perhaps the most frequently cited candidate is Ramses II, also known as Ramses the Great, who ruled from 1279–1213 BCE, nearly 1,800 years after Narmer, the first pharaoh. Ramses II is known for extensive building projects and lasting prosperity during his reign. His long rule and extensive use of labor for constructing monumental architecture, such as the city of Pi-Ramesses, has led some scholars to speculate he might be the pharaoh of the Exodus story.

Another candidate is Ramses II's successor, Merneptah, who ruled from 1213–1203 BCE. The Merneptah Stele, an upright stone, which dates from his reign, contains the earliest known mention of "Israel" outside the Bible and appears to indicate a people located in Canaan around 1200 BCE.

Ramses II had been obsessed with the construction of numerous projects, which required thousands of laborers including slaves, but not slaves in the sense of slaves in ancient Rome or pre-Civil War in America. Large Egyptian state projects like temple building and tomb construction typically included a mix of workers composed of:

- **Skilled Artisans and Workers** who lived in worker villages, such as the famous Deir el-Medina. These workers were not slaves in the traditional sense because they were paid and lived in a structured community with rights and legal protections.

- **Corvée Labor**, which is a form of unpaid, forced labor required by the state for its big projects. These laborers were typically not slaves but rather peasants who owed labor as a form of tax. This system was seasonal and allowed peasants to return to their homes and farms when they were not on the job.

- **Prisoners of War and Slaves,** who were used for particularly strenuous tasks, like mining and quarrying. These individuals had fewer rights and could be considered closer to our modern perceptions of slavery. Egyptian "slaves" often had legal rights, could own property, and even negotiate transactions.

The Israelites would have been laborers in this third category, certainly an unpleasant experience but not as harsh as represented in the movie *The Ten Commandments*. This would mean that Moses, formerly an Egyptian Prince by adoption but also a Divine Educator, made a huge impact on both the Egyptians, which he had abandoned, and the Israelites, which he was leading.

While the biblical account of Moses leading the migration of Hebrews out of Egypt may not be historically accurate, the mythic character of Moses, like that of Adam, certainly represents a Divine Educator during the time of the Israelites who possessed the qualities of a Manifestation of God.

The Merneptah Stele

The Divine Call in the Americas

The world's great wisdom traditions have mentioned by name only a handful of Manifestations Who have appeared to humanity, so we are left to conjecture about the many others not specifically mentioned by Them. We have been told that "the names of some of them are forgotten and the records of their lives lost..."[51] Because our existing world religions originated in the Middle East and South Asia, geographies such as the Americas and Australia are not present in their Writings, but Divine Educators may have appeared to the peoples living in those places as well.

It is a difficult task to decode myths that have been gathering ornamentations and modifications for hundreds or thousands of years. Commonly, one would expect that Divine Educators, over time, would be deified by primitive cultures and shaped into various material beings such as animals, which are common in nature and already had acquired various symbolic meanings in primitive minds.

In the Americas, new research has shown that human cultures existed much earlier than previously thought. Human societies in Mesoamerica date back to at least 7000 BCE, with the earliest inhabitants practicing hunting, gathering, and later, agriculture. The domestication of maize around 4000 BCE marked a significant development, leading to more settled agricultural communities. By 2000 BCE, complex societies such as the Olmecs began to emerge, laying much of the cultural and technological groundwork for later civilizations like the Maya and Aztecs. These societies developed city-states, monumental architecture, ceremonial complexes, and sophisticated artistic and intellectual achievements.

Development of more formalized religions began very early in this timeline, as elsewhere in the world. If we believe the scriptures of various world religions, Divine Educators appeared everywhere in the world at the dawn of civilizations so that no societies would be

---

51   Bahá'u'lláh, *Gleanings from the Writings of Bahá'u'lláh*, page 20.

without God's guidance and could begin the gradual acquisition of spiritual knowledge.

The early teachings in Mesoamerica would have gone through the same syncretistic process as religious beliefs in the rest of the world. In many cases, basic truths would have been transformed from metaphors into literal depictions, concepts adapted to cultural standards, some ideas hijacked for various reasons. A Divine Educator metaphorically described as "the royal Falcon on the arm of the Almighty"[52] may have been thought of as a literal falcon and likely depicted as a bird.

No mention is made in the scriptures of our great wisdom traditions of Quetzalcōātl, but of all the potential candidates in Mesoamerica to be a Divine Educator, it would likely be this deity in Aztec and Mayan mythology.

Quetzalcōātl

Quetzalcōātl is an important deity in Mesoamerican mythology, particularly within Aztec and Toltec cultures, and is known by various names and titles across various regions and languages.[53] Here are some of the names and titles associated with Quetzalcōātl:

- **Quetzalcōātl** - The primary Aztec name meaning "Feathered Serpent" or "Plumed Serpent," combining quetzal (a colorful bird with vibrant feathers) and cōātl (meaning serpent or snake).

- **Gucumatz** - Among the K'iche' Maya, Quetzalcōātl is referred to as Gucumatz, a name that also means "Feathered Serpent."

---

52 Bahá'u'lláh, *Tablets of Bahá'u'lláh*, p. 169.
53 Mary Miller and Karl Taube, *The Gods and Symbols of Ancient Mexico and the Maya*; Miguel León-Portilla, *Aztec Thought and Culture: A Study of the Ancient Nahuatl Mind*; David Carrasco, *Quetzalcōātl and the Irony of Empire: Myths and Prophecies in the Aztec Tradition*.

- **Kukulkan** - The Yucatec Maya also worshipped a Feathered Serpent deity known as Kukulkan, who closely resembles Quetzalcōātl in both name and form.

- **Ce Acatl Topiltzin Quetzalcōātl** - This title refers to a legendary Toltec ruler who was often associated or conflated with the god Quetzalcōātl. "Ce Acatl" means "One Reed," a date in the Mesoamerican calendar, and "Topiltzin" translates as "Our Prince" or "Our Lord."

- **Ehécatl-Quetzalcōātl** - In Aztec mythology, this form combines Quetzalcōātl with Ehécatl, the god of wind. Ehécatl-Quetzalcōātl is often depicted as the god responsible for moving the wind to clear paths for the rain.

- **White Tezcatlipoca** - Within Aztec mythology, Quetzalcōātl is sometimes called the "White Tezcatlipoca" (one of the four Tezcatlipocas), distinguishing him from his "brother" gods.

- **Lord of the Morning Star / Tlahuizcalpantecuhtli** - As a god associated with Venus, the morning star, Quetzalcōātl is sometimes referred to as Tlahuizcalpantecuhtli, meaning "Lord of the Dawn."

In some versions of this myth, Quetzalcōātl, which in the Nahuatl language means "Feathered Serpent," is an apt description of how this figure is often depicted.

Quetzalcōātl depicted as the Feathered Serpent.

In Toltec versions, however, Quetzalcōātl is associated with a legendary priest-king named Ce Acatl Topiltzin Quetzalcōātl, a title that means "Our Lord One Reed Quetzalcōātl," where "One Reed" refers to a date in the Mesoamerican calendar. According to legend, this figure was a human ruler and high priest around 1123 CE in the city of Tula (Tollan), one of the major centers of the Toltec civilization.

Ce Acatl Topiltzin Quetzalcōātl is described as a benevolent, wise and moral leader who opposed human sacrifice, promoted learning, and established the "turquoise age" (ie., golden age) in ancient Tollan. His teachings on morality, art, and knowledge reflected the ideals attributed to Quetzalcōātl as a god. This historical or semi-mythical figure eventually became conflated with the deity Quetzalcōātl, making it difficult to distinguish between the god and the legendary king in later stories.

You may recall that this happened also with Jesus. More than three hundred years after Jesus's death, a conference of Catholic bishops voted to declare him God by creating an entity called the Trinity—God the Father, God the Son, and God the Holy Ghost.

Stone carving of Quetzalcōātl in human form.

In various myths, Quetzalcōātl appears in a human form to teach people essential skills and arts. He is often described as a bearded, white man in long robes. He is credited with introducing practices like agriculture (especially maize cultivation), writing, art, and religious knowledge. In these narratives, Quetzalcōātl takes on the role of a wise teacher or priest, directly interacting with humans and guiding them in ways that elevate their civilization. It is easy to imagine Quetzalcōātl, a human incarnation of the gods, as a Divine Educator, though we have no scriptural confirmation of this.

In the story of his departure in human form, Quetzalcōātl is deceived by Tezcatlipoca, the embodiment of change through conflict. Quetzalcōātl experiences shame after being tricked into drinking pulque (an alcoholic drink), leading him to abandon his people and sail eastward, but he promises to return one day. In this story, he behaves in a very human way, showing emotions like regret, shame and sorrow.

A leading American authority on Quetzalcōātl—Henry B. Nicholson, often referred to as the country's greatest scholar of the Aztec civilization—wrote with academic confidence that Quetzalcōātl was likely a historical person:

> **First, and most importantly, I believe that it is quite possible that there was an "original" Topiltzin Quetzalcōātl, an actual person who lived on this earth but who later apparently became inextricably fused (and confused) with more than one deity—and probably with later rulers as well.[54]**

Nicholson summarized what little is known about Quetzalcōātl's religious forms as learned from sacred indigenous traditions:

> **Under his benevolent rule no human sacrifice was permitted, only that of quail, butterflies, snakes, and large grasshoppers.[55]**

Quetzalcōātl challenged the "sacrificial logic" and militarism of ancient Mexican culture by abolishing the entrenched practice

---

54 Henry B. Nicholson, *Topiltzin Quetzalcoatl: The Once and Future Lord of the Toltecs*, p. 259.

55 Henry B. Nicholson, *Topiltzin Quetzalcoatl: The Once and Future Lord of the Toltecs*, p. 10

of human sacrifice. Quetzalcōātl taught (and exemplified) prayer and penance as essential practices of a functional new religion. And according to a long-held prophetic tradition, Quetzalcōātl insisted he would return one day to reclaim his throne.

In the Aztec ritual calendar, different deities were associated with the cycle-of-year names: Quetzalcōātl was tied to the year Ce Acatl (1 Reed), which correlates to the year 1519. and much of the population believed this would be the year of Quetzalcōātl's return.

> In one of the amazing coincidences of history, the Cortes expedition arrived in the year 1519, known to the Aztecs as the year 1 Reed (ce acatl), which was the birthdate and calendar name of Topiltzin Quetzalcōātl.[56]

Motecuhzoma (Montezuma), the last Aztec emperor of Mexico, tragically mistook the Spanish conquistador, Hernán Cortés, for the return of Quetzalcōātl. The conquest, clearly a collision of two worlds, would one day be reversed, according to the prophecy of Quetzalcōātl's return.

Quetzalcōātl-and-Tezcatlipoca

---

56   David Carrasco, *Daily Life of the Aztecs: People of the Sun and Earth*, p. 216.

There are two interesting parallels between Quetzalcōātl and the named Divine Educators. First, the story of Quetzalcōātl's departure stresses the dangers of intoxication in a land filled with hallucinogenic botanicals like ayahuasca that were most likely used by shamans. Our two most recent world religions—Islam and the Bahá'í Faith—both prohibit followers from using intoxicating substances. Second, the "ascension" of Quetzalcōātl into the heavens after leaving this mortal realm explains why he is often associated with the planet Venus. But more striking is how this tale reflects the account of Jesus's bodily ascension into heaven as found in the New Testament. The Toltecs could not have known about the ascension of Jesus.

Another mysterious commonality exists between Mesoamerica and Egypt, two cultures that also had no direct contact, thus no way of sharing beliefs. Osiris is one of the primary gods in the Egyptian pantheon, known primarily for his role as the god of the Underworld. In Egyptian mythology, among the younger siblings of Osiris were Seth, the god of chaos and war, and Isis, the goddess of healing and rebirth. Isis and Osiris eventually married and became the first queen and pharaoh of Egypt.

While Quetzalcōātl and Osiris are from distinct cultures (Mesoamerican and Egyptian) with no historical connection, they share symbolic and thematic similarities that have led scholars to compare them. Here are some of these points of association between Osiris and Quetzalcōātl:

- **Both embody elements of life and death**. Osiris is directly associated with the afterlife, resurrection, and rebirth, being a god who dies and is resurrected annually in Egyptian mythology. Quetzalcōātl, in some Mesoamerican traditions, is linked to cycles of death and rebirth, particularly through his connection to agriculture, as a god of wind and life, and his legendary promise to return.

- **Both are associated with agriculture and fertility.** Osiris was worshipped as a god of vegetation, particularly important for his association with the Nile's flooding and the growth of crops. Quetzalcōātl, similarly, was considered a god of wind and air, elements vital for rain and thus crop cultivation, and was directly worshipped as a patron of the priesthood and learning but also connected to the earth.

- **Both are seen as cultural heroes** who brought civilization to their people. Osiris is often credited with teaching the Egyptians the arts of civilization, such as agriculture and religious rituals. Similarly, Quetzalcōātl is credited with introducing important cultural and technological advancements to the Mesoamerican peoples, such as the calendar and the knowledge of metallurgy.

- **Similar iconography and symbolism**: The iconography of both deities often involves symbols of regeneration and eternal life. Osiris is often depicted as a mummified king, symbolizing his role in the afterlife and resurrection. Quetzalcōātl is often depicted as a feathered serpent, combining the terrestrial (serpent) and the divine (feathers, symbolizing heavens), embodying spirituality and earthly existence.

- **Both have moral and ethical overtones**: Both deities are associated with moral and ethical teachings. Osiris's story emphasizes justice and the importance of moral integrity in the judgment of the dead. Quetzalcōātl's legends often promote values such as knowledge, spirituality, and foresight.

These themes of life, death, resurrection, cultural advancement, and morality highlight deep and universal human concerns today, reflecting why such figures resonate strongly. But in these early times, those themes were likely not high on the priority lists of these people.

Some experts suggest the similarities likely arise from a shared human experience since there is no direct historical or cultural connections between ancient Egypt and Mesoamerica. If the concept of the appearance of Divine Educators were allowed into their theory-making, the conclusions may be different. The simplest and most compelling explanation for me is that a shared, unified message had been communicated to both cultures. And not only to these two, but many others as well.

The fantastic images of the "Feathered Serpent" may seem too unbelievable to take seriously, but they are no more imaginative than the fanciful depiction of gods in Hindu temples and artwork. Once Divine Educators become wrongly deified so that even Their individual virtues become gods, the important messages They brought to humanity become subverted by the myth-making process.

A relief carving of the Feathered Serpent

Some scholars refuse to consider Quetzalcōātl a religious leader comparable to Buddha or Jesus Christ because "no comparable systemized body of religious doctrine seems to have stemmed from his life or teachings,"[57] only oral traditions. Perhaps these scholars

---

57 Henry B. Nicholson, *Topiltzin Quetzalcoatl: The Once and Future Lord of the Toltecs*, p. 264.

have forgotten that the Patriarch Abraham also left no systemized body of religious doctrine.

Nevertheless, the absence of a body of religious doctrine that was likely lost in the mists of antiquity does not mean it did not exist. Deganawida, the "Great Peacemaker," was considered to be a prophet who counseled peace among the warring tribes of North America but left behind no systematized body of religious doctrine. Like Deganawida, Quetzalcōātl stopped the unnecessary shedding of human blood by ritual or warfare and inaugurated a fresh, vibrant civilization.

Although Quetzalcoatl is not named in Bahá'í Writings, some Bahá'ís recognize in him qualities that make him comparable to Buddha, Zoroaster, Jesus or Muhammad. And they see Bahá'u'lláh as the return of the spirit and power of Quetzalcōātl as well as of all other former Manifestations. Like the metaphor of the "Feathered Serpent" often used to depict Quetzalcōātl, Bahá'u'lláh referred to each prior Manifestation of God as the "royal Falcon."

> I am the Sun of Wisdom and the Ocean of Knowledge. I cheer the faint and revive the dead. I am the guiding Light that illumineth the way. I am the royal Falcon on the arm of the Almighty. I unfold the drooping wings of every broken bird and start it on its flight.[58]

Author Christopher Buck beautifully sums up the belief of many indigenous Bahá'ís in these words that begin by describing the quetzal, a strikingly colored bird:

> The Resplendent Quetzal is crimson-breasted, with iridescent, emerald plumage that shimmers with golden-green to blue-violet light in the sunlight. Baha'u'llah, many Baha'is believe, may be the return of the spirit

---

58 Bahá'u'lláh, *Tablets of Bahá'u'lláh Revealed After the Kitáb-i-Aqdas*, p. 169.

> and power of Quetzalōātl for having brought new teachings that restore the dignity of indigenous peoples with respect for their cultures and sacred traditions, while establishing a connection with the wider world, in a true "unity in diversity"—where the royal Falcon, as the Resplendent Quetzal, radiates spiritual light in the cloud forests of purity and wisdom.[59]

Various historical texts say that Quetzalcōātl spoke of a new religion coming in the thirteenth Toltec Era upon his return from the east. But before he returned, men also would come and conquer the Indians, forcing on them a different religion. But after that, upon Quetzalcōātl's return, all the "ancient glory" would return. He would bring the "advent of a new spiritual order" and return as he had left, from the east across the sea.

One of these Mayan prophetic writings, called the *Chilam Balam of the Itza Maya*, is reproduced below. The Chilam Balam were elite spiritual leaders of the post-Conquest Mayan culture. Their social positions were similar to those of priests. Many of the Mayan towns like Itza had their own Chilam Balam, whose book would take the name of the town. These texts followed the Mayan custom of first predicting their history and then living it. It may be that no other cultures have ever gone so far in this direction.

The *Book of Chilam Balam of the Itza Maya* was a sacred text prepared by generations of priests to record the past and predict the future. The official prophet of each twenty-year rule was the Chilam Balam, or Spokesman of the Jaguar—the Jaguar being the supreme authority charged with converting the prophet's words into fact. The book presents a world of incredible numerological order with a society slowly yielding to Christianity and Spanish political pressure but never surrendering.

---

59 Christopher Buck, *Quetzalcoatl, the "Plumed Serpent,"* available on bahaiteachings.org at https://bahaiteachings.org/quetzalcoatl-the-plumed-serpent/.

When the **Katun 13** Ahau is coming to an end
    [ca. 1844]...
The sign of the true God on high, there will come to us
The **upright beam** [the standard of God], it will
    manifest itself
To **light the world.**
The union ended, envy ended,
When the bearer of the future sign came to us,
The priest lord,
You shall see it from afar
Coming. The fame of the beam [standard] comes
To awaken us. From everywhere
It comes to us. To the power of Itzamna
Approaches our master, Itza.
Your brother is coming now.
Receive your bearded guests from the east,
Bearers of the standard of God.
Receive the word of God which
Comes to us on the **day of resurrection**
Which is feared by all in the world, Lord
You are the unique God who created us
Take advantage of the word of God
Whose sign you raise on high
Whose beam you raise upright
That you raise upright so that it may be seen
It changes the splinters that come out of it
It changes them after the rainbow appears
Shown throughout the world,
It is the sign of the true God of heaven.
That is the one you shall worship, Itzas
You are going to worship its ensigns on high
You are going to worship the true faith
You are going to worship the True God
Believe the word of the One God,
For his word came from heaven,

> And it counsels you, Itzas.
> ***It awakens the world***, makes them believe.
> Within another Katun
> I wept for my words, I, Chilam Balam
> When I explained the word of the True God
> Lord ***forever over the earth***.[60]

The prophecies of Chilam Balam foretell the coming of the bearded guests from the east bearing aloft the "upright beam" beginning in 1844 CE. We know this because the first line of this prophecy begins with the mention of "Katun 13." A Katun is a unit of time in the Toltec calendar equal to 7200 days. This calendar starts at Katun 0, the beginning of the Toltec Era dated 1168 CE. Katun 13, then, runs from 1844 to 1896 as this table shows.

Toltec Era	CE Year
Katun 0	1168 CE
Katun 1	1220 CE
Katun 11	1740 CE
Katun 12	1792 CE
Katun 13	1844 to 1896

This prophecy claims that a new Messenger will come to present the "word" of the "One God" come down "from heaven" which will "light the world" and "awaken" humanity on the "day of resurrection."

The Baha'i Faith began in 1844 CE, so it matches the prophecy. The bearded guests from the east may be Baha'u'llah and his forerunner, the Báb, who come from the east (Persia.) These Manifestations of God brought the message that will "light the world"

---

60 A note attached on this codex reads: "Copied by D. Juan Pio Perez on October 25, 1837..." This segment is excerpted from *The Codex Perez and the Book of Chilam Balam of Maani* translated and edited by Eugene R Craine and Reginald C. Reindorp, University of Oklahoma Press, 1979.

and "awaken" humanity on the "day of resurrection." Referring to this "day of resurrection," the Bahá'í writings explain that with the declaration of the Báb in 1844:

> The Sun of Reality hath appeared and flooded all regions with its glorious light; it has upraised the Standard of Oneness of the world of humanity and summoned all mankind to the refulgent Truth... Awake! Awake! Become mindful!... Ere long this transcendent Light will wholly enlighten the East and West![61]

Other Indigenous Messengers of God

In acknowledgement of the never-ceasing rain of God's progressive revelation to humankind, there have been many messengers who have taught and inspired native and Indigenous peoples.

> Among the bounties of God is revelation. Hence revelation is progressive and continuous. It never ceases. It is necessary that the reality of Divinity with all its perfections and attributes should become resplendent in the human world. The reality of Divinity is like an endless ocean. Revelation may be likened to the rain. Can you imagine the cessation of rain? Ever on the face of the earth somewhere rain is pouring down.[62]

I have no authority to designate indigenous messengers as Manifestations of God, but our most recent wisdom tradition has made the following remarkable letter dated March 22, 1988, from the Bahá'í Faith's Universal House of Justice, a democratically elected international council that oversees the affairs of the Bahá'í world.

---

61 'Abdu'l-Bahá in a Tablet written to Dr. George Augur in Tokyo, *Japan Will Turn Ablaze!*, Bahá'í Publishing Trust of Japan, 1992.
62 Abdu'l-Baha, *The Promulgation of Universal Peace*, p. 378.

> It is, of course, true that new movements of thought, especially in the field of religion, tend to obliterate old ones, or to transform their nature in the eyes of the people ....
>
> The Baha'i attitude to earlier religions... is not that they are false or "heathen," but that, at root, they are all true and that these fundamental truths still persist within them. Baha'is encourage Indians in South America, for example, to see and reverence the profound spiritual truths which are to be found in both their pre-Christian religions and in the Catholicism which, in later centuries, has to varying degrees supplanted or overlaid their archaic faiths. Through the Baha'i teachings, the inner conflict which many still feel between their ancient religions and Christianity is resolved and, at the same time, they are enabled to understand their spiritual unity with the peoples of other continents, such as Buddhists, Hindus and Muslims with whom they will undoubtedly come into contact with increasing frequency.[63]

This letter not only states the manner in which progressive revelation occurs but establishes that there are fundamental truths embedded in each religion, if we could only separate the divinely inspired elements from the manmade. Rather than exterminating older beliefs and traditions, we should consider all with respect and search them for meaning. Bahá'ís recognize that indigenous religions have often been marginalized or suppressed due to colonialism, globalization and religious prejudices. The Bahá'í concept of cultural preservation is guided by a profound belief in unity in diversity, which encourages respect for the traditions and practices of indigenous peoples as part of humanity's spiritual and cultural heritage.

---

63   Letter dated 22 March 1988, written on behalf of the Universal House of Justice to a National Spiritual Assembly.

The writings of our most recent wisdom tradition were largely written to audiences of believers in the former major wisdom traditions. I think this is why the authors refer chiefly to the Founders of those Abrahamic religions. But this does not mean that other religions including indigenous belief systems did not have guidance from Messengers of God. In fact, we are told directly that they did:

> Unto the cities of all nations He hath sent His Messengers, Whom He hath commissioned to announce unto men tidings of the Paradise of His good pleasure, and to draw them nigh unto the Haven of abiding security, the Seat of eternal holiness and transcendent glory.[64]

In this passage, indigenous and folk religions are seen as valid expressions of divine truth tailored to the specific needs of their communities. Their contributions to the global spiritual heritage are deeply valued. Through its principles of unity and respect for diversity, the Bahá'í Faith seeks to harmonize these traditions with a universal vision for the oneness of humanity.

Naturalist and anthropologist Vinson Brown has written about some of the indigenous messengers of God in the Americas and Australia. Though incomplete, here is a partial list of those messengers claimed by various peoples:[65]

- Deganawida (Haudenosaunee/Iroquois);
- White Buffalo Calf Maiden (Lakota);
- Sweet Medicine (Cheyenne);
- Quetzalcoatl (Toltec);
- Viracocha (Inca);
- Ulikron (Panama);
- Chinigchinich (a.k.a. Chinigchinix, of the Tongva

---

64 Bahá'u'lláh, *Gleanings from the Writings of Bahá'u'lláh*.
65 Vinson Brown, *Voices of Earth and Sky*.

people of southern California and northern Baja California).

- Lone Man (of the Mandan and Hidatsa First Nations);
- Breathmaker (of the Seminole and Miccosukee peoples);
- Talking God (Navajo/Diné);
- Gluskap (Wabanaki and other First Nations);
- Wesakechak (Cree);
- Nanabush (Anishinaabe [Ojibway]);
- Bunjil (Australian Aboriginal);
- Rainbow Serpent (Australian Aboriginal).
- Mother Corn (Arikara);
- Kuuchamaa (Kumeyaay);
- Ibeorgun of the Guna people of the San Blas Islands in Panama;
- Tunupa, of the southern Andean and Qollasuyu region near Lake Titicaca;
- Bochica (Nemterequeteba) of the Chibchas in Columbia;
- Wangetsmuna, Kamsa in Southern Colombia;
- Iyatiku (Corn Woman): Acoma Pueblo.

In the conclusion to his work, author Vinson Brown added this coda:

> ...often the culture hero promises that he or one like him will return again when the world gets dark and the Earth needs a Light-bringer. Is not all this evidence suggestive that the Great Spirit has a Great Plan, that He has helped mankind in all parts of the world, as a kind Father should and would, and is preparing them for a day of unity, beauty, honor and glory when the dark

> doings of man shall fade away before the blinding light of a New Teacher?⁶⁶

Navajo Prophecies

The Navajo (or Diné, meaning "the People," as they call themselves) are one of the largest Native American tribes in the United States. Their history is rich and complex, blending oral traditions with archeological and historical evidence. They are believed to have migrated from the northern regions of North America around 1000–1400 CE to settle in present-day Arizona, New Mexico, Utah, and Colorado. Their spiritual beliefs focus on harmony with nature (*hozho*), involving complex ceremonies and deities such as Changing Woman, Talking God, Calling God and various Holy People.

In an interview with author Christopher Buck,⁶⁷ Navajo Bitahni Wayne Wilson explained some Navajo prophecies that are embedded in ancient Navajo chants.

> When I was little, there were many Chanters and Medicine Men. But now, very few remain… In order to understand these chants, you have to really submerse yourself in the environment of that ceremonial setting for your spirit to truly understand what is being recited. They are the words of Talking God and the Holy People, passed down for centuries in their original form. … [T]here is a Chant which explains the coming of the Báb and Bahá'u'lláh.

In her Master's Thesis,⁶⁸ religious studies scholar Linda Covey reported that in 1963, Navajo Annie Kahn had written down the oral

---

66 Vinson Brown, *Voices of Earth and Sky*.
67 https://bahaiteachings.org/navajo-traditions-lead-bahai-faith/.
68 Linda S. Covery, *Diné Becoming Bahá'í: Through the Lens of Ancient Prophecies*," A Masters Thesis submitted to the Graduate College of Missouri State University.

story of the Unity chant passed down from her grandfather. This chant told how someone called "He who is the All-Wise, the all-knowing" brought a kind of "Holy Book" to the Navajo people. Because the Navajo unfortunately could not read or write at the time, the "Great One" gave it to them in chants, which could be more easily remembered. Covey summarized Kahn's interpretation of the chant/prophecy this way:

> The Unity Chant says that a new light will come from the east to send its rays to those few Indians who are watching from the tops of the mesas. The "glorious new light" will be recognized by two signs. The first sign is a nine-pointed star whose points symbolize completeness and the love and unity of all religions, races, and nations... The second sign instructs the Diné [Navajo] to look for a "great chief with twelve feathers" or "twelve great principles."

The "new light" is thought to mean a new divine revelation, as it does in most religious prophecies regardless of source. That this new light comes from the east likely points to the Holy Land (birthplace of three major religions) or Iran (birthplace of two major religions.)

Nine-pointed stars in many forms, of course, are a Bahá'í religious symbol.

The Bahá'í nine-pointed star.

My understanding is that the number nine is significant because the numerical value of the word "Bahá" (in Arabic, "glory") is 9 in Abjad numerology, a system where letters are assigned numerical values. As the highest single-digit number, it encompasses all preceding numbers when they are paired, symbolizing comprehensiveness, unity, perfection and fulfillment. In the Bahá'í context, 9 represents the unity of all religions, all humanity, and all creation.

The "twelve feathers" of Navajo prophecy.

According to Annie Kahn, the "twelve feathers" of the expected "great chief" to come refers to the twelve primary spiritual principles of the Bahá'í Faith, which are:

1. The Oneness of God
2. The Oneness of Religion
3. The Oneness of Humanity
4. The Independent Investigation of Truth
5. The Elimination of Prejudice
6. The Equality of Women and Men
7. Universal Education
8. The Harmony of Science and Religion
9. A Spiritual Solution to Economic Problems

10. The Abolition of Extreme Wealth and Poverty
11. World Peace through a Global Framework of Governance
12. A, Universal Auxiliary Language

Covey covers another Navajo prophecy about the "Warrior Twins" of Navajo mythology who were conceived by the goddess Changing Woman. As young men, the Warrior Twins saved the world by slaying all "Monsters" except for Death, Disease, Hunger, Poverty, and Old Age, and gave the Diné [Navajo] the weapons of sacred ceremonies and prayers to use for healing and the good life.[69] Every major religion has an expectation of a "return" of their spiritual leader, including this traditional Navajo belief of the reappearance of the Warrior Twins, sometimes called the "Monster Slayers," who the Navajo considered divine messengers.

Archival material written by an anonymous Navajo explains that the Monster Slayers were expected to return to the Navajo Nation "reborn by the iniquities of all humankind" and give to all humanity "the spiritual weapons to battle and slay all the Monsters." The anonymous Navajo writer spoke of the return of the Warrior Twins as the "New Day" that would be signaled by "terrible trials for the Diné," but the "Wise Ones" [Holy People] knew that they would see "the death throes of the Old Era" and the birth of the "New Era."[70]

The Navajo belief in the return of their Warrior Twins underscores the universality of progressive revelation worldwide. For the Navajo, this prophecy indeed was fulfilled. Since the dawning of the "New Day" in 1844 with the revelation of the Bahá'í era, the Diné (Navajo have been beset by the arrival of American settlers and soldiers, which inflamed intercultural tensions due to competition for land and resources. The Navajo were subjected to raids, displacement,

---

[69] Maureen Trudelle Schwarz, *Molded in the Image of Changing Woman: Navajo Views on the Human Body and Personhood*, p.24.

[70] All direct quotations in this paragraph are from "Navajo Prophesy and its Fulfillment in the Bahá'í Faith" (private collection;) "Reborn by" indicates that the iniquities of humanity required the return or rebirth of the Warrior Twins.

and military campaigns that culminated in the "Long Walk." In 1864, under the leadership of Kit Carson, the US government forcibly relocated the Navajo to Bosque Redondo, a reservation in eastern New Mexico. Thousands of Navajo were forced to march over three hundred miles, suffering extreme hardship, hunger and death. The Bosque Redondo experiment failed, and in 1868, the Navajo signed a treaty allowing them to return to a portion of their original lands.

The Navajo began rebuilding their society, expanding their reservation through subsequent treaties and purchases. The twentieth century brought new challenges, however, including forced assimilation policies like boarding schools. The Navajo people have endured centuries of hardship but remain a vibrant and resilient community deeply connected to their traditions and ancestral lands. Their emphasis on harmony, oral history, and adaptability continues to shape their identity and contributions to the broader American story.

Our most recent wisdom tradition has set this standard for its own governance and the behavior of its members:

> To discriminate against any tribe because they are in a minority is a violation of the spirit that animates the Faith of Bahá'u'lláh. As followers of God's Holy Faith it is our obligation to protect the just interests of any minority element within the Bahá'í Community. In fact, in the administration of our Bahá'í affairs, representatives of minority groups are not only enabled to enjoy equal rights and privileges, but they are even favored and accorded priority. Bahá'ís should be careful never to deviate from this noble standard even if the course of events of opinion should bring pressure to bear upon them. The principles in the Writings are clear, but usually it is when these principles are applied that questions arise... [71]

---

71 On behalf of the Universal House of Justice, February 8, 1970: *Lights of Guidance*, p. 528.

Chapter 7:
Aliens or Divine Educators?

The theory of ancient astronauts, also known as the ancient alien theory, suggests that extraterrestrial beings visited Earth in prehistoric times and interacted with humans, influencing ancient human technology, architecture and even religion.

Ideas about extraterrestrial visits to Earth can be traced back to the nineteenth century and earlier with authors like Charles Fort, who wrote about strange archaeological findings and speculated that visitors from other planets had influenced ancient civilizations. In the early twentieth century, some scholars and writers began to interpret ancient myths, religious texts, and archaeological discoveries with a new perspective that allowed for possible extraterrestrial contact. This included interpretations of biblical angels and gods from various mythologies as analogies for alien visitors.

The idea of beings from the sky developing a relationship with ancient humans can be found in various mythologies and religious texts globally. These stories often depict gods or celestial beings who descend from the heavens and possess advanced knowledge, sometimes directly interacting with humans. The emergence of the science fiction genre in the early twentieth century set the stage for reinterpreting extraterrestrial influences in a new light. Novelists like

H.G. Wells and early pulp science fiction magazines featured tales of alien visitors and advanced technologies. These colorful stories and vivid illustrations helped reshape public imagination about life beyond Earth.

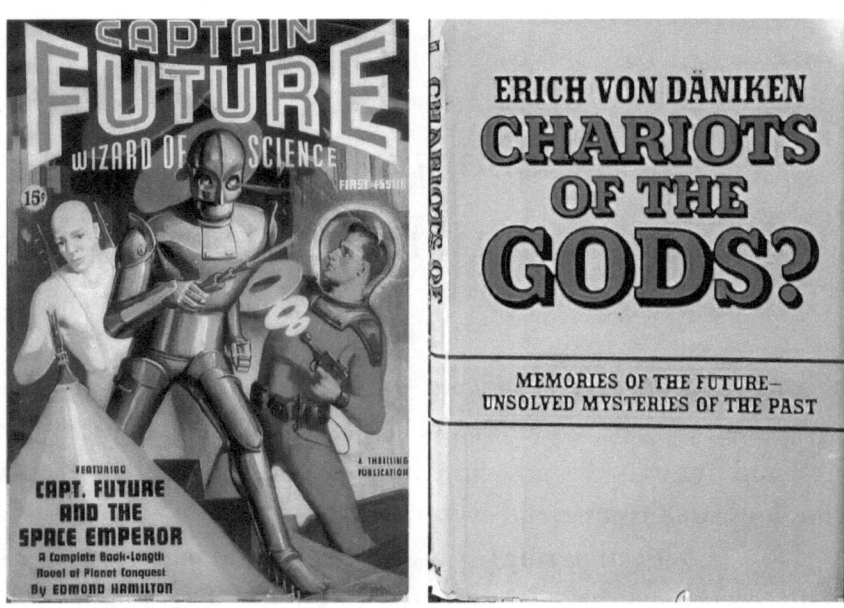

Left: The first edition in 1938 of a pulp science fiction magazine.
Right: The cover of *Chariots of the Gods?* by Erich von Däniken.

The popularity of this theory was given a boost when author Erich von Däniken published his 1968 book *Chariots of the Gods? Unsolved Mysteries of the Past*. In this bestselling book, von Däniken proposed that many ancient technologies and architectural achievements were too advanced for their periods and must have been the result of alien tutelage. He cited examples like the Egyptian pyramids, the Nazca lines in Peru, and the giant stone heads of Easter Island.

After *Chariots of the Gods?* was published, the theory gained widespread attention both in academic circles and popular media. The author's ideas began to be explored and disseminated through documentaries, television series, and public speaking engagements. Then, in the 1970s, Zecharia Sitchin published several books about ancient connections with alien visitors, focusing particularly on his interpretations of Sumerian texts and artifacts. He suggested that an alien race called the Anunnaki from the planet Nibiru had visited Earth thousands of years ago.

Another notable proponent of the theory, Robert K.G. Temple, contributed to the theory with a 1976 book called *The Sirius Mystery* that claimed the Dogon people of Mali possessed knowledge of the Sirius star system that could only have been acquired from extraterrestrial beings.

The theory has been kept alive well into the twenty-first century through various forms of media, notably the History Channel's series *Ancient Aliens*, which debuted in 2009. This series explores many facets of the ancient astronaut theory, bringing it to an even broader audience and weaving it into popular culture, which expanded when the series became available on various streaming platforms like Hulu, Netflix, Disney+ and HISTORY Vault. It has also been syndicated internationally. The success of *Ancient Aliens* reveals the wide appeal of mysteries related to the origin of our species and our past, and the evolution of our religions and technologies.

An ad for the TV series *Ancient Aliens*.

Ancient Aliens Vs. Progressive Revelation

The theory of ancient astronauts and the concept of progressive revelation found in religious writings are quite different in their essence and origins but share some intriguing conceptual similarities.

Transmission of Knowledge

Both concepts involve the transmission of knowledge from a higher, more advanced source to humanity. The ancient astronaut theory suggests that extraterrestrial beings visited Earth in antiquity and shared knowledge or technology with early human civilizations for motives that even sympathetic theorists debate. In our most recent wisdom tradition, progressive revelation refers to the idea that God progressively reveals spiritual and moral guidance to humanity through a series of Divine Messengers, each of whom brings teachings that are suited to the time and place of Their appearance. Clearly stated in scripture, God's motive is to help bring about an ever-advancing civilization.

Evolution of Human Understanding

Both conceptual frameworks propose that human understanding and civilization have evolved over time due to influences that are external and greater than individual human endeavors. For ancient astronaut proponents, this evolution is attributed to extraterrestrial intervention. In the scriptural view, this evolution is seen as a spiritual and moral development guided by successive revelations from God.

Impact on Civilization

Both the theory of ancient astronauts and the concept of progressive revelation suggest that these external inputs have significantly impacted the structure and progress of human civilizations. Ancient astronaut theorists often claim that such interventions explain rapid advancements in technology and culture seen in ancient civilizations. Our latest religious teachings claim that the moral and spiritual teachings brought by Divine Educators shape the social and ethical frameworks of societies.

Cyclical or Periodic Nature

The idea of cycles or periods is evident in both concepts. The ancient astronaut theory often involves recurring visits or influences from extraterrestrials across different times and cultures. Progressive revelation in the Bahá'í Faith involves a continuing cycle of Divine Educators (also called Manifestations of God) who appear throughout human history.

★ ★ ★

Despite similarities, the underlying basis of these concepts is vastly different. One is rooted in interpretations of discovered archeological and textual anomalies, while the other is a theological principle central to a major world religion and suggested by its predecessors. These differences highlight how similar ideas of knowledge and civilization development can arise from very different worldviews and premises.

Interestingly, this book bridges the gap between the two concepts by reinterpreting anomalous archeological and textual discoveries through a perspective that neither grafts scientific biases onto religious concepts nor forces an extraterrestrial paradigm onto strange artifacts and historic texts. This book is an attempt to offer a third alternative, possibly the oldest one, as it dates back to the dawn of civilization—a logical yet spiritual concept of the origins of civilization and religion.

The Problem of Human Interpretations

Everything humans encounter in life is subject to interpretation. What is it? What does it mean? How and why did it come into being? Is it relevant to me or my beliefs? These are important questions, especially when dealing with religion—and also rock art, which holds clues to the roots of religion. These subjects live in a murky land dominated by ambiguity, bias, debate, scarcity of tangible proof, and an abundance of hubris. Rock art, I think, demonstrates this.

Below is a rock painting of a large humanoid figure surrounded by smaller figures. Ancient nomads, the ancestors of the Navajo people, created this larger-than-life scene perhaps seven thousand years ago—about 5000 BCE, two thousand years before the first Egyptian pharaoh, Narmer.[72]

Called the "Holy Ghost" panel, this artwork is the highlight of a vast mural nearly three hundred feet long located in Utah's Horseshoe Canyon. David Sucec, a former professor of painting and art history at Virginia Commonwealth University, has called this mural the "Sistine Chapel" of Utah's Barrier Canyon. The mural features about eighty different figures, and scholars vigorously debate a variety of theories as to its meaning. With no tangible proof of the artists' intent, dispute rages on.

The "Holy Ghost" panel in Utah's Horseshoe Canyon dated to approximately 5000 BEC.

---

72 *Smithsonian Magazine*, available at: https://www.smithsonianmag.com/arts-culture/traces-of-a-lost-people-84026156/.

The rock artists created this panel by filling their mouths with paint tinted with red ochre and then blowing clouds of it onto the sandstone. The ghostly, tall figure is eight feet tall, larger than life. The creation of such a massive mural is akin to putting up a billboard, which no one would do unless there was an important message to announce. Without written text, however, that message remains ambiguous and confusing.

This Holy Ghost panel is important here because the TV series *Ancient Aliens* has presented it as #1 on its list of rock art exemplars that support the theory of extraterrestrials visiting ancient humans. According to that ET theory, the large, ghostlike figure in this panel must an alien because he is bigger and appears to feature the large eyes that contemporary human "witnesses" report aliens as having.

As I look at this panel, I do not see an alien entity. I see a figure revered by the others who surround him, possibly made taller to visually indicate his importance or power. This painting could represent an encounter of humans with a Divine Educator. The large eyes that ancient alien theorists see on the figure's head I interpret as objects that may surround some kind of headdress. The "spacesuit," which some believe is worn by the main figure, I decipher as a furry, animal-skin covering, and the long garments worn by the humans are perhaps shaman ceremonial robes.

I cannot prove my interpretation, ET theorists cannot prove their view, and neither can legions of scholars who disagree with each other verify their interpretations. But that is not the point of this section. Individual verses of the Bible have been assigned thousands of different meanings. There are no witnesses left to provide first-hand testimony to the "miracles" described in any scriptures. No known Divine Educator is alive today. But what we have is a trail of circumstantial evidence left behind in the form of rock art (tough to date and interpret), ancient myths (difficult to reconcile and demythologize), historical records (hard to verify), sacred texts (difficult to authenticate and interpret,) and incomplete knowledge of everything. Thus, facts are always subject to change.)

Nevertheless, we must always search independently for truth with rational thinking and an open mind. A main teaching of the Bahá'í Faith, our most recent great wisdom tradition, is that the first duty for everyone is to investigate reality. What does this mean?

> **It means that man must forget all hearsay and examine truth himself, for he does not know whether statements he hears are in accordance with reality or not. Wherever he finds truth or reality, he must hold to it, forsaking, discarding all else; for outside of reality there is naught but superstition and imagination...[73]**

Truth is relative to the best available information we have at the time. It is always fair to test what we believe and what we have been told. If we find something cannot be reconciled with the facts, it is fair to dismiss that information. If we find something that is not logical or reasonable to be true, it fair to challenge that information by researching the facts. If we discover something for which we cannot fathom a sensible meaning, it is fair to develop a theory that can be further tested against other information.

In this book, I am testing the concept of progressive revelation against available evidence. In the process, I am presenting my personal conclusions about evidence I am finding. It is your duty to examine truth yourself, for as the previous quotation tell us, "outside of reality there is naught but superstition and imagination."

---

73   Abdu'l-Baha, *The Promulgation of Universal Peace*, p. 61.

Chapter 8:
Understanding the Prophets

The language used in the scriptures of the various wisdom traditions can be confusing. We find multiple English-translated terms that refer to prophets—individuals who had a special relationship with God and exhibited keen insights and other gifts. Despite the proliferation of names, however, we learn from our most recent wisdom tradition that there are two kinds of prophets—independent Prophets and dependent Prophets. In the following quotation, 'Abdu'l-Bahá refers to "the second sort of prophets," for which I have assigned the term "dependent Prophets" for ease of reference.

> Universally, the prophets are of two kinds. One are the independent Prophets Who are followed; the other kind are not independent and are themselves followers. The independent Prophets are the lawgivers and the founders of a new cycle... The Manifestations of universal Prophethood Who appeared independently are, for example, Abraham, Moses, Christ, Muhammad, the Báb and Bahá'u'lláh. But the others who are followers and promoters are like Solomon, David, Isaiah, Jeremiah and Ezekiel. For the independent Prophets are founders; They establish a new religion and make new creatures

> of men; They change the general morals, promote new customs and rules, renew the cycle and the Law. Their appearance is like the season of spring, which arrays all earthly beings in a new garment, and gives them a new life. With regard to the second sort of Prophets who are followers, these also promote the Law of God, make known the Religion of God, and proclaim His word. Of themselves they have no power and might, except what they receive from the independent Prophets.[74]

Different Titles for Independent Prophets

In our newest wisdom tradition, the most frequently used term for an independent prophet is "Manifestation of God," but many other terms refer to Manifestations of God appearing on Earth, including Divine Educators, Messengers of God, and Luminaries. This can be confusing, because in the Bahá'í Writings these terms can also refer to "lesser prophets." Because of the cultural and linguistic differences of the places and times of scriptural revelation, other synonyms with similar meanings have been used. Here are some of the most common ones that I believe refer to the concept of Manifestations of God.

Hindu References to Manifestations

- **Avatar** refers to the descent or manifestation of a deity on earth, particularly in the form of Vishnu's Avatars like Krishna and Rama.
- **Saguna Brahman** refers to the aspect of Brahman (the ultimate reality) with attributes, manifesting in forms and deities.
- **Ishvara** refers to the personalized manifestation of God or Supreme Being, often in a deity form (e.g., Shiva, Vishnu).

---

74 'Abdu'l-Bahá, *Some Answered Questions,* pages 164-166; 149-150

- **Darshan** is the experience of seeing a deity or holy person believed to be a form of God's manifestation.

Buddhist References to Manifestations

- **Nirmanakaya**: In Mahayana Buddhism, this refers to the manifestation of the Buddha in a form that interacts with the world.
- **Bodhisattva:** While not God, bodhisattvas are manifestations of enlightened beings who embody divine compassion and assist in guiding others toward enlightenment.

Zoroastrian Reference to Manifestations

- **Fravashi**: Guardian spirits that serve as manifestations of Ahura Mazda's divine protection and guidance.

Jewish References to Manifestations

- **Shekinah** refers to the divine presence of God, particularly in the context of God's dwelling among the people, such as in the Temple or in times of revelation.
- **Malach Yahweh (Angel of the Lord)** is a representation or manifestation of God's presence in a way that interacts with humans (e.g., in the burning bush or encounters with Abraham).
- **Glory of God (Kavod)** is a manifestation of God's majesty and divine presence often depicted as light or cloud (e.g., Exodus 24:17).
- **Messiah** harkens back to the Jewish concept of an expected king of the Davidic line who would deliver Israel from foreign bondage and restore the glories of its golden age.

Christian References to Manifestations

- **Messiah** harkens back to the Jewish concept of an expected king of the Davidic line who would deliver Israel from foreign bondage and restore the glories of its golden age. To many Christians, Jesus was the prophesied messiah of Judaism but was also a Manifestation or "Son" of God (John 11:27).

- **Son of God** is a reference to Jesus in his relationship to God (John 1:34). In the fourth century, this was interpreted to mean Jesus was literally the Son of God, thus God Himself.

- **Savior** refers to Jesus as a Manifestation of God with an emphasis on his ability to save the souls of sinners to prevent eternal damnation.

- **Incarnation** refers to God becoming flesh in the person of Jesus Christ (e.g., John 1:14). The inference is slightly different than "manifestation," however, which proposes that a Manifestation of God is not God incarnate but a perfect reflection of God's attributes.

- **Theophany** is a visible manifestation of God to humans (e.g., burning bush in Exodus 3:2-4).

- **Emmanuel** means "God with us," often used to refer to Jesus as the manifestation of God (Matthew 1:23).

- **Logos** refers to Jesus Christ as the Word (or Logos) of God, the divine reason and the manifestation of God's will (John 1:1).

Islamic References to Manifestations

- **Rasul.** Meaning "Messenger," a Rasul is a prophet who has been given a specific scripture or set of laws to deliver to their people. They are tasked with conveying a divine message.

- **Al-Bashir**. Meaning "Bearer of Good News," this term is used for a messenger who brings glad tidings of salvation, blessings, or divine mercy.

- **Tajalli**: Refers to God's self-manifestation in the world. It is not a physical appearance but rather the idea of God's presence being reflected in creation and revelation.

- **Al-Nur (The Light)**: Refers to God's manifestation as divine light, a symbol of God's guidance and presence (Surah An-Nur, 24:35).

These terms and their meanings provide a glimpse of how different audiences interpreted the words of the Revealers of the Scriptures and their commentators. The variances we find certainly reflect a continuing refinement of this understanding.

In Hinduism, for example, the belief in Avatars like Krishna and Rama illustrates the recurring appearance of divine figures who guide humanity according to its changing needs. In Christianity, this view continues, but the concept of Jesus as the "Word" (Logos) made flesh reflects the idea of a Manifestation of God who brought a new and transformative spiritual message. Islam also recognizes multiple Messengers (*Rasul*) and Prophets (*Nabi*) such as Adam, Noah, Jesus and Muhammad, who were sent at different times with messages relevant to their communities. The Qur'an acknowledges the validity of revelations prior to Muhammad's, as does the Bahá'í Faith.

Other Recognized Manifestations (Independent Prophets)

Earlier, we listed Manifestations, all of Whom directly or indirectly founded a major wisdom tradition still extant (though the light of Zoroastrianism has dimmed considerably.) Several other notable figures, however, have also been acknowledged as Manifestations of God, a station much greater than the host of minor dependent prophets.

Adam

According to our most recent wisdom tradition, Adam was the first Manifestation of God. Regarding Adam's physical existence, Bahá'í teachings offer a flexible perspective. While Adam is acknowledged as a Manifestation of God, Bahá'í interpretations of sacred texts often emphasize symbolic meanings over literal historical details. In this sense, Adam may be understood both as a real person whose reality has been lost to history, and also as a symbolic figure representing the emergence of human consciousness and the beginning of divine guidance to humanity.

This interpretation aligns with the view that religious stories often contain layers of metaphor and spiritual significance beyond literal history. The Bahá'í Faith does not necessarily require a literal belief in the events described in scriptures, such as the parable of Adam in Genesis, allowing for both spiritual symbolism and scientific understanding of human origins.

Though we have no historical information about Adam—which is just a name assigned to the first Manifestation of God to begin the current chain of revelation—there must have been a first One to be given the mission of guiding early humanity and establishing the rudimentary principles of civilization and morality. As a metaphor, Adam represents humanity's collective spiritual history and growth. Thus, Adam began the chain of progressive revelation to humanity. As our most recent Manifestation wrote:

> **Contemplate with thine inward eye the chain of successive Revelations that hath linked the Manifestation of Adam with that of the Báb.**[75]

---

75 Bahá'u'lláh, *Gleanings from the Writings of Bahá'u'lláh*, Section XXXI, p. 74.

Noah

The Bahá'í Faith regards Noah as one of the early Manifestations of God who brought divine guidance to humanity. He is seen as a major prophet who, like other Manifestations, played a pivotal role in advancing human civilization spiritually and morally.

Noah is generally viewed symbolically, especially in the Bahá'í teachings, where the parable of Noah and the Great Flood represents a time of spiritual renewal and the struggle against societal corruption. His mission is considered essential in the process of progressive revelation, where each Manifestation builds upon the teachings of those who came before.

Like Moses, Jesus, Muhammad and others, Noah brought a divine message suited to the needs of his time. His spiritual station is considered equal to other Manifestations because each of these figures reflects the will and attributes of God, guiding humanity according to divine wisdom.

Of interest, however, is the discovery in Iraq of a clay tablet the size of an iPhone Pro covered in cuneiform impressions—the world's oldest known form of writing. Dating back to a period before the Gilgamesh flood legend and around a thousand years before Noah was thought to have lived, this ancient Sumerian tablet is an instruction manual ostensibly provided by the god Enki for the construction of an ark capable of housing many animals in anticipation of a great flood.

Finally translated in 2009 by Dr. Irving Finkel, the "Ark Tablet" specified precise dimensions that would produce a traditional coracle (a round boat made of reeds waterproofed with bitumen) of a massive scale—six meters high and covering an area of 3,500 square meters, nearly two-thirds the size of a football field. If stretched out in a line, the amount of rope prescribed would reach from London to Edinburgh.

> A waterproofed coracle would never sink and being round isn't a problem—it never had to go anywhere: all it had to do was float and keep the contents safe: a cosmic lifeboat.[76]

Was this Ark ever built? Is it possible that this is the source of the myth of Noah's flood and other flood stories around the world? If so, it indicates that the Manifestation referred to as Noah may indeed have had an origin in a time more ancient than thought. If not, these instructions may have been the inspiration for a popular set of myths.

While the historic facts of the biblical Noah's Ark story may not be true, the tale may be based on an earlier remembered event. Almost certainly, its purpose—as with all scripture—was to provide a memorable metaphor for important spiritual truths.

> Noah was sent to a stubborn and rebellious people, who were immersed in a sea of ignorance and heedlessness. For nearly a thousand years, He repeatedly admonished them and exhorted them to follow the right path… By the Ark is meant the Cause of Noah, and by those who were saved in the Ark, those souls are meant who attained the station of certitude and entered the Cause of God.[77]

Even in our modern times, we can understand that the flood symbolizes the consequences of ignoring divine guidance and the transformation brought by the washing away of old traditions and the acceptance of new revelations. Noah's endurance and steadfastness are clearly examples of the trials faced by all Manifestations of God.

---

76 HistoryofInformation.com, available at: https://www.historyofinformation.com/detail.php?id=4060.

77 'Abdu'l-Bahá, *Some Answered Questions*, Chapter 18, p. 79.

Abraham

Abraham can be seen as a foundational figure in the spiritual history of humanity. He is regarded by many as the "Father of Faith" and the progenitor of monotheism in His region. He established the belief in one God, which deeply influenced the missions of later Manifestations, including Moses, Jesus and Muhammad. The Writings of Judaism, Christianity, Islam and the Bahá'í Faith all frequently reference Abraham, highlighting his role in establishing the concept of a covenant between God and humanity. He is honored as a vital link in the chain of divine guidance.

In Christianity, Abraham is revered as a model of faith and obedience. The New Testament often refers to him as a spiritual forefather, and his faith in God's promises is seen as a precursor to the teachings of Jesus. He is considered a key link in the lineage leading to Christ.

In Islam, Abraham (Ibrahim) is highly honored as a prophet and a key figure in establishing the worship of one God. He is considered a "Hanif," someone who maintained pure monotheism before the formal revelations of Judaism, Christianity or Islam. Abraham's willingness to submit to God's will is seen as the ultimate example of faith, and he is directly associated with the Kaaba, a stone building at the center of Islam's most important mosque and holiest site, the Masjid al-Haram in Mecca, which he and his son Ishmael rebuilt, according to Islamic tradition.

While Abraham did not establish an institutionalized religion, his legacy and teachings deeply influenced the formation of the four major monotheistic faiths—Judaism, Christianity, Islam and the Bahá'í Faith. His role as a patriarch and His covenant with God are foundational elements that underpin these religions, making him a central figure in the spiritual history of the Abrahamic traditions.

Dependent Prophets (Minor Prophets)

Dependent (or minor) prophets are terms I use to define those Prophets Who do not have divine authority to initiate a new revelation or religious "dispensation," a divinely appointed era during which a new Manifestation's teachings are in effect. Rather than developing a following of believers, dependent prophets are themselves followers and operate under the authority of the Manifestation of God for their era. This concept originates in Bahá'í teachings.

The primary function of these minor prophets is to propagate, interpret and uphold the teachings of the previous Manifestation so those principles are widely disseminated and applied within society. They act very much like political surrogates do today, representing and promoting the platforms of the candidates they endorse. Unlike the Manifestations they represent, who bring new laws and teachings to suit the evolving needs of humanity, dependent prophets follow the teachings of the Manifestation they serve and have no authority to alter laws or reinterpret teachings. Here are examples of some dependent prophets in various religions.

Judaism

- **Aaron (Harun).** Aaron was the brother of Moses (Musa) and played a significant role as Moses's spokesperson and assistant. He did not establish a new religion but helped Moses convey God's message to the Israelites and was instrumental in maintaining religious practices and teachings. As a dependent prophet, Aaron supported Moses's mission but did not bring any new laws or revelations.
- **Joshua (Yusha).** Joshua was a key figure in leading the Israelites after Moses's death. He helped implement and uphold the laws given to Moses by God but did not bring a new religious dispensation. Joshua is

considered a dependent prophet who helped ensure the survival and continuation of the Mosaic teachings.

- **Elijah (Elias).** In the Bible, Elijah is regarded as a prophet who upheld the worship of God during a time of widespread idol worship among the Israelites. He did not bring new laws but worked to restore the faith of the people in the monotheistic God. Elijah is considered a dependent prophet who worked within the framework of the Mosaic Law, striving to revive adherence to the covenant between God and Israel.

Christianity

- **John the Baptist.** In Christianity, John the Baptist is considered a forerunner of Jesus Christ, preparing the way for his ministry and baptizing followers as a sign of repentance. He did not introduce a new religious dispensation but worked within the existing Jewish framework. John the Baptist is seen as a dependent prophet who acknowledged Jesus as the Messiah and directed people toward him.

- **The Twlelve Disciples**. These individuals were among the first believers in Jesus as the Messiah and were active in evangelizing His message to the greater population.

- **Paul**. The New Testament writer was a missionary and theologian whose dramatic conversion transformed him into a passionate apostle of Christ. A Jew and Roman citizen, he became a tireless church-planter, preacher, and letter-writer.

Islam

- **Ali.** Though Islam does not recognize any "prophets" after Muhammad, Ali, his son-in-law, was both a close companion and the fourth caliph of Islam. He played a pivotal role in early Islamic leadership and is revered as the first Imam in the Shia tradition.

- **Ishmael (Isma'il).** Ishmael is considered a prophet in Islam, particularly revered for his role in the story of Abraham's willingness to sacrifice his son. He upheld the monotheistic teachings of his father, but did not bring a new revelation. Ishmael is a dependent prophet under Abraham, continuing his teachings and playing a foundational role in the lineage of future prophets.

Zoroastrianism

- **Zoroaster's Disciples.** Zoroaster (Zarathustra) is the central figure of Zoroastrianism, a Manifestation of God. His disciples and followers, such as Maidhyoimah and Vishtaspa, are considered to be dependent prophets or spiritual leaders who propagated and reinforced the teachings of Zoroaster. These figures did not bring new religious laws but helped spread the teachings of Zoroaster.

Hinduism

- **Vyasa.** Traditionally considered the compiler of the Vedas and author of the Mahabharata, Vyasa is seen as a sage or *rishi* who played a pivotal role in preserving and organizing the scriptures of Hinduism. He did not introduce new religious laws but reinforced existing Vedic teachings. Vyasa worked within the framework of earlier Vedic revelations.

Notable Figures in the Bábí and Bahá'í Faiths

No figures from early Bahá'í history have been identified as a "dependent" or any other kind of prophet, but there are a number of significant figures who played major roles in the development of these Faiths.

Bábí Faith[78]

- **Quddús (Mullá Muhammad 'Alí-i-Bárfurúshí).** Quddús is considered the foremost of the Letters of the Living, a group of eighteen early followers of the Báb who served in much the same way as the original twelve apostles of Jesus. Quddús was the last and most distinguished member of this group, which collectively helped propagate the Báb's teachings.

  Quddús is regarded as the closest and most important of the Báb's followers. The Báb gave him the title "Quddús," meaning "The Most Holy," and considered him second only to Himself in spiritual rank. Quddús played a leading role in some of the most critical moments of the Bábí movement, including leading the Bábís during the Battle of Fort Shaykh Tabarsí, a significant conflict between the Bábís and the Persian government. His martyrdom at the hands of the authorities became a symbol of devotion and sacrifice within the Bábí community.

- **Táhirih (Fátimih Baraghání).** Táhirih was another of the Letters of the Living and is one of the most prominent female figures in the Bábí movement. She is renowned for her powerful advocacy for women's emancipation, religious reform, and her poetry. Táhirih, also known as "The Pure One," was a fervent disciple of the Báb. She declared her faith in the Báb's teachings and contributed significantly to spreading His message, particularly in Iraq and Persia. She is remembered for her bold and radical actions, including removing her veil publicly in a

---

78 Information about the following figures can be found in: Shoghi Effendi, *God Passes By*, in which these individuals are described as "the most distinguished among [the Báb's] disciples."

gathering of Bábí leaders, symbolizing the break from the old religious traditions and the beginning of a new spiritual era.

- **Mullá Husayn (Mullá Husayn Bushrú'í).** Mullá Husayn was the first of the Letters of the Living and the first person to recognize and accept the Báb's station as a Manifestation of God. He is thus one of the earliest and most important figures in the Bábí Faith. Mullá Husayn is known as the first person to encounter the Báb and declare his faith in Him. He was the one the Báb sent to spread His teachings and to bring other disciples to the Báb's cause. Mullá Husayn played a significant role in the early propagation of the Bábí teachings, traveling extensively to teach others about the new message.

Bahá'í Faith

- **'Abdu'l-Bahá.** In the Bahá'í Faith, 'Abdu'l-Bahá, the son of Bahá'u'lláh, is considered the Center of the Covenant, who was the authorized interpreter of his father's teachings but did not bring new laws or revelations. He is not considered a Manifestation of God or a dependent prophet.[79] He guided the Bahá'í community after Bahá'u'lláh's passing, helping to spread and explain the Bahá'í teachings globally.

- **Shoghi Effendi.** Shoghi Effendi, the Guardian of the Bahá'í Faith, guided the Bahá'í community but did not have the rank of a Manifestation of God and is not considered a dependent Prophet. He clarified and elaborated upon the teachings of Bahá'u'lláh and 'Abdu'l-Bahá to ensure their proper interpretation.

---

79   At the official website of the Bahá'í Faith (http://bahai.org) this statement is made: "Abdu'l-Bahá was not a prophet and at no time claimed to have received direct revelation from God."

Shoghi Effendi, ensured[80] the unity and correct understanding of Bahá'u'lláh's message.

Sages and Spiritual Teachers

Our newest wisdom tradition suggests a third category of enormous importance to the world's spiritual evolution by helping inspire, educate and uplift humanity. Bahá'í teachings recognize that many spiritual leaders and founders of religious or philosophical movements may have been divinely inspired or guided, whether or not they claimed to have a divine station. Examples of such leaders are:

- **Socrates**, a Greek philosopher seen as one who reflected divine wisdom and taught the virtues of justice and the soul's immortality.

- **Plato**, a student of Socrates, is recognized for his philosophical contributions on justice, virtue and the ideal society as well as for the enduring influence of his idea.

- **Aristotle**, a student of Plato, is respected as a luminary whose intellectual contributions informed humanity's understanding of the natural and metaphysical worlds.

- **Zoroaster's disciples** preserved the teachings of Zoroaster and upheld His principles of truth, purity and justice.

---

80 Considering his position as the Guardian of the Bahá'í Faith, Shoghi Effendi wrote in *The World Order of Bahá'u'lláh* this statement: Exalted as is the position and vital as is the function of the institution of the Guardianship in the Administrative Order of Bahá'u'lláh, and staggering as must be the weight of responsibility which it carries, its importance must, whatever be the language of the Will, be in no wise over-emphasized. The Guardian of the Faith must not under any circumstances, and whatever his merits or his achievements, be exalted to the rank that will make him a co-sharer with 'Abdu'lBahá in the unique position which the Center of the Covenant occupies—much less to the station exclusively ordained for the Manifestation of God.

- **Confucius** is viewed as a sage and philosopher who promoted moral and ethical teachings that resonate with the principles of divine guidance.
- **Buddhist Teachers and Sages** helped sustain the teachings of enlightenment, compassion, and the Middle Way.
- **Poets and Mystics**, including Persian poets such as Rumi, Sa'di and Hafiz, are highly regarded for their mystical insights and poetic expressions of divine love and spiritual truths.

I would also include the following in this category:

- **Laozi (Lao Tzu)** is acknowledged for his teachings on harmony, simplicity, and living in accordance with the natural order and spiritual principles.
- **Guru Nanak**, the founder of Sikhism, is recognized as a great spiritual teacher who contributed significantly to the development of religious thought; his teachings are respected for their emphasis on unity and devotion to God.
- **Mahavira**, the key figure in Jainism, is similarly respected for his teachings on non-violence and spiritual discipline.
- **The Dalai Lama**, the spiritual leader of Tibetan Buddhism, is seen as a respected religious leader who emphasizes compassion and peace.

These and many others can be viewed as part of an ongoing process of spiritual enlightenment by contributing to the broader tapestry of religious knowledge and ethical teachings. They expanded human understanding of ethics, metaphysics, and the soul's relationship to higher realities

Different Strokes for Different Folks

Progressive revelation proposes that Divine Educators appear when needed in different geographies to open another revealing chapter in the book of laws and guidance for humanity. In earlier times, however, because these Manifestations appeared on a sparsely populated planet, these ancient Educators spoke to small audiences of locals who had no concept of the world as a globe. The size of a primitive human's world was the distance one could travel by foot or camel in a few days. Communication was generally oral until rudimentary writing was invented in Mesopotamia around 3200 BCE. There were no telephones or flush toilets. Science was synonymous with mythology and folklore. Moral and ethical rules of conduct were largely unknown, and social unrest often governed the camps.

By saying that a new Manifestation of God brings teachings and laws suited to the social, spiritual and intellectual needs of the people of that time, we are not talking about broadcasting a message to the world over satellite TV or the internet. The new message traveled slowly and to a relatively small group of nearby residents who had almost no idea of how the physical world worked. Critical thinking skills were in short supply, so the Educator's message had to be simple. It had to use common, culturally acceptable memes and relevant stories or parables to provoke understanding of concepts the populace had never heard before and struggled to understand. The attention of the audience had to be seized, and so the consequences of disobeying the new guidance had to be stated vividly. As Divine Educators appeared in different parts of the world to people with varying beliefs, traditions, rituals and languages, the fundamental spiritual truths necessarily were explained differently and at varying levels of detail.

The Uneven Roll-out of Revelation

Many of the Manifestations we know today appeared over a period of about five thousand years in a relatively small area from the eastern shore of the Mediterranean to the Ganges. The progression of religious teachings proceeded at a different pace in India than in Persia because the message of Krishna did not reach all the way to the Black Sea region. Inevitably, then, differently evolved strains of teachings developed along different timelines.

To many people, the concept of progressive revelation means that Hinduism evolved through the intervention of Divine Educators into Buddhism, then was transformed by Abraham, Moses, Zoroaster, Jesus, Muhammad the Báb and Bahá'u'lláh. But this would have been impossible. An Indian strain of religion affected by various Divine Educators existed largely as a separate religious milieu comprised mostly of Hindus, Jains and Buddhists. Apparently, some of the Zoroastrian concepts leaked into India causing some evolution of Hinduism and Buddhism.

An Iranian strain began with the appearance of Zoroaster and had some influence on Islam. A Semitic strain began with Abraham and continued later with Judaism, Christianity, Islam, the Babi Faith and the Bahá'í Faith.

These developments complicate the task of discerning the path of progressive revelation through all these various belief systems, each with different Divine Educators who had different allotments of truth to deliver to Their divergent populations at various stages of cultural and intellectual development.

Each of the strains of revelation can be thought of as different schools in various locations. It may take children three years to master the third-grade material in one school, but elsewhere it might take only a year to learn the same lessons.

Chapter 9:
The Essential Oneness of the Manifestations of God

There is a common misperception among those examining the Founders of the world's various wisdom traditions. This view holds that each Prophet-Founder is a separate and competing entity—that they are like individual kings of different nation-states. Yet nothing could be further from the truth.

Hinduism (Bhagavad Gita)

Hinduism, the most ancient wisdom tradition still extant, plainly explains in the Rig Veda:

> They call Him Indra, Mitra, Varuna, Agni, and He is heavenly-winged Garutman; to what is One, sages give many a title—they call it Agni, Yama, Matarisvan. [81]

This scripture states that although God is referred to by different names (Indra, Varuna, Agni, et cetera), these names are merely different aspects or titles of the same ultimate reality. This

---

81 *Rig Veda* 1.164.46

is consistent with the concept that divine Manifestations, though appearing under different names and in various cultural contexts, are ultimately expressions of the same singular divine truth.

Zoroastrianism (Avesta)

Zoroaster speaks of future saviors (Saoshyants) who will come to renew the faith and bring justice and righteousness. This implies a continuity of divine guidance through various ages.

> He is the Saoshyant, and world-renovator, and the righteous judge of the living and the dead, and his helpers are the blessed Immortals, whose thoughts are good, whose words are good, whose deeds are good.[82]

The concept of the Saoshyant can be seen as an early expression of the idea of recurring divine figures or Manifestations who come to renew religion and lead humanity back to righteousness.

Buddhism (Dhammapada)

In Buddhism, the idea of a single God or deity is not readily apparent, but the concept of multiple Buddhas appearing over time to guide humanity is present. This idea suggests that Buddhas, despite appearing in different times, share the same enlightened nature and bring the same essential teachings of truth and liberation.

> The Tathagatas (Buddhas) of the past, present, and future are all the same in nature, and they preach the same Dharma.[83]

---

82 *Avesta, Yasna* 43.11.
83 *Dhammapada.*

Judaism (Hebrew Bible)

The Hebrew Bible speaks of God sending prophets throughout history to guide the people of Israel. While it does not explicitly discuss the unity of prophets in the same way as other religious texts, it does affirm a continuous line of divine guidance through various Prophets.

> The Lord your God will raise up for you a prophet like me from among you, from your fellow Israelites. You must listen to him.[84] — Deuteronomy 18:15 (NIV)

This passage, spoken by Moses, is often seen by religious traditions as foretelling the coming of future Prophets. Christians often interpret this passage as referring to Jesus, while Jews view it as a promise of ongoing prophetic guidance. The passage can also be understood in the broader sense that God's guidance is not confined to a single person or moment in history but continues through successive prophets.

Christianity (New Testament)

In the book of *Revelation*, Jesus speaks about a future time in which He will return with a new name, suggesting that the reality of a new Prophet will be the same spirit of Christ having a human form but called by a different name.

> The one who is victorious I will make a pillar in the temple of my God. Never again will they leave it. I will write on them the name of my God and the name of the city of my God, the new Jerusalem, which is coming down out of heaven from my God; and I will also write on them my new name.[85]

---

84 *Deuteronomy* 18:15 (NIV).
85 *Revelation* 3:12 (NIV).

Jesus also spoke about other shepherds (Manifestations or Divine Educators) coming to guide humanity with the voice of unity:

> And other sheep I have, which are not of this fold: them also I must bring, and they shall hear my voice; and there shall be one fold, and one shepherd.[86]

Islam (Qur'an

Islam also teaches that there is an essential oneness among the Prophets sent by God. The Qur'an makes it clear that all prophets bring the same essential message from God.

> Say: We believe in God and in what has been revealed to us and what was revealed to Abraham, Ishmael, Isaac, Jacob, and the tribes, and in what was given to Moses, Jesus, and the prophets from their Lord. We make no distinction between any of them, and to Him we have submitted.[87]

This verse explicitly states that there should be no distinction made between the Prophets, affirming their unity in delivering God's message. Islam recognizes multiple Prophets, including those from Judaism and Christianity, implying a shared divine mission. Another passage reinforces this idea:

> And for every nation is a messenger. So when their messenger comes, it will be judged between them in justice, and they will not be wronged.[88]

---

86 *John* 10:16 (NIV).
87 *Quran 2:136.*
88 *Qur'an 10:47.*

This suggests that each community or people has received divine guidance through a messenger, reinforcing the idea of the continuity and oneness of divine messengers.

The Bahá'í Faith

One would expect our newest wisdom tradition to provide the clearest and most expansive explanation of the oneness of the Manifestations, and it does. In the words of Bahá'u'lláh, all the Manifestations of God should be regarded as one soul:

> The Bearers of the Trust of God are made manifest unto the peoples of the earth as the Exponents of a new Cause and the Revealers of a new Message. Inasmuch as these Birds of the celestial Throne are all sent down from the heaven of the Will of God, and as they all arise to proclaim His irrefutable Faith, they therefore are regarded as one soul and the same person. For they all drink from the one Cup of the love of God, and all partake of the fruit of the same Tree of Oneness.[89]

'Abdu'l-Bahá, the son of Bahá'u'lláh and interpreter of His teachings, clarified the essential unity of the Manifestations of God, referring to Them as the Prophets of God.

> All the Prophets of God, His well-favored, His holy and chosen Messengers, are without exception the bearers of His names and the embodiments of His attributes. They differ only in the intensity of their revelation and the comparative potency of their light.[90]

The Bahá'í Faith warns against any person or religion favoring one Manifestation over another or assigning any of Them a higher rank.

---

[89] Bahá'u'lláh, *The Kitáb-i-Íqán (The Book of Certitude)*, p. 152.
[90] 'Abdu'l-Bahá, *Selections from the Writings of 'Abdu'l-Bahá*, p. 49.

> Beware, O believers in the Unity of God, lest ye be tempted to make any distinction between any of the Manifestations of His Cause, or to discriminate against the signs that have accompanied and proclaimed Their Revelation. This indeed is the true meaning of Divine Unity, if ye be of them that apprehend and believe this truth.[91]

Bahá'u'lláh explains that while all the Manifestations of God come from the same divine source and are regarded as one soul, their missions and teachings vary according to the needs and circumstances of their time.

> It is clear and evident to thee that all the Prophets are the Temples of the Cause of God, Who have appeared clothed in divers attire. If thou wilt observe with discriminating eyes, thou wilt behold Them all abiding in the same tabernacle, soaring in the same heaven, seated upon the same throne, uttering the same speech, and proclaiming the same Faith. Yet, inasmuch as they have appeared in different dispensations, their utterances differ. In the same way, their missions vary. The light is the same, but the lamps are many.[92]

Pre-existence of Manifestations

The Manifestations or Prophets of God do not become transformed from ordinary human beings into divinely empowered Beings. They are distinct from birth. They pre-exist in the realm of the spirit prior to assuming a human identity—prior even to creation itself—whereas ordinary humans begin at conception.

---

91 Bahá'u'lláh, *Gleanings from the Writings of Bahá'u'lláh*, p. 59.
92 Bahá'u'lláh, *Gleanings from the Writings of Bahá'u'lláh*, p. 52.

> Briefly, the Holy Manifestations have ever been, and ever will be, Luminous Realities; no change or variation takes place in Their essence.[93]

> In the beginning was the Word, and the Word was with God, and the Word was God.[94]

This latter verse from the Gospel of John clearly speaks about the Creative Word of God from which all things are brought into existence. The Greek word *logos* ((λόγος), translated here as "Word," actually has multiple meanings, including "logic" and "reason." In Greek philosophy, *logos* referred to a universal, divine logic, or the "mind of God." Heraclitus described *logos* as a universal underlying principle that is eternally valid. The Stoics believed that logos referred to the reason inherent in matter, which is God. No wonder John in his Gospel wrote that *logos* (reason or logic) was with God, and *logos* (reason or logic) was God (in the sense of being the "mind of God."

This "Word," then, represents God's will and purpose logically manifesting in creation through the laws of physics, which are an inherent part of creation. The "Word" is an expression of divine knowledge and power, a medium through which God communicates His will to humanity. The phrase "the Word was with God" can be understood in the Bahá'í teachings to mean that the Manifestations of God, such as Moses, Jesus, Muhammad, the Báb, and Bahá'u'lláh, are embodiments of the Word with the ability to express His will and purpose to humanity. They are with God in the sense that, like mirrors, they perfectly reflect God's attributes and execute His will, yet they are not God themselves in essence.

Biblical scholars are correct in stating that John also uses *logos* metaphorically to refer to Jesus Christ, but they stop short of the full

---

93 'Abdu'l-Bahá, *Some Answered Questions*, p. 86.
94 The *Bible*, John 1:1 (KJV).

truth. *Logos* apparently refers to *all* the Manifestations of God, as they are all to be regarded as one soul.

The idea that "the Word was God" underscores the profound unity of God's message throughout all religious dispensations. All the great religions are divine in origin, and their core spiritual messages are expressions of the same "Word" or divine truth adapted to the needs and capacities of different peoples and times.

Beyond all the doctrines, mandates, rites and rituals, *logos* (the "Word") is the true power of religion. Bahá'u'lláh explained that through the power inherent in the Word of God, every human infirmity was banished[95], the dying vitality of humanity's belief in God is restored[96], and all of humankind can be illumined by the light of unity[97].

> **Every word that proceedeth out of the mouth of God is endowed with such potency as can instill new life into every human frame.**[98]

Since birth, Manifestations have always known of their Prophethood, and over time they receive intimations of their revelation. They are aware of each other and the part that Each plays in the ongoing enlightenment of humankind. But this does not mean that They are God. The first chapter of John in the New Testament makes this clear by proclaiming that no man—which would include those who knew Jesus—had ever seen God, but that Jesus had testified to God's existence.

> **No man hath seen God at any time; the only begotten Son, which is in the bosom of the Father, he hath declared him.**[99]

---

95 Bahá'u'lláh, *Gleanings from the Writings of Bahá'u'lláh*, 36:3.
96 Bahá'u'lláh, *Gleanings from the Writings of Bahá'u'lláh*, 99.
97 Bahá'u'lláh, *Gleanings from the Writings of Bahá'u'lláh*, 131:3
98 Bahá'u'lláh, *Gleanings from the Writings of Bahá'u'lláh*, 74.
99 The *Bible*, John 1:18 (KJV).

Some sects of Christianity have elevated the station of Jesus to that of God. They zealously quote another passage from the Gospel according to St. John as proof.

> The Word became flesh...

Other Christians disagree and some consider such a belief blasphemous. It is difficult indeed to reconcile an omnipresent God Who has no physical constraints fitting into the finite body of an earthbound human who can occupy just one space at a time. Our latest wisdom tradition elaborates on this point:

> The reality of Christ was the manifestation of God's love. If we claim that the divinity of the Almighty cannot become the reality of man, and cannot become the station of a servant, this is true.[100]

While Jesus certainly manifested divine qualities and like a mirror reflected God's attributes to humanity, He—and no other Manifestation, either—was not a literal incarnation of God, but rather One who revealed the "Word"—the revelation and virtues of God—through example and teachings.

The diversity of opinions about the essential nature of the Manifestations of God may be the greatest source of bigotry and conflict among the world's religions. Much of the turmoil and violence that characterize the saga of human history derives from the bitter contention among religions about who these Beings are and which One should have supremacy over the others. This is unfortunate, because within the reality reflected in all these Manifestations lie the seeds of unity.

> Better is this [unity] for you than all the treasures of the earth, could ye but comprehend it.[101]

---

100 'Abdu'l-Bahá, *Some Answered Questions*, p. 103.
101 Bahá'u'lláh, *The Kitáb-i-Aqdas*, p. 111

Chapter 10:
Knowing an Unknowable God

Taming Humanity's Unbridled Imagination

The boundless curiosity and imagination of humankind has inexhaustible potential. Throughout history, this imagination has blistered sleep and fostered colorful myths and superstitions to explain the unexplainable and inspire the arts, religions and philosophies of people who lack science or critical thinking skills. Chief among these visionary exercises has been numerous fanciful imaginings of a Creator—a God or pantheon or gods—that governs and perhaps guides the world's affairs.

Looking at this from another perspective, science fiction author Arthur C. Clarke pointed out that even technology can mistakenly become an idol of worship:

> Any sufficiently advanced technology is indistinguishable from magic.[102]

---

[102] British science fiction writer Arthur C. Clarke formulated three adages that are known as "Clarke's three laws," of which this one, the third law, is the best known and most widely cited.

Unfortunately, humankind's unbridled imagination has provided endless incorrect solutions for the world's many perplexing problems. To primitive minds, it has also offered wildly implausible beliefs about the nature of reality that are now proven to be, well—*imaginary*.

Certainly, the multitude of competing myths, no matter how memorable, cannot all be accurate in their earnest attempts to explain the vexing reality of our world. In other words, most myths must be wrong. Surely, all the contradictory solutions proposed by creative thinking to solve the problems of the world cannot be successful. Most of them must be wrong. Astonishingly, some ancient stories and beliefs have survived pre-history and remain influential today, which is why many modern buildings have no thirteenth floor. Since everyone "knows," the number 13 is unlucky, why would anyone want to sleep on a clearly dangerous floor?

To folklorists, mythologists, and secular experts in religious studies and scriptural scholarship, the inevitable drift of folkloric tales is inevitable due to the imprecision of oral storytelling, cultural and social influences, and geographic adaptations to the stories. Analyzing incremental changes to determine the influences that contribute to each stage of drift is akin to an archeologist sifting through shards of poverty to spot clues about the nature and evolution of a long-buried society. Such scientific efforts are enormously beneficial to the gaining of knowledge, but one element is usually missing—the possibility of an intervention by an external stimulus such as ancient astronauts or a Supreme Being.

As mentioned earlier, the concept of progressive revelation makes no comment about the recently popularized theory of ancient astronauts, but it does assert that periodic interventions by God—or rather Manifestations of God—explain many of the sudden twists and turns in the revealing of religious Truth and provide essential course corrections to help steer humankind back to a stronger footing in reality. This concept teaches that without periodic interventions by these Manifestations, the wandering evolution of uninhibited beliefs would leave humanity literally unmoored from reality with no moral or ethical signposts to chart a course toward an advancing global society.

> God hath never left Himself without a witness, but hath from the beginning of time to the present day sent down His Prophets unto mankind, who have each been commissioned to acquaint the world with the mysteries of a mighty Day.[103]

> From the beginning of the world until the present time, the divine bounties, the heavenly splendors and the outpouring of the holy spirit have been streaming forth without cessation. The divine Manifestations have been sent down, and the holy Books have been revealed. This unceasing outpouring is evident and manifest as the sun.[104]

These statements from our most recent wisdom tradition affirm the continuous nature of divine guidance through the successive Manifestations of God and reveal how God's spiritual light and guidance have always been present in the world, ensuring that humanity is never left without divine assistance.

Formalized Beliefs About God

There are a vast number of formalized beliefs about the nature of God—too many to catalog here due to the diversity of human cultures and religions. We can organize many of them, however, into several categories and subcategories classified across religious traditions, philosophical perspectives, and theological schools of thought. Here are a few examples:

---

103 Bahá'u'lláh, *Gleanings from the Writings of Bahá'u'lláh*, p. 79.
104 'Abdu'l-Bahá, *Selections from the Writings of 'Abdu'l-Bahá*, p. 58.

- **Monotheism** *(belief in one God)*. This includes the Abrahamic religions (Judaism, Christianity, Islam, the Bahá'í Faith) and Sikhism.

- **Polytheism** *(belief in multiple gods)*. This includes Hinduism, often considered polytheistic, though many Hindus see these deities as manifestations of one ultimate reality called Brahman. This also includes ancient religions such as Greek, Roman, Egyptian, Norse and others, plus Shinto, with its belief in *kami* (spirits or gods associated with nature.)

- **Pantheism** *(God is equivalent to the universe)*. This includes belief systems in which God and the universe are inseparable. Pantheism is also found in some interpretations of Hinduism, Stoicism, and Spinoza's philosophy.

- **Panentheism** *(God is in everything but also transcends it)*. These are beliefs in which God exists in all parts of the universe but is greater than the universe. Panentheism can be found in aspects of Hinduism, Process Theology, and some strands of Christianity.

- **Deism** *(belief in a non-interventionist God)*. This is a belief that God created the universe but does not interfere with it. Deism was a popular belief during the Enlightenment.

- **Dualism** *(belief in two equal but opposing forces)*. This is found in Zoroastrianism (Ahura Mazda vs. Angra Mainyu) and in some interpretations of Gnosticism, and Manichaeism.

- **Agnosticism** *(belief that the nature of God is unknowable)*. Agnosticism can exist alongside various religious traditions or as a standalone philosophical stance.

- **Atheism** *(belief that no God exists)*. While atheism is a non-belief in God, some atheists may hold distinct philosophies about existence, the universe, and spirituality.

- **Non-theism or Transcendental Beliefs**. These comprise beliefs in spiritual principles and the nature of the universe without a creator god (found in some strands of Buddhism.) In Taoism, these beliefs focus on the *Tao* (way or principle) without personifying it as a god.

- **Other Indigenous and Folk Beliefs**. There are numerous indigenous and animistic traditions in which the divine is intertwined with nature, ancestors, and spirits.

- **Mysticism**. Mystic beliefs emphasize direct, personal experiences of the divine, often cutting across multiple religions (e.g., Sufism in Islam, Christian Mysticism, Kabbalah in Judaism).

- **Secular Philosophies**. These include existentialism, humanism, and other schools of thought that may reject or redefine traditional philosophies.

It seems there is nothing—even the idea of God—that humanity's imagination cannot twist and bend into a thousand different configurations to suit the fancies of those doing the imagining. Left alone, this free-for-all invention of gods leaves humanity rudderless and strips the real-life classroom of a meaningful curriculum or wise teachers. This seems hardly a suitable system for intelligent beings seeking guidance in a difficult world. Progressive revelation does not impose beliefs on anyone. Instead, it offers a successful pattern of living and a divine curriculum[105] for moral and ethical growth.

---

105 The term "divine curriculum" was coined by author Edward Price to describe the lessons delivered to humankind by the Manifestations of God on whose

An Unfathomable Essence

All the world's great wisdom traditions acknowledge that humanity cannot hope to understand the full nature of God. The specific cultural differences into which each Manifestation of God appeared has always shaped the context within which an Educator's message would be inserted and understood. In other words, each Manifestation revealed a message suitable for the time, the location, and the capacity of His audience for understanding.

In the Aryan strain of religious development—Hinduism, Zoroastrianism and Buddhism—longstanding cultural currents produced an appreciation for a more meditative approach to understanding a Supreme Being and achieving personal growth. The Abrahamic religions—Judaism, Christianity, Islam and the Bahá'í Faith—allow in various ways for a believer to establish a personal relationship with God despite the obvious difficulties of having a relationship with an entity one can never hope to understand.

With inevitable nuances, the most consistent understanding of God among the great wisdom traditions is that the essence of God is unknowable. Because creation predictably seeks to bond with its Creator, however, the dilemma of how to love an unknowable essence must be solved. Over time, through progressive revelation, the answer emerged, was then lost due to political infighting, and later emerged again in even fuller relief.

Hinduism

Responding to Indian culture and its tolerance for more abstract concepts and a Supreme Being that is less than personal, Krishna delivered a belief system we now call Hinduism that helped people of the time connect more deeply with the divine. The following passage suggests that Brahman (God, or the Supreme Reality) is beyond the

---

Teachings were founded the world's great wisdom traditions. Price is the author of a book series entitled *The Divine Curriculum*.

grasp of the senses and cannot be directly known, emphasizing the unknowable aspect of Brahman.

> That which cannot be seen with the eye, but by which the eye sees: know that alone to be Brahman, the eternal, and not what people here adore.[106]

Hinduism offers both an impersonal and a personal view of the divine. The *impersonal* aspect is captured in the concept of Brahman, the infinite, formless, and ultimate reality that pervades everything. Brahman is presented as beyond all human comprehension and description. This is analogous to the unknowable aspects of God in Judaism, Islam, and the Bahá'í Faith, which teach that God's essence is beyond human understanding.

Hinduism, however, also allows for the worship of other deities like Vishnu, Shiva, and Devi, through whom individuals can personally relate to God. This duality—impersonal Brahman and other personal gods—sets Hinduism apart from strict monotheistic faiths that reject the notion of multiple forms of the divine. It is not known whether these multiple deities first appeared as a consequence of believer's needs for a closer personal connection to Brahman or if the concept of these additional deities arose earlier. In any case, for many Hindus, these numerous deities are viewed more symbolically as memorable metaphors for forces of nature or for specific attributes of Brahman, the Supreme Being. It is reasonable to consider that the more ancient Hindu conception of a complex cosmic order of spiritual beings would gradually be replaced by more symbolic interpretations emphasizing the underlying truths.

Zoroastrianism

In the monotheistic religion of Zoroastrianism, the belief in a Supreme Being centers on Ahura Mazda, the all-knowing, all-

---

106 *Kena Upanishad* 1:6 (Swami Sivananda translation)

powerful and benevolent Creator. But tucked inside this wisdom tradition is the concept of dualism, in which an evil force, Angra Mainyu, is locked in a cosmic struggle with the Creator. Angra Mainyu is viewed as the personification of evil, chaos and destruction, but is not a god on the same level as Ahura Mazda. Zoroastrianism prescribes the worship of Ahura Mazda alone as the supreme deity.

> Ahura Mazda is far beyond the understanding of mortals. His essence is beyond comprehension, and only through His light may humans gain some glimmer of knowledge.[107]

In this passage, Ahura Mazda, the Supreme God of Zoroastrianism, is portrayed as beyond human understanding, indicating the unknowable nature of the divine.

Buddhism

While Buddhism does not focus on a Supreme Being, the following passage implies that the ultimate reality (Nirvana) is beyond the world of form and is unknowable in ordinary terms.

> There is, monks, an unborn, unbecome, unmade, unfabricated. If there were not that unborn, unbecome, unmade, unfabricated, there would not be the case that escape from the born, become, made, fabricated would be discerned. But because there is an unborn, unbecome, unmade, unfabricated, escape from the born, become, made, fabricated is discerned.[108]

At first, this passage may seem inscrutable, but the language becomes clear when clarifying that the phrase "unborn, unbecome, unmade, unfabricated" can only refer to the ultimate reality, which

---

107 Zoroastrian scriptures *(Bundahishn, and Zand-i Vohuman Yasht)*
108 *Udana* 8:3 (Pali Canon, Theravāda tradition).

is beyond all conditioned phenomena and the realm of ordinary comprehension. It implies that this reality cannot be understood in terms of the usual categories of existence and non-existence, which are shaped by worldly experience. Thus, it suggests that the supreme truth or reality transcends human concepts and is unknowable in conventional terms.

Judaism

Judaism emphasizes that God is wholly transcendent and beyond human understanding. While God is involved in the world and engages with humanity through covenants and revelation (as seen in the Torah), the true essence of God is beyond human comprehension. This parallels beliefs in Islam and the Bahá'í Faith in which God is also seen as utterly beyond human understanding though still accessible through divine guidance.

> My thoughts are not your thoughts, neither are your ways My ways, declares the Lord. As the heavens are higher than the earth, so are My ways higher than your ways and My thoughts than your thoughts.[109]

This passage implies that God's nature and ways are beyond human comprehension, suggesting that God's full essence is unknowable to human beings.

Although Judaism presents God as unknowable, the Hebrew Bible also presents Him as a personal God who engages with people through covenants (agreements), direct commandments and prophecy while remaining ultimately mysterious in nature. In contrast, Hinduism (in its highest conception of Brahman) and Buddhism (with its focus on Nirvana) often describe the divine or ultimate reality in more impersonal terms.

Most biblical scholars question the historicity of many Old Testament stories in which God seems to direct successful military

---

109 *Isaiah* 55:8-9 (NIV).

actions (the Fall of Jericho); empowers a would-be king (David and Goliath); confuses the language of a wayward society (Tower of Babel); destroys cities because of their wickedness (the destruction of Sodom and Gomorrah); proves his superiority to false prophets (sending fire to consume a sacrifice on Mount Carmel); saves a repentant prophet from the belly of a fish (Jonah and the Whale); helps the Israelites escape a pursuing Egyptian army (The Parting of the Red Sea); cleanses the earth of evil by flooding it (Noah's Ark).

These stories demonstrate how the Bible portrays God as actively involved in human history, intervening in powerful ways to fulfill His purposes, guide His people, and shape the course of history. It is impossible to know whether these stories were meant as parables to help make an unknowable God more accessible to the relatively simple people of the day, just as we are not sure who authored these books of the Old Testament. Many of the stories were clearly derived from earlier myths. What we know for sure is that Judaism taught that God is unknowable.

Christianity

Christianity affirms belief in one God but uniquely holds the doctrine of the Trinity, which teaches that God is three entities in one. This is different from Judaism, Islam, Zoroastrianism, and the Bahá'í Faith, which all maintain that God is one entity and indivisible. Many sects within Christianity view the three parts of the Trinity—the Father, the Son, and the Holy Spirit—as distinct from each other yet fully one in their combined essence. This concept is complex and mysterious, reflecting the idea that God's true nature is ultimately beyond human comprehension. The question for many people, including Christians, is this—if God is unknowable, how did the Council of Nicaea in AD 325 understand the triune nature of God's essence well enough to vote in favor of declaring that Jesus was God?

> Oh, the depth of the riches both of the wisdom and knowledge of God! How unsearchable are His judgments and His ways past finding out![110]

This biblical verse expresses the belief that God's wisdom and judgments are beyond human comprehension, indicating the unknowability of God's nature.

Interestingly, the Christian doctrine of the Trinity was not original. It harkens back to a much more ancient Hindu trinity, which consists of Brahman (the creator), Vishnu (the preserver), and Shiva (the destroyer). In certain Hindu traditions, however, Krishna is not just seen as an Avatar or co-equal of God, but as the Supreme Being Himself.

The idea of God incarnating into human form is also not unique. Variations of this concept can be found in:

- **Ancient Greek and Roman Mythology**. In these mythologies, gods frequently took human form to interact with mortals, sometimes for benevolent purposes, other times for personal reasons or interference in human affairs. Zeus (Greek), aka Jupiter (Roman) was notorious for taking human form to seduce mortal women. Examples include the story of Leda, whom Zeus visited in the form of a swan, or Europa, whom Zeus abducted while disguised as a bull. Dionysus, the god of wine and revelry, was often described as walking among mortals in human form, teaching the art of wine-making and participating in festivals.
- **Buddhism (certain interpretations)**. In Buddhism, there is a concept of bodhisattvas and Buddhas manifesting in human form to teach and guide others.

---

110 *Romans* 11:33 (KJV).

Buddhas (enlightened beings) are sometimes seen as divine figures who descend to help humanity, such as Gautama Buddha himself. In Mahayana Buddhism, there are examples of celestial Buddhas or bodhisattvas taking earthly forms to save sentient beings. Avalokiteshvara, the bodhisattva of compassion, is believed by some to incarnate in various forms to aid those in need, including the Tibetan belief in the Dalai Lama as an earthly incarnation of Avalokiteshvara.

- **Egyptian Mythology.** In Ancient Egypt, the Pharaoh was often regarded as the physical incarnation of a god, particularly the god Horus; later, Amun-Ra. Pharaohs were seen not just as political leaders but as divine beings who represented the gods on Earth. This concept of divine kingship intertwined the religious and political roles of the pharaoh, who was considered both a deity and a ruler. For example, Osiris, the god of the afterlife, was believed to incarnate in the deceased pharaohs as part of the cycle of death and rebirth, further associating the ruler with divine status.

- **Shamanism.** In various indigenous religious traditions, such as shamanism among Native American, Siberian, or Amazonian peoples, it is believed that certain shamans or spiritual leaders can become possessed by gods or spirits, which act as incarnations or vessels for the divine. The divine or spiritual beings work through the shaman to perform healing, guide the community, or bring divine messages to the people. In these traditions, the shaman's body becomes a temporary home for the divine during rituals or sacred ceremonies.

- **Taoism**. In Taoism, certain immortals (known as *Xian*) or gods are believed to have taken on human form to guide humanity toward spiritual wisdom or balance with the Tao (the Way). These divine beings sometimes descend to teach, heal, or protect humans. One famous example is Laozi, the founder of Taoism, who is sometimes viewed in religious Taoism as an incarnation of the *Tao* itself, though this is more symbolic than literal.

- **Shinto**. In Shinto, the traditional religion of Japan, gods or spirits (called *kami*) are believed to incarnate in physical forms, including humans. Certain individuals, such as the emperor, have historically been considered living embodiments of *kami*. The Japanese emperor was traditionally considered to be a descendant of the sun goddess Amaterasu, thus becoming a divine figure on Earth. Additionally, *kami* are believed to dwell within natural elements, animals, or even people, reflecting a deep connection between the divine and the material world in Shinto practice.

Islam

Tawhid, or the belief in the absolute oneness of God, is a central tenet of Islam. Muslims believe that Allah (God) is utterly indivisible—without partners, associates or incarnations. This strict monotheism is similar to Judaism, Zoroastrianism and the Bahá'í Faith.

By contrast, Christianity introduced the doctrine of the Trinity, in which God is understood to exist as three entities (the Father, the Son and the Holy Spirit) combined into one essence. No wonder, then, that Islam and Christianity, both with roots that go back to Abraham and revere the teachings of Jesus, have sparred ferociously for centuries. The Christian Trinity is viewed by Muslims as blasphemous.

In Islam, Allah is completely transcendent (beyond the physical world) and immanent (close to creation), but His transcendence is emphasized. Allah is described as unknowable in essence, and humans can only know His will, not His true nature.

> Vision perceives Him not, but He perceives all vision; and He is the Subtle, the Acquainted.[111]

The focus on Allah's transcendence is similar to Judaism and the Bahá'í Faith. For both, God's essence is beyond human understanding.

Bahá'í Faith

The Bahá'í Faith shares the strict monotheism of Judaism, Christianity, Islam, Sikhism, and Zoroastrianism, believing in one God who is the creator of all things. Bahá'ís believe that God is eternal, all-knowing, and all-powerful, much like the descriptions of God in these other faiths. However, the Bahá'í Faith emphasizes the oneness of God in a way that includes all religions, teaching that the same God has been revealed in different ways through different Manifestations throughout history.

This belief in one God aligns closely with Islam and Judaism, which also emphasize God's unity, and contrasts with the Christian doctrine of the Trinity, in which God is understood to exist in three entities (the Father, the Son, and the Holy Spirit). The Bahá'í Faith rejects the Trinity, instead seeing Jesus Christ as a Manifestation of God rather than an incarnation of God.

In the Bahá'í Faith, God is described as unknowable in His essence. Bahá'u'lláh, the founder of the Bahá'í Faith, wrote:

> To every discerning and illuminated heart it is evident that God, the unknowable Essence, the Divine Being, is immensely exalted beyond every human attribute, such as corporeal existence, ascent and descent, egress and regress.[112]

---

111 *Qur'an* 6:103).
112 Bahá'u'lláh, *Gleanings from the Writings of Bahá'u'lláh*, section LXXXIV).

This concept of God's unknowability is central to the Bahá'í Faith and closely mirrors the beliefs in Islam, Judaism, and Zoroastrianism, where God's essence is beyond human comprehension. The following passage further reinforces the idea that God's essence is completely beyond the grasp of human understanding, even for philosophers and prophets.

> As to the reality of the Divine Essence, it is transcendent, beyond all comprehension, and far above every description. The human mind cannot grasp it and the power of thought cannot encompass it. From time immemorial, it has been, and will continue to remain, in the loftiest heights of sanctity and purity. All the philosophers are bewildered in their attempt to understand it, and the wise are perplexed in comprehending its reality.[113]

The Bahá'í Faith, our newest wisdom tradition, deeply respects Christianity and its Figures, including Jesus. Its teachings clarify the traditional doctrinal of the Trinity by emphasizing that God is singular and cannot be divided into different persons or essences. Distinctions between God the Father, God the Son, or God the Holy Spirit are seen as symbolic rather than literal divisions within God's essence. Jesus is one of the Manifestations of God, not God incarnate in human flesh.

> The reality of Christ was a clear mirror, and the Sun of Truth—that is, the Essence of Divinity, the divine Being—was resplendent in this mirror. In other words, all the perfections, bounties, and splendours of the Sun of Truth were visible and apparent in the reality of Christ. If we say that the Sun is visible and manifest in the mirror, we do not mean that the Sun itself has

---

[113] 'Abdu'l-Bahá, *Some Answered Questions*, p. 295.

> descended from the heights of its sanctity and indwelt within the mirror; rather, it has become manifest and resplendent therein with all its perfections and attributes.[114]

In this analogy, Jesus (the mirror) reflects the divine attributes of God (the Sun), but Jesus is not literally God Himself. The Sun remains in its lofty place while the mirror perfectly reflects its light. This explanation emphasizes the distinction between God and Jesus while honoring the role of Christ as a divine Manifestation.

In the New Testament, Jesus is sometimes referred to as God's "only begotten Son." In the Bahá'í Faith, a deeper meaning is attributed to this reference, as might be expected from a later Manifestation of God. In Bahá'í thought, all the Manifestations of God are "sons" in the sense that They reflect God's light and attributes. Jesus is called the "only begotten Son" to highlight the unique significance of His mission in the history of Christianity and human history.

The term "begotten," is not taken literally, which would give it an unintended sexual connotation, but metaphorically as a way of indicating the closeness and intimacy of Jesus's relationship to God. It signifies that Jesus was chosen by God for a specific purpose, just as other Manifestations are chosen in their own contexts.

Other Manifestations of God were likewise given special titles of honor to signify their special mission or spiritual qualities. Some examples are:

- **Krishna**: *"Hari."* Many titles have been bestowed upon Krishna, including "Hari," which has multiple meanings, including ""Remover of Sins and Afflictions," and "Bringer of Light to the Darkness of Ignorance."

---

114 'Abdu'l-Bahá, *Some Answered Questions*, 2014 edition, p. 118.

- **Zoroaster**: *"Bearer of the Fire"* (or *"Light of God"*). In Zoroastrianism, Zoroaster (Zarathustra) is associated with fire and light, symbolizing divine illumination and purity. He is often referred to as the "Bearer of the Fire" or "The Light of God", representing the divine truth and wisdom he brought to humanity. The fire in Zoroastrianism symbolizes spiritual enlightenment. Zoroaster's role as the one who bears this divine light emphasizes his mission to guide humanity toward truth, righteousness, and the worship of Ahura Mazda (God). This title is always viewed symbolically.

- **Buddha:** *"The Enlightened One."* While the title "Enlightened One" is used in Buddhism itself to refer to Buddha's attainment of nirvana (spiritual awakening), the Bahá'í Faith views Buddha as an illuminator of divine truth who reflected God's attributes of wisdom and compassion. No one would apply this reference exclusively to Buddha.

- **Abraham**: *"Friend of God."* Abraham is often referred to as the "Friend of God" (in Arabic: *Khalil Alláh*), emphasizing his special relationship of closeness and trust with God. This title reflects Abraham's role as the father of monotheism and the one through whom God's covenant with humanity was reaffirmed. This title highlights the deep intimacy and faith he had with God, symbolizing his mission to establish a belief in the oneness of God that would influence the Abrahamic religions—Judaism, Christianity, Islam, and the Bahá'í Faith. No one has ever proposed that Abraham was the only friend of God.

- **Moses**: *"Interlocutor of God"* (*Kalim Alláh*). Moses is often referred to as the "Interlocutor of God" or "He who spoke with God" (in Arabic: *Kalim Alláh*), highlighting his unique role as the one who directly communicated with God and received divine law. This title emphasizes the special way in which Moses was given the Torah and the covenant between God and the Israelites. This title reflects Moses's mission to establish a divine legal framework and guide the Israelites to freedom, symbolizing his pivotal role in history. No one has ever claimed that Moses was the only Manifestation or Prophet who spoke with God.

- **Muhammad**: *"Seal of the Prophets" (Khatam al-Nabiyyin)*. In Islamic and Bahá'í theology, Muhammad is known as the "Seal of the Prophets" (in Arabic: *Khatam al-Nabiyyin*). This title emphasizes His unique role in bringing the final revelation of God's will, referred to as the "Seal," which would end a religious dispensation known as the Prophetic Era and begin a new dispensation with the advent of the Báb.

- **The Báb**: *"The Gate."* The Báb, who was the forerunner of Bahá'u'lláh, is known by the title "The Gate" (in Arabic: *Báb*). This title reflects His role as the one who prepared the way for Bahá'u'lláh, similar to how John the Baptist is seen as the forerunner to Jesus. The Báb's mission was to open the spiritual gate to a new era of revelation and prepare humanity for the coming of Bahá'u'lláh. The Báb's title signifies His unique mission as the intermediary between past religious dispensations and the Bahá'í era, marking the transition to a new cycle of the fulfillment of prophecy.

- **Bahá'u'lláh**: *"The Glory of God,"* Bahá'u'lláh, the founder of the Bahá'í Faith, is referred to as the "Glory of God" (in Arabic: *Bahá'u'lláh*). His title reflects His role as the Manifestation who ushers in a new era of global unity, justice, and spiritual renewal. Bahá'u'lláh's mission is seen as unique in its global scope, bringing a message meant to unite all of humanity in the age of maturity. Bahá'u'lláh also referred to Himself as the "Promised One of All Ages," indicating His fulfillment of prophecies from various world religions. This title emphasizes His special role in bringing to fruition the expectations of previous religious dispensations.

Chapter 11:
Mirrors That Reflect God

On earlier pages, we have given a summary of the qualities and missions of the Manifestations of God, which we often refer to as Divine Educators. In this chapter, I will be quoting from passages revealed by our most recent wisdom tradition, which provide more detail than previous revelations about the nature of the Divine Educators Who incrementally increase our knowledge of God and divine realities.

Dual Nature

The Manifestations of God possess a dual nature—human and divine. As humans, They possess human attributes such as physical bodies and emotions. They can experience sorrow, pain and love. They can be injured, become ill and die. This human aspect helps them relate to humanity and personally demonstrate how one can apply virtues to all circumstances of human life. Their physical realities anchor them in the material world, enabling them to be accessible and relevant to the people and societies they encounter.

> The Holy Manifestations have three planes. One is the physical reality, which depends upon matter; the body of the Manifestation comes into being through the union of father and mother.[115]

---

115 'Abdu'l-Bahá, Some Answered Questions, p. 153

While They possess human attributes and live as humans, Their human nature is pure and free from the flaws and limitations that characterize ordinary people. This is why Christians refer to Jesus as "without sin." This exaltation above human imperfections applies equally to all the Manifestations of God.

> **The human temple that hath been the vehicle of such a revelation [of the Manifestations] is, under all conditions, regarded as utterly remote from, and immeasurably exalted above, all human imperfections.**[116] (Gleanings, p. 67)

Though human, Manifestations of God also have a divine nature, meaning that They reflect God's attributes, such as love, mercy, justice and wisdom. This divine nature does not make them God or a vessel in which God resides, however, since there is but one God who is unknowable and cannot be divided or constricted in any way. The "divine nature" of the Manifestations means that They *mirror* God's will. We can come to know and understand God by knowing and understanding his Manifestations.

> **These sanctified Mirrors… are but expressions of Him Who is the Invisible of the Invisibles.**[117] (The Kitáb-i-Íqán, p. 99)

> **These sanctified Mirrors, these Day Springs of ancient glory, are one and all the Exponents on earth of Him Who is the central Orb of the universe, its Essence and ultimate Purpose.**[118] (Gleanings, p. 47)

---

116 Bahá'u'lláh, *Gleanings from the Writings of Bahá'u'lláh*, p. 67.
117 Bahá'u'lláh, *The Kitáb-i-Íqán*, p. 99.
118 Bahá'u'lláh, *Gleanings from the Writings of Bahá'u'lláh*, p. 47.

The human nature of the Manifestations is not obliterated by their divine nature. They remain human while perfectly reflecting divine attributes.

> In the Holy Manifestations of God, the divine perfections are infinite, but the individual reality is not transformed into the Reality of Divinity itself. It remains human.[119]

Despite Their human experiences, the Manifestations all possess divine knowledge and authority. Consider that Jesus performed miracles, Muhammad revealed the Qur'an, and Bahá'u'lláh authored a vast body of scripture while in exile.

> He Who is the Day Spring of Truth is, no doubt, endowed with an all-encompassing knowledge.[120]

Oneness in Essence and Purpose

The Manifestations of God serve as intermediaries between the unknowable essence of God and humanity. Each is uniquely suited to Their time but reflects the same divine truths. Their unity exists on a spiritual level, but They remain distinct in Their physical lives and historical missions.

> The Manifestations of God are united on the level of reality and differentiation exists only in the conditions of their individual lives.[121]

The Manifestations are unified in Their role as channels of divine guidance, but this does not imply They share the same soul or are the same person.

---

119 'Abdu'l-Bahá, *Some Answered Questions*, p. 153.
120 Bahá'u'lláh, *Gleanings from the Writings of Bahá'u'lláh*, p. 52.
121 'Abdu'l-Bahá, *Some Answered Questions*, p. 153.

> **They all abide in the same Tabernacle, soar in the same heaven, are seated upon the same throne, utter the same speech, and proclaim the same Faith.**[122]

In the Bible, Jesus told us, "I am the way, the truth, and the life: no man cometh unto the Father, but by me.[123] In those words, Jesus was inviting humanity of His era to follow Him. But He was also referring all humanity to all other Manifestations of God past and future, Who all "abide in the same Tabernacle, soar in the same heaven, are seated upon the same throne, utter the same speech, and proclaim the same Faith."[124]

> **The lamps are many, but the light is one.**[125]

Many people become confused by the different names, varying human personalities and unique missions of the Manifestations, imagining Them to be spiritually distinct also.

> **...as they all arise to proclaim His irresistible Faith, they therefore are regarded as one soul and the same person. For they all drink from the one Cup of the love of God, and all partake of the fruit of the same Tree of Oneness.**[126] (Italics added.)

Nevertheless, it is still correct to look at Jesus and say, "I see God," because Jesus was a mirror in which we can see God's perfections. When one sees the sun in a mirror, one can see, "Look, here is the sun." But the sun itself is not physically in the mirror. Only its reflection can be seen.

---

122 Bahá'u'lláh, *Gleanings from the Writings of Bahá'u'lláh*, p. 52.
123 *The Bible*, John 14:6.
124 Ibid,.
125 Bahá'u'lláh, *Gleanings from the Writings of Bahá'u'lláh*, p. 66.
126 Bahá'u'lláh, *The Kitáb-i-Íqán*.

> The reality of Christ was a clear mirror, and the Sun of Reality – that is to say, the Essence of Oneness, with divine attributes – was shining and manifest in it.[127]

Unity of Goals

Manifestations of God all have the same overall goals.

Awaken Humanity's Spiritual Potential

To begin, They aim to awaken humanity's spiritual potential, fostering inner transformation and the discovery of divine virtues within every individual. At the dawn of civilization, this awakening process starts with a primer on the spiritual nature of humankind as it differs from animals.

> The purpose of the one true God, exalted be His glory, in revealing Himself unto men [through His Divine Educators] is to lay bare those gems that lie hidden within the mine of their true and inmost selves.[128]

Establish Unity

The Manifestations all promote unity among individuals, communities, and nations, transcending differences to establish harmony and peace.

> The purpose of the religion of God is to create unity and concord amongst the peoples of the world; make it not the cause of dissension and strife.[129]

---

127 'Abdu'l-Bahá, *Some Answered Questions*, p. 114.
128 Bahá'u'lláh, *Gleanings from the Writings of Bahá'u'lláh*, p. 287.
129 Bahá'u'lláh, *Tablets of Bahá'u'lláh*, p. 129.

Achieve an Ever-Advancing Civilization

The teachings of the Manifestations are intended to advance human civilization, fostering justice, understanding, and collective well-being.

> The purpose underlying the revelation of every heavenly Book, nay, of every Divinely-revealed verse, is to endue all men with righteousness and understanding, so that peace and tranquillity may be firmly established amongst them.[130]

Renew and Tailor Spiritual Guidance

The Manifestations renew divine guidance for each era, educating humanity in spiritual, intellectual, and practical ways to ensure holistic progress. This guidance is renewed as old guidance becomes outdated and is tailored to the unique needs of those who need guidance and have the enhanced capacity to understand deeper truths.

> Know of a certainty that in every Dispensation the light of Divine Revelation hath been vouchsafed unto men in direct proportion to their spiritual capacity.[131]

> The Prophets of God have appeared at various times among men, and each one has given a teaching that was suitable to the capacity of the age in which He appeared.[132]

---

130 Bahá'u'lláh, *Gleanings from the Writings of Bahá'u'lláh*, p. 206.
131 Bahá'u'lláh, *The Kitáb-i-Íqán*, p. 66.
132 'Abdu'l-Bahá, *Some Answered Questions*, p. 155.

Different Missions

Although each Manifestation has the same goals, each also has a unique mission, and these missions are different depending on the cultural development, the intellectual capacities, and the needs of the era in which each appears. Here is one way to summarize those missions.

Abraham: Foundation of Monotheism

Abraham's mission was to establish the belief in one God and lay the foundation for future religious systems.

> Abraham... directed His gaze towards the Kingdom of the Almighty, and, while in the land of His enemies, arose with divine authority and set the foundations of the Faith of God.[133]

Moses: Lawgiver and Nation-Builder

Moses's main task was to deliver the Ten Commandments and the Mosaic Law, providing spiritual and social order for the Israelites.

> He Who conversed with God [Moses]... promulgated the laws of God and dispelled the darkness of ignorance.[134]

Krishna: Love and Kindness

Krishna's message was one of love and kindness.

> The Message of Krishna is the message of love. All God's prophets have brought the message of love. None has ever thought that war and hate are good. Everyone agrees in saying that love and kindness are best.[135]

---

133 Bahá'u'lláh, *The Kitáb-i-Íqán*, p. 15.
134 Bahá'u'lláh, *Epistle to the Son of the Wolf*, p. 29
135 'Abdu'l-Bahá, *Paris Talks*, p. 199.

Zoroaster: Purity and Order

Zoroaster's main task was to teach humanity about the duality of good and evil and emphasize purity of thought, word and deed.

> The firetemples of the world stand as eloquent testimony to this truth. In their time they summoned, with burning zeal, all the inhabitants of the earth to Him Who is the Spirit of purity.[136]

Buddha: Enlightenment and Compassion

Buddha's mission was to awaken humanity to the path of detachment, mindfulness and compassion.

> The founder of Buddhism was a precious Being Who established the oneness of God.[137]

Jesus Christ: Love and Redemption

Jesus taught the primacy of love, mercy, and forgiveness, emphasizing inner transformation.

> By sacrificing Himself... a fresh capacity was infused into all created things. Its evidences, as witnessed in all the peoples of the earth, are now manifest before thee.[138]

Muhammad: Social and Spiritual Order

Muhammad appeared as a Manifestation of God to unify the Arabian tribes under the worship of one God and reveal the Qur'án, establishing a comprehensive spiritual and legal system. Bahá'u'lláh said this:

---

[136] Bahá'u'lláh, *The Tabernacle of Unity*.
[137] 'Abdu'l-Bahá, *Some Answered Questions*, Part 4.
[138] Bahá'u'lláh, *Gleanings from the Writings of Bahá'u'lláh*, XXI

> What explanation can they give concerning that which the Seal of the Prophets (Muḥammad)—may the souls of all else but Him be offered up for His sake—hath said?: "'Ye, verily, shall behold your Lord as ye behold the full moon on its fourteenth night.[139]

The Báb: Herald of a New Era

The Báb's mission was to prepare humanity for the coming of Bahá'u'lláh and initiate a new cycle of divine revelation.

> This is the Dayspring of the Revelation of God, did ye but know it. This is the Dawning Place of the Cause of God, were ye to recognize it.[140]

Bahá'u'lláh: Unity and Global Civilization

Bahá'u'lláh's mission is to unite humanity and lay the foundations for a global civilization based on justice, unity and universal principles.

> So powerful is the light of unity that it can illuminate the whole earth.[141]

One and the Same

The various Manifestations may differ in their names, human distinctions and missions, but all are Mirrors perfectly reflecting the same divine light and attributes of God so humanity can glimpse the unknowable. Despite the passion with which the followers of one wisdom tradition or another may promote "their" Manifestation

---

139 Bahá'u'lláh, *Epistle to the Son of the Wolf*.

140 This passage appears in the section titled "The Declaration of the Báb," which is a tablet written by Bahá'u'lláh in honor of the Báb. The online version can be found at: https://www.bahai.org/library/authoritative-texts/bahaullah/days-remembrance/

141 Bahá'u'lláh, *Gleanings from the Writings of Bahá'u'lláh*, p. 288.

as the greatest or most important, or the last one ever to appear, humanity has been encouraged to view all the Manifestations as one and the same in their divine essence, which transcends distinctions of time and culture. This perspective underlies the concept of progressive revelation, in which the same divine truth is revealed anew in successive ages to guide humanity's spiritual and social evolution.

> **No distinction do We make between any of His Messengers. They all have but one purpose; their secret is the same secret.**[142]

> **Regard ye not the Person of the Manifestation, but fix your gaze upon the light that shineth through Him. They are all but one person, one soul, one spirit, one being, one revelation.**[143]

> **[The] attributes of God are not, and have never been, vouchsafed specially unto certain Prophets, and withheld from others. Nay, all the Prophets of God… are but one soul and one spirit, the first and the last, the beginning and the end… They only differ in the intensity of their revelation, and the comparative potency of their light.**[144]

---

142 Bahá'u'lláh, *Gleanings from the Writings of Bahá'u'lláh*, p. 78.
143 Bahá'u'lláh, *The Kitáb-i-Íqán*, p. 142.
144 Bahá'u'lláh, *The Kitáb-i-Íqán*, p. 153.

Chapter 12:
Our Latest Wisdom Tradition

Before we can continue, we must become familiar with our latest wisdom tradition, which appeared less than two centuries ago. Called the Bahá'í Faith, according to its scriptures, it is not a competing religion to other established wisdom traditions; rather, it is the next stage of an unfoldment of divine revelation, a deep well from which all wisdom traditions have drawn their inspiration.

The Bahá'í Faith proposes that all existing major wisdom traditions have taught in various ways the concept of progressive revelation. Because the Bahá'í Faith presents the most comprehensive and detailed explanation of progressive revelation and its goals, the rest of this book will compare the scriptures of each older wisdom tradition with each other and with the Bahá'í writings to discover the truth of this assertion. For this reason, it is necessary to begin with a description of the Bahá'í Faith and its two Manifestations of God, which may be unfamiliar territory for many readers. Without this fundamental knowledge, we may miss many important clues for discovering the truth of progressive revelation.

Two Manifestations

The Bahá'í Faith is a monotheistic wisdom tradition founded by the appearance of two Manifestations of God, the first one known as the

Báb (an Arabic term meaning the "Gate") and Bahá'u'lláh, (an Arabic term meaning "Glory of God").

The Babi Faith

In the early nineteenth-century, as Christians in America were expecting the imminent "second coming" of Jesus, there was simultaneously great anticipation among Muslims in Persia that an Islamic messiah known as the Qa'im would finally return. Persia was ruled by rigid Islamic orthodoxy, socio-economic stagnation, brutal clerical dominance, and intimidating misogyny due in large part to extremist misunderstandings of the Qur'an. The penalty for heresy or apostasy was death.

Into this harsh religious climate, on the evening of May 22, 1844, a 24-year-old merchant named Siyyid `Alí-Muhammad Shirazi boldly declared that he was the promised Qa'im, a divinely inspired figure who would prepare the way for a greater Manifestation of God He referred to as "He whom God shall make manifest." This second Manifestation would appear in the year nine, the young man announced publicly. This referred to the year 1853, which was nine years after this young man declared Himself the Qa'im.

> **In the year nine, ye will attain unto all good.**[145]

Increasingly referred to as the Báb, this Divine Educator began revealing spiritual and social teachings intended to renew religion and reform Persian society, documenting them into two books called the *Persian Bayán* and the *Arabic Bayan*. Within several years, this charismatic young man attracted over a hundred thousand followers, provoking the powerful Islamic regime to begin a campaign of vicious persecution. More than twenty thousand of the Báb's followers, known as Babís, perished in a series of massacres throughout the country.

---

145 The Báb, *Persian Bayán*, Vahid 2, Chapter 7.

Finally, in 1850, just six years after his declaration, the Báb was imprisoned and finally killed by firing squad. The first attempt at His public execution was by a firing squad composed of 750 soldiers in three ranks of 250 each. This large number was not only a reflection of the seriousness with which the Persian authorities viewed the Báb's teachings and the threat they believed He posed to the established order, but it was also part of the dramatic and highly public nature of His execution.

Astonishingly, the first volley of shots only cut the ropes from which the Báb and a devout follower surnamed Anis were hanging. A second attempt by a different firing squad carried out their mission successfully. The execution was reported in the *London Times*.

Today, Bahá'ís consider the Báb to be both an independent Manifestation of God and the forerunner of Bahá'u'lláh, one of the Twin Founders of the Bahá'í Faith.

Transition to the Bahá'í Faith

The second Manifestation of the Bahá'í Faith, Whom the Báb referred to as "He whom God shall make manifest," was born as Mírzá Husayn-`Alí Núrí in 1817 into a noble and wealthy Persian family. As a child, He showed unique spiritual insight and became a prominent follower of the Báb, though He was two years older. In His mid-20s, He declined a life of privilege and became one of the leading disciples of the Báb.

After the execution of the Báb, the disheartened Bábí community continued to be persecuted. At a conference of Bábís near the small village of Badasht, Mírzá Husayn-`Alí Núrí took the title Bahá'u'lláh ("Glory of God"). Though He was a nobleman, Bahá'u'lláh was deemed an apostate and eventually arrested, beaten, and thrown into an infamous dungeon in Tehran called the *Síyáh-Chál* ("Black Pit"). The pit was a discarded cistern converted into a dungeon. Three flights of steep stairs descended into an area with no light and no functioning latrine. The reeking, rat-infested chamber was filled with up to 150 male prisoners.

In 1852, while burdened by heavy chains in this dungeon, He received a vision of a Maiden who revealed that He was the Manifestation of God prophesied by the Báb. The year 1852 was the year nine on the lunar calendar. Bahá'ís see this as a literal fulfillment of the Báb's prophecy: "In the year nine, ye will attain unto all good."

About His vision in the dungeon, Bahá'u'lláh later wrote:

> She was imparting to both My inward and outer being tidings which rejoiced My soul, and the souls of God's honoured servants. Pointing with her finger unto My head, she addressed all who are in Heaven and all who are on Earth saying: "By God! This is the best beloved of the worlds, and yet ye comprehend not. This is the Beauty of God amongst you, and the power of His sovereignty within you, could ye but understand.[146]

Some scholars have described parallels between this maiden and Sophia, the personification of wisdom in Hellenistic philosophy and religion, Platonism, Gnosticism and Christian theology.

After four months of incarceration in the Black Pit, Bahá'u'lláh and his entire family were banished from his native land, the beginning of forty years of exile and further imprisonment. He was first sent to Baghdad, where He and His companions stayed for ten years while attracting a large number of followers,

In 1863, on the eve of His further banishment to what is now Turkey and then to the Holy Land, Bahá'u'lláh finally publicly declared that He was the Universal Messenger of God foretold by the Báb.

In 1868, Bahá'u'lláh arrived in the Holy Land with about seventy family members and followers. He and his family had been sentenced by Ottoman authorities to perpetual confinement in the penal colony of Acre, a peninsula off the shore of what is now

---

146 Bahá'u'lláh, *Summons of the Lord of Hosts*, p. 5

northern Israel. Entire families were sentenced with offenders in those days.

The order of confinement was never lifted, but because of a growing recognition of Bahá'u'lláh's outstanding character, He eventually was able to move outside the walls and onto the mainland. He lived His final years at a country home called Bahjí, where He passed away and was interred in 1892. For Bahá'ís, His shrine at Bahjí the holiest place on earth.

During the forty years of His exile, Bahá'u'lláh revealed a series of books, tablets and letters that today form the core of the holy writings of the Bahá'í Faith. Comprising the equivalent of about one hundred volumes, the writings of Bahá'u'lláh describe the nature of God and the purpose of human existence, specify new religious laws in keeping with contemporary society, and outline a vision for creating a peaceful and prosperous global society.

Succession Plan

Bahá'u'lláh recognized a major problem in previous religions—disruption of the unity of each Faith caused by disputes over leadership when the Founder died due to a lack of unambiguous succession planning. To resolve this issue, Bahá'u'lláh left explicit instructions to assure the continuity of guidance and leadership by establishing a line of succession, referred to as the Covenant.

- **'Abdu'l-Bahá.** In His will, Bahá'u'lláh appointed His oldest son, 'Abdu'l-Bahá, as the authorized interpreter of His teachings and Head of the Faith. Throughout the East and West, 'Abdu'l-Bahá became known as an ambassador of peace, an exemplary human being, and the leading exponent of a new Faith. According to the official Bahá'í website for the United States, during World War I, when a blockade threatened the lives of many civilians in Haifa, Israel, 'Abdu'l-Bahá saved them from starvation by anticipating the need for food prior to the war and teaching the villagers how to grow corn and store it properly, then giving it to Haifa civilians in need from every nation. In 1920, 'Abdu'l-Bahá was knighted at the residence of the British Governor in Haifa at a special ceremony.[147]

- **Shoghi Effendi.** Appointed Guardian of the Bahá'í Faith in 'Abdu'l-Bahá's Will and Testament, 'Abdu'l-Bahá's eldest grandson, Shoghi Effendi, spent thirty-six years systematically nurturing the development, deepening the understanding, and strengthening the unity of the Bahá'í community, as it increasingly grew to reflect the diversity of the entire human race.[148]

- **The Universal House of Justice.** Since the passing of Shoghi Effendi, the development of the Bahá'í Faith worldwide has been guided by the Universal House of Justice. In His book of laws, Bahá'u'lláh ordained this institution of the Faith, instructing it to exert a positive influence on the welfare of humankind, promote education, peace and global prosperity, and safeguard human honor and the position of religion. The nine members of the Universal House of Justice are democratically elected every five years by the members of the Bahá'í national administrative bodies around the world.[149]

Religious Innovations

Although the Bahá'í Faith teaches the concept of progressive revelation, in which Divine Educators throughout human history have maintained the continuity of spiritual teachings revealed by God, some distinctive innovations set apart the Bahá'í Faith from

---

147 http://bahai.us/the-knighting-of-abdul-baha/.
148 https://www.bahai.org/beliefs/bahaullah-covenant
149 https://www.bahai.org/the-universal-house-of-justice

all previous religions. These unique features were revealed by the most recent Manifestation of God as consistent with the needs of a contemporary society.

- **Unambiguous continuity of authority.** For the first time in religious history, a Manifestation of God, in clear and unambiguous language, provides for the authorized interpretation of His Word, and ensures the continuity of the divinely appointed authority that flows from the Source of the Faith's teachings.

- **No clergy.** The Baha'i faith has no clergy because it emphasizes the principle of equality among all believers, believing that individuals can directly access God without the need for an intermediary or priestly class to interpret scripture or mediate between them and the divine, and potentially insert personal beliefs that may lead to disunity and schism. Every Baha'i is considered capable of understanding and practicing their faith independently.

- **No outside donations.** The Bahá'í Faith does not accept financial contributions for its own purposes from non-Bahá'ís. Financial support of the Bahá'í Faith is a bounty reserved by Bahá'u'lláh to His declared followers. This bounty imposes full responsibility for financial support of the Faith on the believers alone.

- **Authentic, handwritten scriptures.** Serious issues exist regarding the authenticity and provenance of scriptures of most of our wisdom traditions. Not so with the Bahá'í Faith. Most Bahá'í writings are original manuscripts written by the Báb or Bahá'u'lláh, occasionally dictated to an amanuensis and approved by the Manifestation.

Teachings of the Bahá'í Faith

The Bahá'í Faith affirms the spiritual principles of all previous religions, as we shall see. Since Divine Educators are also sent to expand humanity's knowledge of God, we should expect clarification on some principles and even some new truths to be revealed. Central to all the principles taught by the Bahá'í Faith are these three assertions:

The oneness of God

There is only one God. Though He is unknowable, He has sent various Manifestations of His essence to humanity. They act as Divine Educators and as mirrors of God's qualities and virtues so we may catch a glimpse of Him reflected in Them. One can draw closer to God through prayer, meditation, study of the holy writings of all the great wisdom traditions, and through service to humankind.

> As our knowledge of things, even of created and limited things, is knowledge of their qualities and not of their essence, how is it possible to comprehend in its essence the Divine Reality, which is unlimited? ... Knowing God, therefore, means the comprehension and the knowledge of His attributes, and not of His Reality. This knowledge of the attributes is also proportioned to the capacity and power of man; it is not absolute.[150]

The oneness of religion

There is only one religion, which God reveals progressively to humankind through His Manifestations Who serve as Divine Educators. Outward differences between the religions are due to the exigencies of the time and place in which each religion was revealed and to the natural devolution of teachings caused by humanity.

---

150 'Abdu'l-Bahá, *Some Answered Questions*, pp. 220–21.

> The divine religions embody two kinds of ordinances. One is those which concern spiritual verities and are founded upon morality. These are essential and one and the same in all religions. The other kind are those which pertain to material things and change in each prophetic cycle in accordance with the exigencies of the time.[151]

The oneness of humanity

All people are equal in the sight of God. Their unity transcends all divisions of race, nation, gender, caste and social class.

> Ye are the fruits of one tree, and the leaves of one branch. Deal ye one with another with the utmost love and harmony, with friendliness and fellowship.[152]

Major Spiritual Principles of the Bahá'í Faith

The major principles of the Bahá'í Faith affirm, clarify or expand upon the principles of previous religions. In some cases, new spiritual principles are asserted because the need for them has arisen or humanity's ability to comprehend them has improved. Some major spiritual principles are:

- The requirement for each person to *independently search after truth*, unfettered by superstition, tradition or coercion.[153]

- The *condemnation of all forms of prejudice* whether based on religion, race, class, ethnicity, national origin, gender or age.

---

151 'Abdu'l-Bahá, *The Promulgations of Universal Peace*, p. 197
152 Bahá'u'lláh, *Epistle to the Son of the Wolf*, p. 288.
153 A deep study of this principle can be found in the following book: Massoud Kazemzadeh and Gary Lindberg, *The Soul of Humanity: How rational thinking can save us from the chaos of blind faith*, https://geni.us/souls_speak.

- The essential *harmony of science and religion* despite our adequate lack of understanding of either, which gives rise to false conclusions about both.

- The *equality of women and men*, the two wings on which the bird of humankind is able to soar.

- The introduction of worldwide *compulsory education*, which is necessary to erase the plague of ignorance that afflicts the world.

- The *abolition of the extremes of wealth and poverty*, the cause of so much misery for about one-quarter of the Earth's population who live in poverty, half of which are children.[154]

- The elevation of work performed in the spirit of service to the spiritual rank of worship.

- The *exaltation of justice* as the ruling principle in human society, and of religion as a bulwark for the protection of all peoples and nations.

- The accomplishment of a *permanent and universal peace* as the supreme goal of all humankind.

All these principles are presented in detail in the book *Humanity Coming of Age: How a mature, global civilization can emerge from the chrysalis of despair*,[155] which I coauthored with Massoud Kazemzadeh, PhD.

---

154 See Social Income report at https://socialincome.org/en/int/world-poverty-statistics-2024.

155 Massoud Kazemzadeh and Gary Lindberg, *Humanity Coming of Age: How a mature, global civilization can emerge from the chrysalis of despair*, https://geni.us/HumanityComingofAge; see also, Massoud Kazemzadeh and Gary Lindberg, *The Soul of Humanity: How rational thinking can save us from the chaos of blind faith*, https://geni.us/soulhumanity.

PART TWO

Acknowledging God's Educators

Chapter 13: What's In a Name?

How should we refer to the Manifestations of God? By their given name or full name? By a title They adopted or was awarded Them by God or Their faithful? By the numerous metaphors or other signifiers that obviously point to Them? In the various scriptures, all of these references are used to define specific Manifestations, and each carries a special significance that helps us understand the intended subject of the reference. Here is a short study of the names of our recognized Manifestations of God upon Whom existing wisdom traditions were founded and actively exist today.

Abrahamic Religions

Abrahamic Faith

In the pre-Judaic religion of Abraham—who is a recognized Manifestation of God and a central figure in Judaism, Christianity, and Islam—He is referred to by various names, titles, and metaphors. These references, some implied, reflect his spiritual role, attributes, and significance. Here is a breakdown of these names and metaphors, along with their meanings:

Abram (אַבְרָם) – "Exalted Father"

"Abram" in Hebrew means "Exalted Father" or "High Father" and was Abraham's original name as recorded in the Book of Genesis: "Terah became the father of Abram, Nahor, and Haran; and Haran became the father of Lot."[156] As a name, Abram signified His importance and stature even before God made a covenant with him.

Abraham (אַבְרָהָם) – "Father of a Multitude"

As part of the Covenant made with Abram, God changed Abram's name to Abraham, in Hebrew meaning "Father of a Multitude" or "Father of Many Nations" as recorded in Genesis: "No longer will you be called Abram; your name will be Abraham, for I have made you a father of many nations."[157] This new name reflects Abraham's new role as the patriarch of the Hebrew people (eventually these became the Jews descended from Isaac), Arabs (descended through Ishmael), and others.

Friend of God (Khalíl Alláh in Islam)

This metaphorical title highlights Abraham's unique closeness and trust in God. In the Old Testament, we find this reference in the words of God Himself (italics added): "But you, Israel, my servant, Jacob, whom I have chosen, you descendants of Abraham *my friend*."[158] And in the New Testament, James emphasized this relationship: "Abraham believed God, and it was credited to him as righteousness, and he was called *God's friend*."[159] In Islam, Abraham is also referred to as *Khalíl Alláh* (خَلِيلُ ٱللَّٰه), meaning "the Friend of God," in the Qur'an.

---

156 The *Bible*, Genesis 11:27.
157 The *Bible*, Genesis 17:5.
158 The *Bible*, Isaiah 41:8, (NIV).
159 The *Bible*, James 2:23.

The Patriarch

The term "patriarch" refers to a founding father or leader of a people. Abraham is regarded as the first patriarch of the Jewish faith. The patriarchal lineage in Genesis begins with Abraham, Isaac, and Jacob (the "Patriarchs of Israel"). In Christianity, Abraham is viewed as the spiritual patriarch of all who have faith according to Paul in his letter to the Galatians: "Understand, then, that those who have faith are children of Abraham."[160] The Bahá'í Faith honors Abraham as the Patriarch of the Abrahamic religions—Judaism, Christianity, Islam and the Bahá'í Faith—which have shaped much of their histories and are part of one progressive revelation, with each Manifestation of God building on the foundation laid by Abraham: "All the Prophets of God proclaim the same Faith. They are the channels of God's one eternal religion, which has been revealed and renewed from age to age."[161]

The Righteous (Believer in God)

Abraham is also portrayed as a model of righteousness and unwavering faith in God according to the Hebrew Bible: "Abram believed the LORD, and He credited it to him as righteousness."[162] In the New Testament, Abraham's faith is celebrated as a model for Christians: "Against all hope, Abraham in hope believed and so became the father of many nations."[163]

The Father of the Faithful

This title signifies Abraham's role as the spiritual father of all who believe in God regardless of ethnicity or nation. In the New Testament, Paul refers to Abraham as the father of those who live by faith: "So then, those who rely on faith are blessed along with

---

160 The *Bible*, Galatians 3:7.
161 Bahá'u'lláh, *Gleanings from the Writings of Bahá'u'lláh*.
162 The *Bible*, Genesis 15:6.
163 The *Bible*, Romans 4:18.

Abraham, the man of faith."¹⁶⁴ For Christians, Abraham's faith and trust in God serve as the foundation for understanding faith. The Bahá'í Faith also recognizes Abraham as the "Father of Faith (italics added): "Abraham, as you know, was the *Father of Faith* among the Prophets of God and arose with a great mission."¹⁶⁵

Prophet

Abraham is recognized in the Old Testament as a Prophet, someone who speaks on behalf of God. "Now return the man's wife, for he is a prophet, and he will pray for you and you will live."¹⁶⁶ In Islam, Abraham is revered as Ibráhím (إِبْرَاهِيمُ), a prophet and messenger of God, and one of the most important figures in the Qur'an. The Bahá'í Faith recognizes Him as a prophet of the highest rank, a Manifestation of God: "The holy Manifestations of God, the Source of grace and bounty, have been as the clouds and Abraham was the herald of truth."¹⁶⁷

Founder of Monotheism

This important title from the Bahá'í Faith highlights Abraham's pivotal role in introducing and establishing the belief in one God, which became foundational for subsequent religious traditions. According to the Bahá'í Faith (italics added): "The *Founder of monotheism* was Abraham; it is to Him that this concept can be traced..."¹⁶⁸

The Father of Isaac and Ishmael

Abraham is frequently identified through his two sons—Isaac (ancestor of the Israelites) and Ishmael (forefather of the Arabs). Regarding Isaac, we find this reference in Genesis: "Sarah became

---

164 The *Bible*, Galatians 3:9.
165 Bahá'u'lláh, *The Kitáb-i-Íqán* (The Book of Certitude.
166 The *Bible*, Genesis 20:7.
167 'Abdu'l-Bahá, Some Answered Questions.
168 'Abdu'l-Bahá, *Selections from the Writings of 'Abdu'l-Bahá*, Ch. 25.

pregnant and bore a son to Abraham in his old age."¹⁶⁹ And regarding Ishmael: "Hagar bore Abram a son, and Abram gave the name Ishmael to the son she had borne."¹⁷⁰

Conclusion

The titles of Abraham highlight his extraordinary spiritual role as a patriarch, Prophet, and a symbol of faith and unity across Judaism, Christianity, Islam, and the Bahá'í Faith. These titles emphasize his foundational contributions to monotheism, his covenant with God, and his exemplary faith and obedience. Abraham's titles underscore his universal significance as a unifying figure in the spiritual history of humanity and a critical link in the chain of progressive revelation that culminates in the teachings of Bahá'u'lláh.

Judaism

Most people know the story of Moses, the Founder of Judaism, Whose life was saved when he was put into a chest and cast into the river to prevent Him from being killed by the Egyptian Pharaoh. Citing the words of God, the Qur'an tells us: "…We inspired your mother, saying, 'Put him into the chest, then cast it into the river, and the river will throw it on the bank, and there an enemy of Mine and an enemy of his will take him.'"¹⁷¹ Fulfilling this expectation, the daughter of the Pharaoh discovered the infant alive and adopted Him.

Moses was raised as an Egyptian Prince until He decided to help His people, the enslaved Hebrews, leave Egypt in a mass migration called the Exodus. Moses was called by various names and metaphors including:

---

169 The *Bible*, Genesis 21:2.
170 The *Bible*, Genesis 16:15.
171 *Qur'an* 20:38-39, Sahih International.

Moses (Moshe in Hebrew

Moses's Egyptian stepmother gave the infant the name Moses, meaning "drawn out [of the water]," which refers to Moses being saved as an infant from the Nile River. According to the Old Testament: "She named him Moses, saying, 'I drew him out of the water.'"[172]

The Servant of God

Moses is described as God's humble and devoted servant, fulfilling God's will. The Book of Deuteronomy tells us: "And Moses the servant of the LORD died there in Moab, as the LORD had said."[173] Christianity also tells us in the New Testament that: "Moses was faithful as a servant in all God's house, bearing witness to what would be spoken by God in the future."[174] The Bahá'í Faith upholds this title, seeing servanthood as an integral part of Moses's role as a Manifestation of God—one who perfectly exemplifies servitude to God and delivers divine guidance to humanity.

Prophet and Messenger of God

Moses is recognized as both a Prophet (one who receives divine revelation) and a Messenger (one who conveys God's laws). According to the Hebrew Bible: "The LORD would speak to Moses face to face, as one speaks to a friend."[175] The Qur'an agrees in these words: "And mention Moses in the Book. He was truly sincere, and he was a messenger and a prophet."[176] Bahá'í's see Moses as a Manifestation of God who revealed the Mosaic Law and established the covenant of God with the Israelites.

---

172 The *Bible*, Exodus 2:10 (NIV).
173 The *Bible*, Deuteronomy 34:5 (NIV).
174 The *Bible*, Hebrews 3:5 (NIV).
175 The *Bible*, Exodus 33:11 (NIV).
176 *Qur'an* 19:51, Sahih International.

The Lawgiver

This title, used by many and implied in scripture, identifies Moses as the One through whom God revealed the Ten Commandments and the Mosaic Law. The Book of Exodus tells us: "And the LORD said to Moses, 'Come up to Me on the mountain and stay here, and I will give you the tablets of stone, with the law and commandments I have written for their instruction.'"[177] The New Testament agrees, stating: "For the law was given through Moses; grace and truth came through Jesus Christ."[178] Bahá'ís affirm Moses's role as the Lawgiver but emphasize that divine laws are progressively revealed as well by subsequent Manifestations, such as Jesus, Muhammad, and Bahá'u'lláh.

Shepherd of His People

Moses spent forty years as a shepherd after fleeing Egypt for the first time. According to Exodus: "Now Moses was tending the flock of Jethro his father-in-law, the priest of Midian, and he led the flock to the far side of the wilderness and came to Horeb, the mountain of God."[179] This passage sets the stage for Moses's spiritual role as a shepherd of God's people, which the New Testament builds upon by emphasizing his leadership and faith. Eventually, Moses, like a shepherd, guided the Israelites out of slavery and through the wilderness. According to the Psalm, "You led Your people like a flock by the hand of Moses and Aaron."[180]

Intercessor

Moses is depicted as an intermediary between God and His people, interceding on their behalf. The Old Testament reveals: "But Moses

---

177 The *Bible*, Exodus 24:12 (NIV).
178 The *Bible*, John 1:17 (NIV).
179 The *Bible*, Exodus 3:1 (NIV).
180 The *Bible*, *Psalm* 77:20 (NIV)

sought the favor of the LORD his God. 'LORD,' he said, 'why should Your anger burn against Your people?'"[181] And in the Qur'an, we find: "Moses said, 'My Lord, expand for me my breast [with assurance] and ease for me my task.'"[182] The Bahá'í Faith views the role of intercession as a hallmark of *every* Manifestation of God, including Moses, who bridged the gap between God and humanity.

Precursor of Future Manifestations

Moses foretold the coming of a future Prophet in the Book of Deuteronomy: "The LORD your God will raise up for you a prophet like me from among you, from your fellow Israelites. You must listen to him."[183] Christians view this as a prophecy about Jesus. Bahá'ís, however, see this prophecy as a continuation of progressive revelation applying to all subsequent Manifestations of God including Jesus, Muhammad, the Báb, and Bahá'u'lláh.

Conclusion

The titles of Moses highlight his profound spiritual role as a Prophet, Lawgiver, and Deliverer, reflecting his significance in Judaism, Christianity, Islam, and the Bahá'í Faith. These titles encapsulate his mission to guide humanity, establish divine laws, and lead his people toward liberation and unity. Moses is a central figure in the process of progressive revelation, embodying divine wisdom and guidance that prepared humanity for subsequent teachings from other Manifestations of God. His titles affirm his pivotal role in establishing monotheism and advancing human civilization.

Christianity

The name Jesus was called when growing up was not Jesus Christ. His given name was likely Yeshua (עוּשִׁי) in Hebrew—or Yehoshua,

---

181 The *Bible*, Exodus 32:11 (NIV).
182 *Qur'an* 20:25-26, Sahih International.
183 The *Bible*, Deuteronomy 18:15 (NIV).

which means "God is salvation." In Aramaic, the common language spoken in Jesus's region, His name would have sounded similar to "Yeshua." During His upbringing in Nazareth, people likely would have called him "Yeshua bar Yosef" (Jesus, son of Joseph) to identify Him by his father's name, a custom in Jewish society.

The word "Christ" comes from the Greek word Χριστός (Christos), which means "the anointed one," a similar meaning to that of the Hebrew title "Messiah" (הַמָּשִׁיחַ). Jesus was not called "Christ" during His early life. His followers started adding that title to his name after Jesus's ministry began. Especially after His crucifixion and resurrection, His followers began to refer to Him as "Jesus the Christ" or simply "Jesus Christ" to express their belief that He fulfilled the Jewish prophecies of the Messiah. The title gained prominence in early Christian communities because the Gospels and epistles were written in Greek. Consequently, "Christ" (Χριστός) became central to describing the role of Jesus as the Messiah.

Here are some of the common names, titles and metaphors used to refer to the Manifestation of God we know of as Jesus:

Jesus as the Messiah (Christ)

"Messiah" comes from the Hebrew word *Mashiach*, meaning "anointed one," and the Greek word *Christos* (Christ). In the New Testament, we find this account affirming that Jesus was identified to many as the Messiah and called Christ: "The woman said, 'I know that Messiah (called Christ) is coming. When He comes, He will explain everything to us.' Then Jesus declared, 'I, the one speaking to you—I am He.'"[184]

The Qur'an explicitly refers to Jesus as the Messiah in such verses as this: "[The angels said,] 'O Mary, indeed Allah gives you good tidings of a word from Him, whose name will be the Messiah, Jesus, the son of Mary—distinguished in this world and the Hereafter

---

184 The *Bible*, John 4:25–26 (NIV).

and among those brought near [to Allah].'"[185] Islam's understanding of the meaning of Messiah, however, differs from the Hebrew interpretation. For Muslims, the Messiah's role was to guide the Israelites, confirm the teachings of previous prophets and bring new divine guidance.

The Bahá'í Faith also affirms Jesus as the Messiah, fulfilling Jewish prophecies of the "anointed one" who would bring salvation. However, Bahá'ís see Jesus's mission as primarily a spiritual leadership, not political deliverance. Like Islam, though, Bahá'ís believe that, as a Manifestation of God, Jesus also brought new guidance to humanity.

The Son of God

"Son of God" is a title that emphasizes Jesus's divine origin and unique relationship with God. The Book of Matthew quotes God as saying: "And behold, a voice from heaven said, 'This is my beloved Son, with whom I am well pleased.'"[186] This and similar New Testament verses are a cornerstone to the eventual declaration of Christianity in the fourth century CE that Jesus was in fact God—the second entity within a holy trinity that, as a whole, comprises God.

Islam honors Jesus as one of the greatest prophets and messengers of God but not as divine, calling the Christian concept of the trinity a "shirk" (associating partners with God), a fundamental violation of monotheism. By the term "Son of God," many Muslims believe the meaning refers to Jesus's miraculous creation. The Qur'an states: "Indeed, the example of Jesus to Allah is like that of Adam. He created Him from dust; then He said to him, 'Be,' and he was." In Islam, Jesus's miraculous creation does not make Him God any more than Adam's creation made Him God.

The Bahá'í Faith interprets "Son of God" symbolically rather than literally. Jesus is the "Son of God" in a symbolic and spiritual sense, representing His closeness to God and His role as a perfect

---

185 Qur'an 3:45, Sahih International
186 The *Bible*, Matthew 3:17 (ESV).

reflection of divine attributes. The title "only begotten Son"[187] signifies Jesus's unique mission and purity but is not viewed as exclusive or literal. "Only begotten" comes from the Greek word "monogenes," which can mean "unique" or "one of a kind" rather than "exclusive." Consequently, for many Bahá'ís, this title symbolically emphasizes Jesus's unique spiritual mission as a Manifestation of God and His special relationship with God. Jesus, then, is not literally divine or an incarnation of God but is a Manifestation of God, a perfect mirror reflecting God's will and attributes.

The Son of Man

"Son of Man" is a title Jesus often used for Himself, emphasizing His human nature and the fulfillment of prophecy found in Daniel 7:13–14. In a New Testament passage, Jesus uses this title to explain that while he is human, He still has profound spiritual authority: "But I want you to know that the Son of Man has authority on earth to forgive sins."[188] Bahá'ís agree that Jesus used this term to signify His dual role: human and divine. Like all Manifestations of God, Jesus revealed God's attributes while living a human life.

The Redeemer

"Redeemer" is a title emphasizing Jesus's role in delivering humanity from sin as explained in the Gospel of Luke: "For the Son of Man came to seek and to save the lost."[189] Bahá'ís interpret redemption spiritually. Jesus "redeemed" humanity by renewing divine truth and guiding people toward salvation through His teachings. The Bahá'í writings clarify this: "Christ sacrificed Himself for the life of the world. He bestowed the splendor of His divine reality upon mankind. Through His mercy and compassion, He became the ransom of the reality of man." Here, the word "ransom" is clearly

---

187 The bible, John 3:16 (KJV).
188 The *Bible*, Mark 2:10 (NIV).
189 The *Bible*, Luke 19:10 (NIV).

used symbolically, referring to the way that Jesus's love and sacrifice liberated humanity from spiritual darkness.

The Word (Logos)

Jesus is sometimes referred to as the "Word of God," indicating His divine revelation and role as God's creative command, A New Testament verse tells us that: "In the beginning was the Word, and the Word was with God, and the Word was God."[190] In the Qur'an, we learn that: "Christ Jesus, the son of Mary, was (no more than) a Messenger of Allah, and His Word, which He bestowed on Mary, and a spirit proceeding from Him."[191] Bahá'ís fully affirm this concept, recognizing Jesus as the "Word of God" (a divine Manifestation who reveals God's will through His words and actions).

The Lamb of God

"Lamb of God" is a metaphor for the sacrificial role Jesus played in redeeming humanity's sins, according to its use in the Gospel of John: "Look, the Lamb of God, who takes away the sin of the world!"[192] The Bahá'í Faith acknowledges Jesus's sacrificial role but sees it primarily as a spiritual sacrifice that renewed humanity's faith. Bahá'ís reject the doctrine of original sin, which would require the forgiveness of sins for all humanity, believing that humans are born noble with the capacity for good and that sin is not inherited but is the result of human choices and the struggle between spiritual and material inclinations.

The Light of the World

"The Light of the World" is a title signifying Jesus as the source of spiritual enlightenment, as mentioned by Jesus in the Gospel of John: "I am the light of the world. Whoever follows me will never walk in

---

190 The *Bible*, John 1:1 (NIV).
191 Qur'an 4:171, Yusuf Ali.
192 The *Bible*, John 1:29 (NIV).

darkness, but will have the light of life."[193] For most Bahá'ís, Jesus is regarded as a divine light-bearer, illuminating humanity with God's teachings during His dispensation, just as all Manifestations of God do. As Bahá'u'lláh initiated new religious dispensation, Bahá'ís believe, He became the "Light of the World" for this age fulfilling Jesus's promise of His return and bringing teachings for the unity and progress of humanity in modern times. Both are Manifestations of God, reflecting the same divine light at different times in human history.

The Alpha and Omega

This is a title found in the Book of Revelation signifying Jesus as the beginning and the end, emphasizing His eternal spiritual significance. "I am the Alpha and the Omega, the First and the Last, the Beginning and the End."[194] Alpha and Omega are the first and last letters of the Greek alphabet, symbolizing the beginning and the end. Some Christian sects believe this Bible verse teaches that Jesus is the last prophet to appear on earth, the final Manifestation—except for the repeat performance of Jesus's Second Coming.

Bahá'ís generally recognize the eternal significance of Jesus as a Manifestation of God, but they believe this title applies to all divine Manifestations who successively reveal the eternal Word of God. They believe that all Manifestations, including Jesus, Muhammad, the Báb and Bahá'u'lláh share the same spiritual reality. Each one is the "Alpha and Omega" in their respective ages. Each represents the beginning of a new cycle of divine revelation as well as the completion of God's message for that era.

Bahá'u'lláh affirms this principle: "The Bearers of the Trust of God are made manifest unto the peoples of the earth as the Exponents of a new Cause and the Revealers of a new Message... They are regarded as one soul and the same person."[195]

---

193 The *Bible*, John 8:12 (NIV).
194 The *Bible*, Revelation 22:13 (NIV).
195 Bahá'u'lláh, *The Kitáb-i-Íqán* (The Book of Certitude), p. 153.

The Good Shepherd

"The Good Shepherd" is a metaphor for Jesus's role as a guide and protector of His followers as used in the Gospel of John: "I am the good shepherd. The good shepherd lays down his life for the sheep."[196]

Bahá'ís affirm this metaphor as reflecting Jesus's role as a divine teacher and protector, guiding humanity toward God. Note, however, that Moses is also referred to as the "shepherd of his people." We should expect that certain titles and metaphors indicate something specific about the recipients—in this case, that they are Manifestations of God. In a sense, all the Manifestations are good shepherds by leading Their flock (humanity) toward the truth of God, showing a willingness to sacrifice Themselves for the sake of Their followers, and unifying humanity under the guidance of love and truth.

Bahá'u'lláh wrote: "Regard men as a flock of sheep that need a shepherd for their protection. This, verily, is the truth, the certain truth."[197]"

Conclusion

The titles of Jesus reflect the profound spiritual significance of His mission, identity, and role in divine revelation. Each title encapsulates an aspect of His divine purpose, emphasizing His connection to God, His role in humanity's spiritual journey, and His impact on history. They also underscore His divine connection, highlight His mission as the Savior and bringer of spiritual renewal, reflect His leadership and eternal authority in guiding humanity to God, and affirm His fulfillment of prophecy and universal significance.

---

196 The *Bible*, John 10:11 (NIV).
197 Bahá'u'lláh. *Gleanings from the Writings of Bahá'u'lláh*, p. 335.

Islam

These are ten important names, titles and metaphors referring to Muhammad, Who revealed the Qur'an and founded Islam.

Muhammad – The Praised One

In Arabic, the name Muhammad means "the praised one" or "worthy of praise." The Qur'an tells us: "Muhammad is not the father of any one of your men, but he is the Messenger of Allah…"[198]
Traditionally, Christianity does not recognize Muhammad as a Prophet, viewing revelation as completed by Jesus Christ. However, some Christian scholars acknowledge Muhammad's historical significance. The Bahá'í Faith, however, praises this Manifestation of God in these words: "Muhammad, the Messenger of God, arose in the desert of Ḥijáz like the sun and illumined the whole world."[199]

The Seal of the Prophets
(خَاتَمُ النَّبِيِّينَ, Khatam an-Nabiyyin)

According to the Qur'an, Muhammad is the "Seal of the Prophets," signifying the finality of His mission in Islam. "Muhammad is … the Seal of the Prophets, and Allah has full knowledge of all things."[200] Christians traditionally interpret the concept of "Seal of the Prophets" as incompatible with their belief in Jesus as the "final" Word of God.

The Bahá'í Faith acknowledges Muhammad as the Seal of the Prophets in the sense of having closed the prophetic Adamic cycle of religious dispensations. According to Bahá'í writings, Bahá'u'lláh inaugurated a new cycle of divine revelation that recognizes Muhammad as a true Manifestation of God in the previous cycle: "It is evident that the followers of Muhammad are the true worshipers of the one God, for they have acknowledged and testified that He is

---

198 *Qur'an* 33:40, Sahih International.
199 'Abdu'l-Bahá, *Some Answered Questions*, p. 23.
200 *Qur'an* 33:40, Sahih International.

that 'Seal of the Prophets' foretold in all the sacred books."[201]

The Messenger of God
(رَسُولُ ٱللَّٰهِ, Rasul Allah)

According to Islamic texts, Muhammad is the Messenger of God tasked with delivering the Qur'an, in which we find this passage: "Muhammad is the Messenger of Allah. And those with him are firm against the disbelievers and compassionate among themselves."[202] Christians recognize Muhammad as a historical figure but do not accept Him as God's messenger, and many Christians consider Him a false prophet. Bahá'í writings, however, tell us that: "Muhammad… brought divine civilization to the Arabian Peninsula and called men to the unity of God."[203]

The Prophet (ٱلنَّبِي, Nabi)

Muhammad is often referred to as simply "The Prophet," emphasizing His role in guiding humanity through divine revelation. In recording the words of God to Muhammad, the Qur'an explains the purpose behind His mission: "O Prophet, indeed We have sent you as a witness and a bringer of good tidings…"[204] Bahá'í writings tell us: "That noble soul, the Prophet Muhammad, was a Manifestation of divine guidance and mercy, calling people to the unity of God."[205]

The Light (نُور, Nur)

Muhammad is described as a "light," symbolizing His role in dispelling spiritual darkness: "A light has come to you from Allah and a clear Book [the Qur'an]."[206] In the following passage of Bahá'í

---

201 Bahá'u'lláh, *Kitáb-i-Íqán*, p. 20.
202 *Quran* 48:29, Sahih International.
203 'Abdu'l-Bahá, *Some Answered Questions*, p. 24.
204 *Quran* 33:45, Sahih International.
205 'Abdu'l-Bahá, *The Promulgation of Universal Peace*, p. 371.
206 *Quran* 5:15, Sahih International.

scripture, 'Abdu'l-Bahá wrote: "When the light of Muhammad shone forth in their midst, however, they became so radiant as to illumine the world."[207]

The Unlettered Prophet
(النَّبِيُّ الأُمِّيّ, Al-Nabi al-Ummi)

Muhammad is sometimes referred to as "the Unlettered Prophet," underscoring His lack of formal education and the miraculous nature of the Qur'an, which uses this reference: "Those who follow the Messenger, the unlettered prophet, whom they find written in what they have of the Torah and the Gospel..."[208] Bahá'í writings recognize this characteristic as a sign of Muhammad's divine mission: "Incline your ears to the words of this unlettered One, wherewith He summoneth you unto God, the EverAbiding. Better is this for you than all the treasures of the earth..."[209]

The Mercy to All Creation
(رَحْمَةٌ لِلْعَالَمِين, Rahmat lil-'Alamin)

In the Qur'an, Muhammad is described as a "Mercy to all creation" or to "all the worlds," emphasizing His compassion and mercy: "And We have not sent you, [O Muhammad], except as a mercy to the worlds."[210] Bahá'ís would affirm this title, recognizing Muhammad's teachings as a source of spiritual mercy for humanity.

Ahmad (أحمَد) – The Most Praised

"Ahmad" is another name for Muhammad, meaning "the most praised." The Qur'an tells us: "And [mention] when Jesus, the son of Mary, said, 'O Children of Israel, indeed I am the messenger of Allah to you... bringing good tidings of a messenger to come after

---

207 'Abdu'l-Bahá, *Tablets of the Divine Plan*, p. 33.
208 *Quran* 7:157, Sahih International.
209 Bahá'u'lláh, *Gleanings from the Writings of Bahá'u'lláh*, p. 98.
210 *Quran* 21:107, Sahih International.

me, whose name is Ahmad.'"²¹¹ Some Christian scholars have linked this to Jesus's promise of the Paraclete²¹², but this remains a point of debate. I believe this verse refers to Muhammad, as Ahmad is another form of His name.

The Warner
(نَذِير, Nadhir)

Muhammad is described as a "Warner," one who warns people about turning away from God: "Indeed, We have sent you with the truth as a bringer of good tidings and a warner."²¹³

The Beloved of God
(حَبِيبُ اَللّٰهِ, Habib Allah)

The title "Beloved of God" signifies Muhammad's close spiritual relationship with God. It is widely used in Islamic poetry and devotion, emphasizing Muhammad's love for God and His exalted station.

Conclusion

The titles of Muhammad highlight His prophetic mission, reflect his divine connection, fulfill prophecies in earlier scriptures, and emphasize his moral example. Collectively, they affirm Muhammad's central role in Islamic theology, His transformative impact on humanity and His enduring relevance as a spiritual exemplar. They also signify Muhammad's divine station as a Manifestation of God who prepared humanity for the coming of Bahá'u'lláh.

The Bahá'í Faith – The Báb

The Báb was born on October 20, 1819, in Shiraz, Persia (modern-day Iran), into a respected merchant family. His full name, 'Alí-

---

211 *Quran* 61:6, Sahih International.
212 The *Bible*, John 14:16.
213 *Quran* 2:119, Sahih International.

Muḥammad Shirazi, indicates His place of birth and lineage. The Baháʼí Faith considers Him to be a Manifestation of God as well as the herald, or forerunner, who prepared the way for the coming of another Manifestation, Baháʼuʼlláh, whom the Báb called "He Whom God shall make manifest." There are many titles and metaphorical references to Him, some of which are listed below:

The Báb
(الباب) The "Gate"

The "Báb" literally means the "Gate" in Arabic, symbolizing His role as the gateway to "He Whom God shall make manifest" (Baháʼuʼlláh) and to a new spiritual dispensation. In His prolific writings, the Báb sometimes referred to Himself as the Gate of God: "I am the Gate of God and none shall enter His Kingdom except through Me."[214] This echoes a well-known biblical passage: "Knock, and the door will be opened to you."[215] Baháʼís interpret this passage from Matthew as a metaphorical prophecy fulfilled by the Báb, as the "door" or "gate" to a new era of spiritual knowledge. Baháʼís believe the Báb fulfilled prophecies in the Qurʼan about a forerunner or herald, such as: "And [by] the heaven containing pathways."[216] The "pathway" here symbolizes the Báb as a gateway to divine knowledge.

"The Qaʼim"
(قائم) He Who Arises

In Shiʼa Islam, the Qaʼim (or "He Who Arises") is the awaited prophetic figure from the family of the Prophet Muhammad Who would arise to bring justice. The Báb explicitly claimed this title, asserting He was the promised Qaʼim: "I am the Qaʼim whom you have been awaiting for one thousand years."[217] The Qurʼan alludes

---
214 The Báb, *Selections from the Writings of the Báb*, p. 9.
215 The *Bible*, Matthew 7:7 (NIV).
216 *Quran* 51:7.
217 The Báb, Persian *Bayán* 2:7.

to the Qa'im in verses that describe the coming of One Who will establish justice: "We wished to confer favor upon those who were oppressed in the land and make them leaders and make them inheritors."[218]

The Primal Point
(نقطة أولى, Nuqta-yi-Úlá)

The Báb referred to Himself as the "Primal Point," the point from which a new spiritual cycle begins following the closure of the Adamic cycle of religious dispensations. This reflects His role as the initiator of a new religious era. He wrote: "I am the Primal Point from which have been generated all created things."[219] The Manifestation of God Who followed a few years later wrote about the Báb: "Verily He is the King of the Messengers and His Book [the Báyán] is the Mother Book did ye but know."[220]

The Remembrance of God
(ذكر الله, Dhikr Alláh)

The Báb referred to Himself as "The Remembrance of God," a title often used in Islamic and Qur'anic contexts for those who call humanity to divine worship. The Qur'an stated:
"Indeed, it is We who sent down the message [remembrance], and indeed, We will be its guardian."[221] The Báb interpreted this title as applying to Himself in the context of His divine mission.

The Point of the Bayán

The Báb's seminal work, called the Bayán (meaning "Exposition"), is His primary revelation. Shoghi Effendi, the Guardian of the Bahá'í

---

218 *Qur'an* 28:5, Sahih International.
219 The Báb, *Selections from the Writings of the Báb*, p. 51.
220 Bahá'u'lláh, *Tablet of Ahmad,* (see at https://www.bahaiprayers.org/ahmad.htm.)
221 *Quran* 15:9, Sahih International.

Faith, said this: "The Bayán deriveth all its glory from 'Him Whom God shall make manifest.' All blessing be upon him who believeth in Him and woe betide him that rejecteth His truth"[222]

The Herald of Bahá'u'lláh

The Báb described His mission as preparatory, heralding the coming of Bahá'u'lláh, the Promised One. Bahá'u'lláh, the Manifestation of God Who followed the Báb, acknowledged: "That which was ordained hath been revealed, that which had been promised hath been fulfilled."[223]

Conclusion

The titles of the Báb hold profound symbolic and spiritual significance. They highlight His dual mission as both an independent Manifestation of God and the herald of Bahá'u'lláh. These titles reflect His fulfillment of Islamic prophecies, His station as a gateway to divine truth, and His role in inaugurating a new era of spiritual transformation. For Bahá'ís, the Báb's titles are a testament to His pivotal role in the continuity of progressive revelation, linking the prophetic traditions of the past with the universal teachings of Bahá'u'lláh.

The Bahá'í Faith –Bahá'u'lláh

Bahá'u'lláh (1817–1892), born Mírzá Husayn-'Alí Núrí in Tehran, Persia, was the founder of the Bahá'í Faith. Born into a noble family, He rejected wealth and power to dedicate His life to the spiritual renewal of humanity. A follower of the Báb, Bahá'u'lláh declared in 1863 that He was "He Whom God shall make manifest" as foretold by the Báb. His teachings emphasize unity, peace, and justice, calling for the oneness of humanity and religions. Despite enduring exile,

---

222 Shoghi Effendi, *Shoghi Effendi, The Dispensation of Bahá'u'lláh* (excerpt from *The World Order of Bahá'u'lláh*), p. 100.

223 Bahá'u'lláh, *Epistle to the Son of the Wolf*, p. 135.

imprisonment, and persecution, His writings form the foundation of the Bahá'í Faith, which aims to build a global civilization rooted in spiritual and material progress.

There are many titles and metaphorical references to Him, some of which are listed here:

Bahá'u'lláh
(بهاء الله) The "Glory of God," or the" Splendor of God"

The title "Bahá'u'lláh" (an Arabic term meaning "the Glory of God" or the "Splendor of God") was first associated with Mírzá Husayn-'Alí Núrí by the Báb, the founder of the Bábí Faith, who revered Him as a central figure among His followers. Bahá'u'lláh formally declared His mission as "He Whom God shall make manifest" in the Ridván Garden near Baghdad, Iraq. From this point forward, He became widely recognized as Bahá'u'lláh. This name encapsulates Bahá'u'lláh's mission to reveal God's glory and unify humanity under divine teachings. It aligns with prophecies in various scriptures about the coming of the "Glory of God" and other similar references such as "His glory," "The glory of the Lord," "My glory" (when God is speaking,) et cetera.

This is relevant when we consider a specific verse in Revelation where Jesus refers to being given a new name upon his return, a reference to a different material identity and title.

> "Him that overcometh will I make a pillar in the temple of my God... and I will write upon him the name of my God... and I will write upon him *my new name.*"[224] (Italics added.)

Jesus does not reveal that new name, but chapters 21 and 22 of the Book of Revelation do. These chapters refer to the descending

---

224 The *Bible*, Revelation 3:12 (KJV).

of the city of God (a metaphor for divine revelation) from heaven, and then describe its distinct features. To emphasize the clarity of the verses that tell us the new name of Jesus, the prophecies from those chapters that specify the title "glory of God" or similar phrases will be repeated here twice, the second time substituting "Bahá'u'lláh" (the Arabic translation of the phrases) for the English translation of the original Hebrew, Greek or Aramaic words.

> And he [an angel] carried me away in the Spirit to a mountain great and high, and showed me the Holy City, Jerusalem, coming down out of heaven from God. It shone with **the glory of God**…[225]

> And he [an angel] carried me away in the Spirit to a mountain great and high, and showed me the Holy City, Jerusalem, coming down out of heaven from God. It shone with ***Bahá'u'lláh***…

The prophecy continues:

> I did not see a temple in the city, because the Lord God Almighty and the Lamb [Jesus] are its temple. The city does not need the sun or the moon to shine on it, for **the glory of God** gives it light, and the Lamb is its lamp. The nations will walk by its light, and the kings of the earth will bring their splendor into it.[226]

> I did not see a temple in the city, because the Lord God Almighty and the Lamb [Jesus] are its temple. The city does not need the sun or the moon to shine on it, for ***Bahá'u'lláh*** gives it light, and the Lamb is its lamp. The

---

225 The *Bible*, Revelation 21:10–11 (NIV).
226 The *Bible*, Revelation 21:22–24 (NIV).

> nations will walk by its light, and the kings of the earth will bring their splendor into it.

In other words, Bahá'u'lláh fulfills the preceding prophecy. Another prophecy from the Psalms points to the Glory of God as being predicted by all religions.

> The heavens [all religions] declare **the glory of God**...[227]

> The heavens [all religions] declare **Bahá'u'lláh**...

Many prophecies speak of a universal spread of glory (*Bahá*) to the farthest reaches of our planet depicting *Bahá* as a sun that never sets.

> For the earth will be filled with the knowledge of **the glory of the Lord** as the waters cover the sea.[228]

> For the earth will be filled with the knowledge of **Bahá'u'lláh** as the waters cover the sea.

Isaiah expands on this theme:

> And **the glory of the Lord** will be revealed, and all mankind together will see it.[229]

> And **Bahá'u'lláh** will be revealed, and all mankind together will see it.

Some prophecies point specifically to the Glory of God as a person and not just an attribute of God. These examples show how

---

[227] The *Bible*, Psalm 19:1 (NIV).
[228] The *Bible*, Habakkuk 2:14 (NIV).
[229] The *Bible*, Isaiah 40:5 (NIV).

the attribute of glory is personified as a more direct reference to a Manifestation of God. The first example from Acts in the New Testament presents the story of the stoning of Stephen, which includes this verse:

> But Stephen, full of the Holy Spirit, looked up to heaven and saw **the glory of God**, and Jesus standing at the right hand of God.[230]

> But Stephen, full of the Holy Spirit, looked up to heaven and saw ***Bahá'u'lláh***, and Jesus standing at the right hand of God.[231]

In the Gospel of John, Jesus reveals a new name He will be given:

> Then Jesus said, "Did I not tell you that if you have faith, you will see **the glory of God**?[232]

> Then Jesus said, "Did I not tell you that if you have faith, you will see ***Bahá'u'lláh***?

Some prophecies indicate that the glory of God entered the court or the temple. In these examples, the term "gate" may be referring to the Báb, as that is His primary title:

> Then the man brought me by way of **the north gate** to the front of the temple. I looked and saw **the glory of the Lord** filling the temple of the Lord, and I fell facedown.[233]

---

230 The *Bible*, Acts 7:55 (NIV).
231 The *Bible*, Acts 7:55 (NIV).
232 The *Bible*, John 11:40 (NEB).
233 The *Bible*, Ezekiel 44:4 (NIV).

> **Then the man brought me by way of *the Báb* to the front of the temple. I looked and saw *Bahá'u'lláh* filling the temple of the Lord, and I fell facedown.**

Some prophecies seem to talk about the declaration of the coming Manifestation, as in this verse from Isaiah.

> **And *the glory of the Lord* shall be revealed, and all flesh shall see it together, for the mouth of the Lord has spoken.**[234]

> **And *Bahá'u'lláh* shall be revealed, and all flesh shall see it together, for the mouth of the Lord has spoken.**

This prophecy from Ezekiel clearly shows that "the glory of God" refers to a person according to the statement "His voice was like…" Note also that this person is coming from the east as Bahá'u'lláh came from Persia, which is east of the Holy Land.

> **And behold, *the glory of the God of Israel* was coming from the east. His voice was like the sound of many waters, and the earth shone with His glory.**[235]

> **And behold, *Bahaullah* was coming from the east. His voice was like the sound of many waters, and the earth shone with His glory.**

Here is another example that is even clearer in depicting the Báb as the herald of Bahá'u'lláh, who enters the temple "through the Báb."

---

234 The *Bible*, Isaiah 40:5 (ESV).
235 The Bible, Ezekiel 43:2 (ESV).

> ***The glory of the Lord*** entered the temple through the gate ***facing east***.. ⁵ Then the Spirit lifted me up and brought me into the inner court, and ***the glory of the Lord*** filled the temple.²³⁶

> ***Bahá'u'lláh*** entered the temple through ***the Báb*** facing east. ⁵ Then the Spirit lifted me up and brought me into the inner court, and ***Bahá'u'lláh*** filled the temple.

In the verse above, a gate facing east in religious texts is significant to Bahá'ís as it is seen as a prophetic symbol pointing to the birthplace of the Bahá'í Faith, Persia, located to the east relative to the Holy Land. Also, scriptural references to the east in various religious texts are often seen as prophetic symbols of new spiritual guidance.

In this next verse, we find a prayer for the global recognition of the Glory of God fulfilled in Bahá'u'lláh's mission. The name and the phrase "filling of the earth with glory" resonate with the meaning of Bahá'u'lláh's title and His teachings for achieving global unity. "Light" is an alternative translation of the word "glory."

> Blessed be ***His glorious name*** forever; may the whole earth be filled with ***His glory***! Amen and Amen.²³⁷

> Blessed be ***Bahá'u'lláh*** forever; may the whole earth be filled with ***His light***! Amen and Amen.²³⁸

Other titles and metaphorical referenced for Bahá'u'lláh can be found in the sacred texts of many religions. For example, in the Bahá'í writings we find these titles:

---

236 The *Bible*, Ezekiel 43:4–5 (NIV).
237 The *Bible*, Psalm 72:19 (ESV).
238 The *Bible*, Psalm 72:19 (ESV).

The Promised One of All Ages

Bahá'u'lláh identifies Himself as the fulfillment of the promises of all religions regarding the advent of a Promised One: "This is the King of Days, the Day that hath seen the coming of the Best-beloved, Him Who through all eternity hath been acclaimed the Desire of the World."[239]

The Ancient of Days

The title "the Ancient of Days" reflects the eternal and preexistent nature of Bahá'u'lláh's spiritual reality (italics added): "Magnified be Thy Name, O Lord my God! Thou art in truth the *Ancient of Days*, the Lord of all creation, and the Educator of all beings."[240]

He Whom God Shall Make Manifest

This title originates from the Báb, who prophesied the coming of Bahá'u'lláh as the Promised One of the Bayán: "All things are created through Me, and all things are returned unto Me. Yet I am but a letter out of that most mighty volume, a dewdrop out of that limitless ocean, the first to adore Him Whom God shall make manifest."[241]

The Most Great Name

Bahá'u'lláh's revelation is often referred to as the "Most Great Name," symbolizing the ultimate manifestation of God's guidance: "The Most Great Name beareth Me witness! How great is My blessedness; for ye have been summoned by Me and have attained unto My Presence, and have heard the melodies of the songs of My glory."[242] This passage identifies Bahá'u'lláh as the bearer of the Most Great Name, representing divine authority and power.

---

239 Bahá'u'lláh, *Gleanings from the Writings of Bahá'u'lláh*, p. 12.
240 Bahá'u'lláh, *Prayers and Meditations*, p. 268.
241 The Báb, *Selections from the Writings of the Báb*, p. 50.
242 Bahá'u'lláh, *Gleanings from the Writings of Bahá'u'lláh*, p. 136.

Blessed Beauty

This title reflects Bahá'u'lláh's role as the embodiment of divine light and attributes: "O King! I was but a man like others, asleep upon My couch, when lo, the breezes of the All-Glorious were wafted over Me and taught Me the knowledge of all that hath been... The heavens of the Divine Revelation were cleft asunder and the angels of God were seen descending. The eye of the Lord's Majesty beheld; the Blessed Beauty appeared in the form of a mortal man."[243]

The Divine Educator

This title highlights the role of Bahá'u'lláh role, as well as the role of other Manifestations, as a teacher who brings spiritual and moral enlightenment. "The Prophets and Messengers of God have been sent down for the sole purpose of guiding mankind to the straight path of truth."[244]

The Christian Bible also refers frequently to the "Glory of God" and other phrases referring to the Arabic name "Bahá'u'lláh." Here are other terms used in the New Testament to refer to Bahá'u'lláh.

The Comforter/Paraclete

"But the Comforter [sometimes translated as *Paraclete*], which is the Holy Spirit, whom the Father will send in my name, he shall teach you all things."[245] Bahá'ís see this as a prophecy of Bahá'u'lláh's mission to bring spiritual truth and enlightenment to humanity.

---

243 Bahá'u'lláh, *The Hidden Words*, Arabic No. 6.
244 Bahá'u'lláh, *Gleanings from the Writings of Bahá'u'lláh*, p. 78.
245 The *Bible*, John 14:26.

The Spirit of Truth

"When the Spirit of truth comes, he will guide you into all truth."[246] Bahá'ís associate this with Bahá'u'lláh's role in guiding humanity into a new era of divine knowledge.

Judaism also offers titles and metaphors that refer to Bahá'u'lláh. These include:

The King of Glory

"Who is this King of glory? The Lord of hosts, he is the King of glory."[247] Bahá'ís interpret this as a metaphor for Bahá'u'lláh's divine authority.

The Branch of the Lord

"In that day the Branch of the Lord shall be beautiful and glorious."[248] Bahá'ís associate this title with Bahá'u'lláh as the one who fulfills the promise of spiritual renewal.

The Lord of Hosts

"Thus saith the Lord of hosts: Yet once, it is a little while, and I will shake the heavens, and the earth."[249] Bahá'ís see Bahá'u'lláh as fulfilling this prophecy through His transformative teachings.

Islam also use titles that refer to Bahá'u'lláh, such as:

The Return of the Spirit of Islam

Bahá'u'lláh is seen as fulfilling the Quranic promises of divine guidance and renewal, such as in this verse: "And you will surely know the truth of its information after a time."

---

246 The *Bible*, John 16:13.
247 The *Bible*, Psalm 24:10.
248 The *Bible*, Isaiah 4:2.
249 The *Bible*, Haggai 2:6.

The Great Announcement
(Naba'u'l-A'zam)

Bahá'ís associate this Quranic phrase with Bahá'u'lláh's revelation. "Of what do they question one another? About the great announcement."[250]

Conclusion

The titles and metaphors referring to Bahá'u'lláh across sacred texts emphasize His role as a Manifestation of God and the fulfillment of long-awaited prophecies. These titles, such as "The Glory of God," "The Spirit of Truth," and "He Whom God Shall Make Manifest," symbolize His mission to bring unity, peace, and divine guidance to humanity in a new era of spiritual enlightenment. These interpretations reflect the Bahá'í concept of progressive revelation, where each Manifestation fulfills and builds upon the teachings of earlier prophets.

Aryan Religions

Hinduism

Lord Krishna, one of the most revered deities in Hinduism, is regarded as an Avatar (incarnation) of Vishnu and a central figure in the spiritual traditions of India. His names, titles, and metaphorical references reflect His divine attributes, roles, and significance in Hindu theology, particularly as described in texts like the Bhagavad Gita, Mahabharata, and the Puranas. Below is a list of prominent references associated with Krishna beginning with His name and various titles:

---

250 *Qur'an* 78:1–2.

Krishna
(कृष्ण) – The All-Attractive One

Krishna means "the all-attractive one", reflecting His magnetic personality and divine charm. This name underscores His ability to attract souls to God and lead them toward liberation. "Fix your mind on Me, be devoted to Me, sacrifice to Me, and bow down to Me. You shall surely come to Me. I promise you because you are dear to Me."[251]

Jagannatha
(जगन्नाथ) – Lord of the Universe

Jagannatha is a title emphasizing Krishna's universal sovereignty and divine omnipresence. The title is associated with the famous Jagannath Temple in Puri, India. "The Lord of the universe sustains all living beings."[252]

Hari
(हरि) – The Remover of Sins

Krishna is called Hari as the remover of sins and dispeller of darkness. "One who chants the name of Hari with devotion is freed from the cycle of birth and death."[253]

Ranchor
(रणछोड़) – The Abandoner of War

Ranchor refers to Krishna's strategic retreat from battle during certain episodes, symbolizing His wisdom in avoiding unnecessary conflict. It also implies that he was a seeker of unity among people, the only antidote for continuing wars.

---

251 *Bhagavad Gita* 18:65.
252 *Bhagavata Purana* 10.90.48.
253 *Bhagavata Purana* 6.2.9.

Achyuta
(अच्युत) – The Infallible One

This title emphasizes Krishna's divine perfection and constancy. "You are the eternal, imperishable, and supreme divine Being, the ultimate refuge of all."[254]

Parthasarathi
(पार्थसारथी) – Charioteer of Arjuna

Refers to Krishna's role as the charioteer of Arjuna during the Kurukshetra War, where He served as a guide and mentor. "That Blessed Lord, assuming the role of Arjuna's charioteer, spoke to him words of wisdom."[255]

Sat-Chit-Ananda
(सत्-चित्-आनन्द) – Being, Consciousness, Bliss

This title describes Krishna's eternal and divine nature as the embodiment of existence (*Sat*), consciousness (*Chit*), and bliss (*Ananda*).

Govinda
(गोविन्द) – Protector of Cows and Giver of Joy

The title Govinda refers to Krishna's role as the protector of cows, a sacred animal in Hinduism, and as a giver of spiritual joy. Krishna's life as a cowherd in Vrindavan is central to this title. "He who removes the distress of the cows and the devotees and fulfills their desires is called Govinda."[256]

---

254 *Bhagavad Gita* 11:18.
255 *Bhagavad Gita* 1:24.
256 *Vishnu Purana* 5.1.23.

Madhava
(माधव) – Descendant of the Madhu Clan

Madhava refers to Krishna's lineage, but also means "sweetness" emphasizing His divine and loving nature. "O Madhava, Lord of fortune, You are the eternal guardian of dharma."[257]

Vasudeva
(वासुदेव) – Son of Vasudeva

Refers to Krishna's lineage as the son of Vasudeva, but also signifies the divine consciousness present in all beings. "I am the Self seated in the hearts of all creatures. I am the beginning, the middle, and the end of all beings."[258] The reference to being the beginning and the end is echoed in the later words of Jesus and Bahá'u'lláh.

Yadava
(यादव) – Descendant of the Yadu Dynasty

Yadava refers to Krishna's ancestry as a member of the Yadu dynasty, underscoring His earthly heritage.

Murari
(मुरारी) – Slayer of the Demon Mura

Krishna as the slayer of demons symbolizes His role as the destroyer of evil forces and protector of righteousness. "Murari, the slayer of the demon Mura, protects the virtuous and destroys the wicked."[259]

Shyam
(श्याम) – The Dark-Hued One

Shyam refers to Krishna's dark complexion, symbolizing His enigmatic and all-encompassing divine nature. "O Shyam, who is

---

257 *Bhagavad Gita* 1:14.
258 *Bhagavad Gita* 10:20.
259 *Vishnu Purana* 4.15.4.

dark as a monsoon cloud, yet radiates divine effulgence!" The dark monsoon cloud is a traditional metaphor used to describe Krishna's *Shyam* (dark) skin, which contrasts with His radiant divinity. This dual imagery is prominent in devotional traditions and *bhajans*, where Krishna's physical appearance symbolizes the paradox of His human form containing divine light.

Keshava
(केशव) – The Beautiful One

Keshava refers to Krishna's beauty, but also signifies Him as the slayer of the demon Keshi. "Hail Keshava, the slayer of Keshi, who is the protector of the world."[260]

There are several metaphorical representations of Krishna as well. These include:

The Flute Player

Krishna's flute symbolizes divine love, which calls souls toward God and spiritual unity. The sound of Krishna's flute represents the call of divine love, which transcends material attachments and draws the soul toward God. "When Krishna played His flute, the sound was so sweet that it attracted the *gopis*[261], drawing their minds entirely toward Him. Their attachments to worldly life vanished, and they came running to Him, forgetting everything else."[262]

The Butter Thief

Krishna as the metaphorical Butter Thief highlights His playful, innocent nature and His ability to "steal" hearts through divine love. Krishna's act of stealing butter represents the way He captures the

---

[260] *Vishnu Sahasranama.*

[261] In Hinduism, the word gopis in the plural refers to the group of cowherd women who possess devotion toward Krishna.

[262] *Bhagavata Purana* 10.29.4.

pure devotion of His devotees. Butter, symbolizing the essence of milk, signifies the purity of the human heart. "Stealing butter from the homes of the *gopis*, Krishna, the child of Nanda, delighted in play. He revealed His divinity even in these playful acts, stealing not just butter, but the hearts of the *gopis*."[263]

The Cosmic Dancer

Krishna's dance signifies the rhythm of the cosmos, symbolizing creation, preservation, and destruction in harmony. It represents the cosmic order, with His divine play harmonizing the forces of the universe. Krishna's dance shows His role as the sustainer of balance and protector of His devotees. "Krishna danced in joy, holding Govardhana mountain aloft as an umbrella to protect His devotees from the wrath of Indra. The rhythm of His steps became the heartbeat of the earth itself."[264]

Conclusion

Krishna's titles and the metaphors referring to Him encapsulate His roles as a protector, guide, cosmic sustainer, and divine lover of humanity. They convey His profound influence on spiritual thought, highlighting His universal appeal as a symbol of divine love, wisdom, and cosmic balance.

Krishna's role as a nurturer of souls and protector aligns with the mission of every Manifestation of God Who provides spiritual guidance and ensures the moral and social well-being of humanity. Similar to Moses as a lawgiver or Jesus as the Good Shepherd, many of Krishna's titles emphasize His role in providing divine care and spiritual sustenance suited to His era. Krishna as *Parthasarathi* (Charioteer of Arjuna) in the Bhagavad Gita symbolizes His role as a guide or educator who provides timeless spiritual principles, just as

---

263 *Bhagavata Purana* 10.9.8.
264 *Bhagavata Purana* 10.25.19.

Jesus delivered the Sermon on the Mount or Muhammad revealed the Quran, with each addressing humanity's needs in their respective eras.

His role as *Jagannatha* (Lord of the Universe) and the Cosmic Dancer aligns with the concept of Manifestations of God as maintainers of spiritual and moral order in the world. Like Krishna, each Manifestation addresses humanity's collective spiritual needs, balancing societal harmony and individual enlightenment. Titles like *Achyuta* (The Infallible One) and *Sat-Chit-Ananda* (Being, Consciousness, Bliss) reflect Krishna's eternal and divine nature. The concept of progressive revelation affirms that all Manifestations reflect the same divine reality, appearing in different forms (Krishna and Jesus, for example) and different times to guide humanity.

Zoroastrianism

Zoroaster (known as Zarathustra in the ancient Avestan language) was an Iranian prophet and the founder of Zoroastrianism, one of the world's oldest monotheistic religions. He likely lived around 1200–1000 BCE, though some estimates place him earlier. Born in Persia, he received a divine revelation from Ahura Mazda (Wise Lord), advocating the worship of one God and a dualistic struggle between good (*Spenta Mainyu*) and evil (*Angra Mainyu*). His teachings, preserved in the Avesta (especially the Gathas), emphasize truth, righteousness, and free will. Zoroaster's influence shaped not only Zoroastrianism but also other major religions. His various names and titles are listed below:

Zarathustra/Zoroaster
(زردشت/Ζωροάστρης)

Zoroaster's name means "Golden Light" or "He Who Leads with Camels," reflecting His historical and spiritual significance. "Through the tongue of Zarathustra, Ahura Mazda [God] spoke the holy words."[265]

---

265 *Yasna 31.6*, Avesta.

Spitama
(Belonging to the Spitama Clan)

This title indicates Zoroaster's noble lineage. "Zarathustra Spitama declared the eternal truths revealed by Ahura Mazda [God]."[266]

The Prophet of Ahura Mazda [God]

Zoroaster is referred to as the Prophet or chosen Messenger who revealed God's divine wisdom. "Him who is the prophet of Mazda, we worship and revere, Zarathustra Spitama."[267]

Friend of Righteousness (Ashavan):

This reflects His dedication to *asha* (truth and cosmic order). "Zarathustra is the friend of righteousness, the chosen of Ahura Mazda [God] to lead humanity."[268]

The Bearer of the Flame

Zoroaster is metaphorically described as one who brings the divine flame of enlightenment and truth to humanity. "With the flame of truth, Zarathustra spreads light to dispel falsehood."[269]

Divine Teacher

This title emphasizes Zoroaster's role in teaching humanity about moral choice and devotion to Ahura Mazda [God]. "Zarathustra teaches us to choose the path of *asha*, the path of wisdom and light."[270]

The Divine Sower

This is a metaphor for Zoroaster planting the seeds of righteousness.

---

266 *Yasna* 46.15, Avesta.
267 *Yasna* 43.1, Avesta.
268 *Yasna* 33.6, Avesta.
269 *Bundahishn* 30.2.
270 *Yasna* 31.22, Avesta.

"Like the sower of a fertile field, Zarathustra brings forth the harvest of truth."[271]

Conclusion

Zoroaster (or Zarathustra) is revered as the founder of Zoroastrianism and a prophet of Ahura Mazda, the Wise Lord. His names and titles reflect his divine mission, moral teachings, and spiritual significance. Zoroaster's titles and metaphors highlight His role as a Manifestation of God who revealed eternal truths while addressing the needs of His time. These titles help us understand progressive revelation by illustrating the unity of God's messengers, the continuity of divine guidance, and the advancement of spiritual teachings throughout human history. Each Manifestation, including Zoroaster, contributes to humanity's collective moral and spiritual progress.

Zoroaster's titles—such as "Prophet of Ahura Mazda [God]"—connect Him to a shared divine mission with other Manifestations. The title "Friend of Righteousness" (*Ashavan*) reflects Zoroaster's alignment with truth (*asha*) and the cosmic order, themes echoed in the teachings of all Manifestations of God. Metaphors such as "Divine Sower" and "Bearer of the Flame" symbolize spiritual renewal and enlightenment, a central purpose of progressive revelation. Zoroaster "planted the seeds" of truth, just as Krishna in Hinduism and Moses in Judaism established systems of moral and societal order.

Zoroaster's teachings about the battle between good and evil, free will, and devotion to Ahura Mazda [God] helped shape human understanding of morality and divine justice. These principles laid a foundation for later revelations, such as the Ten Commandments in Judaism and the Quran's ethical guidance in Islam. In progressive revelation, each successive revelation builds upon earlier teachings to advance humanity's spiritual evolution.

---

271 *Visperad* 22.7, Avesta.

Chapter 14:
Chain of Custody

Linked by Prophecy

The concept of progressive revelation relies on the existence of a conclave of Divine Educators Who all possess the same "divine essence" to incrementally teach God's truth to humankind. One would expect these Manifestations, who are Custodians of divine knowledge, to also have knowledge of each other. Since Their messages contain the same truths—but in varying degrees of intensity, cultural appropriateness and detail—we might find in their teachings some prophecies of former Manifestations or Those to come in the future. Beginning with Hinduism, we find an abundance of such references that define a chain of custody to an ever-expanding body of knowledge about God and His process of updating guidance to humanity as the world continuously changes.

What is Prophecy?

To most people, prophecy is often linked to predictions about future events, most vividly two that have been widely popularized in mass media—the end of the world and the coming appearance of another Prophet/Messiah. In some cases, these two topics are interlinked, such as the belief that the Second Coming of Jesus will signal the end of the world.

The idea of prophecy as a supernatural feat of fortune telling that identifies the prophet as either God's messenger or an occultist misses the point. In fact, religious prophecies are often notoriously misleading, cloaked as they are in mysterious symbolism that can be easily misinterpreted unless one holds an authentic Rosetta Stone for unlocking their secrets.

In the second century, adherents of Montanism, a splintered Christian community in today's Turkey, believed the second coming of Jesus to be imminent based on visions and interpretations of the available texts written by the sect's leader, Montanus. Many Montanist-Christian communities were nearly abandoned when believers migrated to the villages of Pepuza and Tymion where the heavenly Jerusalem was believed to soon descend.

In 1831, based on prodigious study of biblical prophecies, religious leader William Miller began preaching that the end of the world as we know it would occur with the second coming of Jesus Christ in 1843. He attracted around a hundred thousand followers who believed they would ascend to heaven when the date arrived. After the 1843 prediction failed to materialize, Miller recalculated his math and determined the world would actually end in 1844. Believer Henry Emmons wrote, "I waited all Tuesday, and dear Jesus did not come... I lay prostrate for 2 days without any pain—sick with disappointment."

As has been proven countless times, relying on scriptural prophecies to reveal details about specific future events is a futile exercise because this is not the intent of prophecy. We will never be able to interpret symbols that refer to future events without knowing the unknowable details of those future events. Before predicted events have occurred, we cannot know them, so the symbolism remains an enigma until the prophecy is fulfilled. When looking backward after a prophesied event has occurred, however, we can sometimes understand how that event fulfills a particular prophecy.

So, if prophecies are relatively ineffective in predicting useful details about coming events, what is their value? Clearly, their value is in:

- Their theological messages, which inform us about God and his Manifestations.
- The managing of expectations about the future, which can foster preparedness and goal-setting.

Theological Messages

In the ancient Hindu religion, prophecies often include theological statements that teach about God's relationship with humanity, such as:

> For the protection of the good, the destruction of the wicked, and the establishment of dharma [righteousness], I manifest myself in every age.[272]

Speaking with the authoritative voice of God, the Avatar Kalki here describes God's vow to protect humanity and continue providing guidance through Manifestations of Himself.

In Zoroastrianism, a similar relationship with humanity is described, indicating that a chief function of prophecy is to help humanity be aware of the presence of God. In this passage, the foretold Manifestation of God is called:

> ...the Saoshyant, who makes the world progress to perfection; he will bring righteousness for all the material worlds, and deliver the truth to the people.[273]

In the Bible, God is described as telling the people of Israel that He is a forgiving God Who, at a future time, will make a new covenant with the Israelites.

---

272 *Bhagavad Gita* 4.8
273 Avesta, *Zamyad Yasht* 19.88-96

> "The days are coming," declares the Lord, "when I will make a new covenant with the people of Israel and with the people of Judah. It will not be like the covenant I made with their ancestors when I took them by the hand to lead them out of Egypt, because they broke my covenant, though I was a husband to them," declares the Lord. "This is the covenant I will make with the people of Israel after that time," declares the Lord. "I will put my law in their minds and write it on their hearts. I will be their God, and they will be my people."[274]

Theologically, this prophecy establishes that God is forgiving and the Hebrews will soon be bound by God's new laws. These will be different from the old laws because circumstances have changed.

Symbolism in Prophecies

Symbolism in prophecies can be vague and hard to interpret without knowledge of common uses of the symbolism within the same text or cohesive group of manuscripts. The New Testament of the Bible, for example, is rich in symbolism. The symbols often represent spiritual truths, future events or theological concepts. To understand symbolism, it may be useful to read several passages along with the most common interpretations according to many Christian theologians.

Prophecy 1

> Then I saw a Lamb, looking as if it had been slain, standing at the center of the throne, encircled by the four living creatures and the elders. The Lamb had seven horns and seven eyes, which are the seven spirits of God sent out into all the earth.[275]

---

274 The Bible, *Jeremiah* 31:31–33 (NIV)
275 The Bible, *Revelation* 5:6–7 (NIV)

Conventional Christian interpretation asserts that the Lamb represents Jesus Christ as the sacrificial Savior, who redeemed humanity through His death and resurrection. Use of the term Lamb signifies that Jesus fulfilled the Old Testament prophecies about the Messiah being the "Lamb of God" as mentioned in John 1:29. The "seven horns" symbolize perfect power, and the "seven eyes" represent perfect knowledge and the omnipresence of the Spirit of God.

Prophecy 2

> A great sign appeared in heaven: a woman clothed with the sun, with the moon under her feet and a crown of twelve stars on her head. She was pregnant and cried out in pain as she was about to give birth.[276]

A Christian interpretation of this passage explains that the "woman" usually represents God's people (Israel or the Church.) The "sun" signifies divine glory, righteousness, or God's presence, the "moon" symbolizes subservient powers, and the "twelve stars" represent either the twelve tribes of Israel or the twelve apostles.

This imagery, then, symbolizes the spiritual struggle and the emergence of God's kingdom through the work of the Messiah. The birth represents Christ's and consequently the Church's mission to spread divine teachings.

Prophecy 3

> Now learn this lesson from the fig tree: As soon as its twigs get tender and its leaves come out, you know that summer is near. Even so, when you see all these things, you know that it is near, right at the door.[277]

---

276 The Bible, *Revelation* 12:1–2 (NIV)
277 The Bible, *Matthew* 24:32–33 (NIV)

The figurative image of the fig tree, according to many Christians, represents signs and events that precede the coming of God's kingdom. The budding leaves symbolize the coming of divine fulfillment. This passage, then, encourages believers to watch for spiritual signs and remain prepared for the fulfillment of God's promise.

Prophecy 4

> At that time the kingdom of heaven will be like ten virgins who took their lamps and went out to meet the bridegroom. Five of them were foolish, and five were wise.[278]

In this prophecy, the bridegroom represents Jesus Christ. The virgins represent humanity, with the wise virgins symbolizing the prepared and faithful, the foolish ones symbolizing those who were unprepared for the coming of God's kingdom. The story continues, explaining that the foolish virgins ran out of oil for their lamps, so they left to buy more oil. The bridegroom, Jesus, came while they were absent and the doors to the marriage feast and by the time they returned the doors were closed to them. The prophecy embedded into this parable underscores the importance of spiritual readiness and vigilance in anticipation of divine judgment.

Acknowledgments

Because all the Manifestations of God possessed divine knowledge, each would have been aware of the master plan we call progressive revelation and the role that all the Manifestations would play in this continuous unfolding of the one true religion of God. The spiritual truths these Divine Educators revealed to humanity, then, must be consistent, as they all came from the same source. One would assume also that each Manifestation would acknowledge His

---

278 The Bible, *Matthew* 25:1–13.

predecessors and prepare humanity for the Manifestations to follow. Such scriptural acknowledgements of past or future Manifestations would certainly help verify and illuminate the concept of progressive revelation.

Unfortunately, many of these scriptural records have disappeared, and those that exist are almost impossible to authenticate. There are also complicating issues such as possible mistranslations, copying errors by scribes, political skirmishes over which manuscripts to canonize, even contradictory understandings of how God may have rendered certain texts free of error and tamper-proof. However, despite these obstacles, we must venture on by searching known scriptures from each of our major wisdom traditions for clues in prophetic passages.

Chapter 15:
Prophecies in the Abrahamic Religion

Historians place the birth of Abraham in the early Bronze Age circa 2000–1800 BCE. Jewish traditions and biblical genealogies place it circa 1813 in the Jewish calendar. Since he left no formalized religion with codified teachings, there are no scriptures from Him that can be studied. What we know about Abraham we have learned from Judaism and Christianity in the Bible and from Islam in the Qur'an.

Scholars believe Abraham was born in Ur of the Chaldees, a city in Mesopotamia (modern-day Iraq) during the rise of city-states and kingdoms amidst a polytheistic religious environment. According to later scriptures, Abraham received a message from God declaring the truth of one God, not many, and charging Him with the responsibility to teach this truth broadly, particularly to his multitude of descendants. According to the book of Genesis in the Bible:

> The Lord had said to Abram, 'Go from your country, your people, and your father's household to the land I will show you. I will make you into a great nation, and I will bless you; I will make your name great, and

> you will be a blessing. I will bless those who bless you, and whoever curses you I will curse; and all peoples on earth will be blessed through you.[279]

Did God, in this passage, promise to make Abraham the "father" of many nations? Some biblical scholars interpret this passage as a prophecy of the universal impact of Abraham's descendants, including the emergence of monotheistic religions—Judaism, Christianity, Islam and the Bahá'í Faith—which infers that the Manifestations who founded these religions were the progeny of Abraham.

This concept of a divine bloodline is relevant because it is stressed in the scriptures of several wisdom traditions.

The Christian Lineage

Two New Testament genealogies of Jesus trace His ancestry back to Abraham. In the book of Matthew, we learn:

> This is the genealogy of Jesus the Messiah, the son of David, the son of Abraham: Abraham was the father of Isaac, Isaac the father of Jacob, Jacob the father of Judah and his brothers...[280]

The Gospel of Luke also traces Jesus's lineage back to Abraham but follows a different path, suggesting a combination of legal (both adoptive and dynastic) and biological (genetic) lineage.

> ...the son of Jacob, the son of Isaac, the son of Abraham...[281]

The Matthew genealogy can be considered the legal lineage of Jesus because it connects Him to Joseph, whom Christians believe

---

279 The *Bible*, Genesis 12:1–3.
280 The *Bible,* Matthew 1:1-2 (NIV).
281 The Bible, Luke 3:34 (NIV)

was Jesus's adoptive father. In Jewish tradition, legal inheritance—including the right to kingship—could pass from adoptive or legal parents. By tracing Jesus's lineage through Solomon to King David, Matthew underscores the right of Jesus to the David throne as prophesied when God delivered the following message to David, a direct descendant of Abraham:

> **When your days are over and you rest with your ancestors, I will raise up your offspring to succeed you, your own flesh and blood, and I will establish his kingdom. He is the one who will build a house for my Name, and I will establish the throne of his kingdom forever. I will be his father, and he will be my son...[282]**

This genealogy connects Jesus to traditional Jewish Messianic expectations. The phrase "I will be his father, and he will be my son" stresses the prophetic importance of Joseph being an adoptive father of a son born of the virgin Mary, Jesus's biological mother, otherwise God could not make that prophecy about Jesus being his son.

In Luke, the genealogy takes a slightly different path—through Jesus's mother Mary rather than through Joseph. This is clear when Luke refers to Jesus as "the son, as was supposed, of Joseph." This odd phrasing may imply that Luke's genealogy in truth reflects Mary's ancestry but formally attributes it to Joseph because of the patriarchal norms of the time.

Many scholars believe that, although Luke listed Heli as Joseph's father,[283] Heli was actually Mary's father. Thus, Heli was Joseph's father-in-law, not his father. Another theory holds that Luke traces an alternate lineage of Joseph through a "levirate" marriage, a practice in which a man marries his deceased brother's widow to preserve the family line.

---

282 The Bible, 2 Samuel 7:12–14
283 The *Bible*, Luke 3:23.

Either way, of course, Luke's genealogy emphasizes Jesus's biological descent through Mary. It also explains why Luke's genealogy had to trace Jesus's lineage through David's son Nathan rather than through Solomon as Matthew did. This emphasizes Jesus's connection to humanity as a whole.

If all of this seems complicated… it is. In ancient Jewish tradition, lineage was crucial for establishing identity and legitimacy. Both the Matthew and Luke genealogies confirm that Jesus was a direct descendant of Abraham through both His mother's and His adoptive-father's lineage. By presenting these two genealogies, the Gospels affirm Jesus's dual connection to the Jewish people and to all humanity.

The Islamic Lineage

The Qur'án implicitly traces the lineage of the Prophet Muhammad back to Abraham specifically through Abraham's son Ishmael (*Ismā'īl* in Arabic). While the Qur'an does not provide a detailed genealogical record, it emphasizes the spiritual and ancestral connection between Muhammad and Abraham, highlighting their shared mission of monotheism and submission to God (*Islam*).

In the Qur'an, we learn that after building the Kaaba, the central focus of Islamic worship in Mecca, Abraham and Ishmael dedicated it to God with these words.

> Our Lord, accept [this] from us. Indeed You are the Hearing, the Knowing. Our Lord, and make us both submissive to You and [raise] from our descendants a nation submissive to You. And show us our rites and accept our repentance. Indeed, You are the Accepting of Repentance, the Merciful. Our Lord, and send among them a messenger from themselves who will recite to them Your verses and teach them the Book and wisdom and purify them. Indeed, You are the Exalted in Might, the Wise.

The italics were added to highlight a prayerful request from a Manifestation of God and his son to send another Manifestation Who will teach wisdom and purify humankind. This was more an affirmation of God's promise of the universal impact on humanity that would result from Abraham's progeny.

Muslims generally regard this request as a prophecy fulfilled by Muhammad. But it seems to me more of an archetypal request for divine guidance not limited to Muhammad but extending to future Manifestations who would "recite verses," "teach wisdom," and "purify" humanity. The Báb and Bahá'u'lláh likewise fulfilled this prophecy by delivering new divine verses (the *Báyán* and the *Kitáb-i-Aqdas* respectively) and various other teachings to guide humanity in a new age.

The Bahá'í Lineage

The two Manifestations of the Bahá'í Faith—the Báb and Bahá'u'lláh—were both descendants of Abraham, tracing their lineage through different branches of Abraham's family. While it is not a requirement for a Manifestation of God to descend from Abraham—indeed, Manifestations who appeared before Abraham could not be descendants—this connection holds deep symbolic significance. It reflects the roles of these two Divine Educators in fulfilling the Abrahamic covenant with God and fixing Their place within the broader framework of progressive revelation so that all who could comprehend would see it.

The Báb, born as Siyyid `Alí Muhammad Shirazi, was a *Siyyid*, meaning a direct descendant of Muhammad. His lineage is traditionally traced back to Abraham through his son Ishmael. While skipping some generations, the Báb's genealogy reads like this:

Abraham → Ishmael → Adnan → Quraysh → Hashim → Abdul Muttalib → Muhammad → The Báb.

This lineage entitled the Báb to wear the traditional green turban, which publicly identified him as a descendant of Muhammad. It also tied the Báb directly to the Abrahamic tradition of monotheism and emphasized His role as a spiritual heir to the covenant of Abraham and the fulfillment of Islamic prophecies about the coming of the Mahdí.

Bahá'u'lláh, born as Mírzá Husayn, was of noble Persian lineage, descending from Abraham through Keturah, Abraham's third wife and then through the ancient Zoroastrian imperial houses and Yazdigird III, the last Sassanid emperor of Persia. This lineage situates Bahá'u'lláh within the Abrahamic tradition. With some skipping of generations, Bahá'u'lláh's lineage appears like this:

Abraham and Keturah → Yazdigird III → Mirzá Buzurg → Bahá'u'lláh.

Significance of Abrahamic Descent

Abraham's covenant with God (Genesis 12:1-3, Qur'án 2:124) promised that his descendants would be a source of blessings for all nations. Both the Báb and Bahá'u'lláh fulfilled this promise. The Báb prepared the way for Bahá'u'lláh, renewing divine guidance within the Islamic context. Bahá'u'lláh brought a universal message of unity, fulfilling the promise of Abraham's descendants and bringing blessings to all humanity.

The Abrahamic descent of the Báb and Bahaullah aligns with prophecies in Judaism, Christianity, and Islam about the appearance of divinely guided figures from Abraham's line. The lineage also reflects the continuity of divine revelation, connecting the Báb and Bahá'u'lláh to earlier Manifestations such as Moses, Jesus, and Muhammad, while marking the culmination of the Abrahamic dispensation with a universal message.

Looking Forward

According to the Pentateuch (the first five books of the Hebrew Bible), Abraham knew that the Hebrews would become enslaved for a long period of time. In Genesis, God told him:

> Know for certain that for four hundred years your descendants will be strangers in a country not their own, and that they will be enslaved and mistreated there. But I will punish the nation they serve as slaves, and afterward they will come out with great possessions.[284]

This prophecy outlines the enslavement of the Israelites in Egypt and their eventual liberation due to the emergence of a deliverer. While Abraham is not described as foreseeing Moses specifically, this covenant indicates that God had already planned the liberation and exodus of Abraham's descendants. Later wisdom traditions also view Moses as the fulfillment of this divine promise. The long period of Israelite captivity is confirmed in the book of Exodus:

> Now the length of time the Israelite people lived in Egypt was 430 years. At the end of the 430 years, to the very day, all the LORD's divisions left Egypt. Because the LORD kept vigil that night to bring them out of Egypt, on this night all the Israelites are to keep vigil to honor the LORD for the generations to come.[285]

The vigil prescribed in this passage refers to the Passover meal, for which the book of Exodus delivers specific instructions. The discrepancy between the 400 years of captivity mentioned in Genesis and the 430 years mentioned in Exodus may be due to a translation issue. In the Greek Septuagint, which was heavily employed by New Testament writers, the text of Exodus 12:40 explicitly reads "in Egypt and Canaan," not simply "in Canaan." The Samaritan Pentateuch also supports this reading. Consequently, if Abraham lived in Canaan for thirty years before Egypt enslaved His people, the longer duration of captivity would have been used in Exodus.

---

284 The *Bible*, Genesis 15:13–14.
285 The *Bible*, Exodus 12:40–42.

Chapter 16:
Zoroastrian Prophecies

This wisdom tradition is one of our oldest monotheistic religions. Zoroastrian tradition places Zoroaster's birth approximately 6,000 years before Alexander the Great, which would be circa 6400 BCE, but that is highly unlikely. Linguistic analysis of Zoroaster's hymns, the Gathas, suggests he lived between 1500 BCE and 1200 BCE, several centuries after Abraham. Scholars believe that Zoroaster lived in Central Asia or eastern Iran, a region associated with the early Indo-Iranian peoples.

Saoshyants

In Zoroastrianism, Manifestations of God, also known as Divine Educators, are referred to as Saoshyants (literally "one who brings benefit"). Sometimes, a Saoshyant is referred to as a "benefactor." According to known Zoroastrian writings, Saoshyants come to renew the world, restore righteousness (*asha*), and bring humanity to spiritual perfection. These prophecies reflect the Zoroastrian understanding of divine intervention in human history to ensure the ultimate triumph of good over evil, a principle explicitly upheld by all the wisdom traditions with the possible exception of Buddhism.

Zoroastrianism points to the dawning of a new religious age in the mid-nineteenth century following the gradual decay and disintegration of a future religion referred to as the Arabian Faith—obviously a reference to Islam, though neither it nor its predecessor, Christianity, had yet appeared.

> When a thousand years have passed from the Arabian Faith, such will be its condition, due to division and disunity, that even if presented to its Founder, He won't recognize it.[286]

Within another two hundred years, it is prophesied, another Manifestation would appear and be referred to as Húshídar to revive the teachings of Islam after its spiritual decline.

> When one thousand two hundred-odd years have elapsed from the Arabian Faith, Húshídar will be raised to prophethood.[287]

Húshídar, in this prophecy, must be referring to the Báb, the forerunner of Bahá'u'lláh in founding the Bahá'í Faith, which followed Islam. The Báb appeared about 1,200 years after the birth of Islam. The name Húshídar provides an additional clue. The name combines two Persian words which could be interpreted as "Bearer of Wisdom" or "Bearer of Understanding." The Báb, whose title means the "Gate," in fact serves as the Gateway to Wisdom and Understanding through whom seekers of truth and tranquility can gain access to the City of God.

Another prophecy attributed to Zoroaster delivers a similar message.

---

286 Suhráb, E., *Mábádi-i-Estediá* (Persian) Thran, Bahá'í Era 130, p. 251.
287 Nuqabá'í, H., *Bishárát-i-Kutub-i-Ásmání* (Persian) Tíhran, Bahá'í Era 124, p. 94.

> When a thousand two hundred and some years have passed from the inception of the religion of the Arabian and the overthrow of the Kingdom of Iran and the degradation of the followers of My religion, a descendant of the Iranian kings will be raised up as a Prophet.[288]

This prophecy must refer to Bahá'u'lláh because He too appeared 1200 "and some years" after the inception of Islam. This was the year 1280 AH on the Islamic calendar, which began with the Hijrah, the founding of the first Islamic community in Medina. Bahá'u'lláh was a descendant of Iranian Kings—specifically, the Sasaniyan Dynasty, which was overthrown by Islamic armies in about 651 CE. The defeat, interestingly, led to the dispersion and degradation of the Zoroastrians. Thus, all five requirements of this prophecy were fulfilled by Bahá'u'lláh.

Húshídar and the following Manifestation represent stages in a progressive divine plan remarkably similar to what we have been calling progressive revelation. These Manifestations, sometimes referred to as Saoshyants, are spiritual leaders who help humanity gradually overcome the forces of evil (*druj*) and align with righteousness (*asha*). Their missions align with the Zoroastrian concept of divine intervention occurring in cycles, bringing humanity nearer to the arrival of something close to what the Christians call the Kingdom of God on Earth ("a state of complete order," as Zoroastrian scripture puts it). These figures underscore the continuous guidance offered by Ahura Mazda (God) and highlight the collaborative role of humanity in achieving cosmic renewal.

By clearly prophesying the Báb and Bahá'u'lláh, Zoroaster also confirms the validity of Their predecessors, Jesus and Muhammad, who are specifically affirmed as Manifestations by the Bahá'í Faith.

---

288 Ferraby, John, *All Things Made New*, London: Ruskin House, 1957, p. 171.

Zoroastrian Priests and Young Jesus

One of the most famous Bible stories is the New Testament account of the three Magi who followed a star to find the infant Jesus and deliver gifts. The account is in the Gospel of Matthew.

> After Jesus was born in Bethlehem in Judea, during the time of King Herod, Magi from the east came to Jerusalem and asked, "Where is the one who has been born king of the Jews? We saw his star when it rose and have come to worship him."

> When King Herod heard this, he was disturbed, and all Jerusalem with him. When he had called together all the people's chief priests and teachers of the law, he asked them where the Messiah was to be born. "In Bethlehem in Judea," they replied, "for this is what the prophet has written:

> 'But you, Bethlehem, in the land of Judah, are by no means least among the rulers of Judah; for out of you will come a ruler who will shepherd my people Israel.'"

> Then Herod called the Magi secretly and found out from them the exact time the star had appeared. He sent them to Bethlehem and said, "Go and search carefully for the child. As soon as you find him, report to me, so that I too may go and worship him."

> After they had heard the king, they went on their way, and the star they had seen when it rose went ahead of them until it stopped over the place where the child

> was. When they saw the star, they were overjoyed. On coming to the house, they saw the child with his mother Mary, and they bowed down and worshipped him. Then they opened their treasures and presented him with gifts of gold, frankincense, and myrrh.

> And having been warned in a dream not to go back to Herod, they returned to their country by another route.[289]

This story requires some additional information to understand. The Magi were a priestly caste in ancient Persia associated with the Zoroastrian religion.[290] They were principally scholars, astronomers, and interpreters of dreams and omens, trained in the religious and scientific traditions of their time. As Zoroastrians, they were predisposed to look for divine signs in the heavens and to align their observations with their religious worldview.

Zoroastrianism places significant emphasis on celestial phenomena, interpreting them as messages from Ahura Mazda (the supreme God). This explains the Magi's obsession with observing and interpreting any newly observed star. As we have seen, Zoroastrianism also contains prophecies of a future savior (*Saoshyant*), born of a virgin, who would bring salvation to the world.

Following the Babylonian Exile in the sixth century BCE, Jewish communities lived in Persia and Babylon, facilitating cultural and religious exchange. The Magi might have been aware of Jewish prophecies about a coming Messiah, such as the following prophecy attributed to Moses:

---

289 The *Bible*, Matthew 2:1–12 (NIV).

290 In Herodotus, *The Histories* (Book 1, Section 101), Herodotus describes the Magi as a hereditary priestly caste of the Medes and Persians, responsible for performing religious rituals and interpreting celestial events. See also: Raymond E. Brown, *The Birth of the Messiah*; and John Dominic Crossan, *Who Killed Jesus?*

> A star shall come out of Jacob, and a scepter shall rise out of Israel.[291]

It is astronomically possible that a new star had appeared in the heavens around the time of Jesus's birth. The exact date of His birth has not been determined, but it has been placed between 7 BCE and 2 BCE based on historical and scriptural clues. Two astronomical events during this period could scientifically explain the appearance of a new star-like light in the sky during that period.

The earlier of the two events was a planetary conjunction. This kind of event occurs when two or more planets appear very close to each other in the sky, creating a bright effect that looks like a star. In 7 BCE, there was a planetary conjunction of Jupiter—which in the legendary history of Rome symbolizes kingship—and Saturn—the seventh planet in astrology, which was symbolized the Jews because they celebrated the Sabbath, the seventh day of the Jewish week. This rare conjunction easily could have been taken for the Star of Bethlehem. It occurred in the constellation Pisces, which was often linked with Israel in ancient astrology, potentially making the conjunction even more significant to the Magi.

The second astronomical candidate was a "guest star"—likely a nova—recorded by Chinese astronomers in 5 BCE. It was visible for about seventy days and could match the description of the Star of Bethlehem.

The Magi's search for the newborn king brought them to Jerusalem, where they likely made inquiries about where such a child might be found. These inquiries reached Herod's ears. Before summoning the Magi, Herod consulted the Jewish chief priests and scribes to identify the prophesied birthplace of the Messiah. These religious men pointed to Bethlehem, based on Hebrew scripture in Micah 5:2, which foretells the Messiah's birth in that town.

---

291 The *Bible*, Numbers 24:17.

> But you, Bethlehem Ephrathah,
>   though you are small among the clans of Judah,
> out of you will come for me
>   one who will be ruler over Israel,
> whose origins are from of old,
>   from ancient times.[292]

Herod secretly summoned the Magi to learn more about the timing and details of the star they had seen. This secrecy suggests Herod's intent to manipulate them without arousing public suspicion. His ulterior motive was to eliminate the threat of an infant "Jewish king" arising to threaten his rule.

The Magi's search for the newborn "savior" was made easier by learning of the town in which the child would likely be found. The Magi found Jesus and gave him gifts of gold (symbolizing kingship), frankincense (an aromatic resin used for religious ceremonies; it represents divinity and worship), and myrrh (an ingredient in the holy anointing oil used for consecrating kings; it symbolizes suffering and sacrifice, which anticipates Jesus's crucifixion.)

Warned in a dream not to return to Herod, the Magi took another route home. Deprived of their report on Jesus's location, Herod was forced to launch his "Massacre of the Innocents," as it is commonly referred.

> When Herod realized that he had been outwitted by the Magi, he was furious, and he gave orders to kill all the boys in Bethlehem and its vicinity who were two years old and under, in accordance with the time he had learned from the Magi.[293]

According to the Matthew account of the Magi, Jesus is called a "child," not an infant, and Herod's cruel decree targeted boys up

---

292 The *Bible*, Micah 5:2 (NIV)
293 The *Bible*, Matthew 2:16.

to two years old to be killed. Also, the mention of the Magi visiting Jesus in a house[294] suggests that some time had passed since his birth. It is unlikely that the Magi encountered Jesus the night of his birth as depicted in nativity scenes.

After the Magi visited Jesus in Bethlehem, an angel appeared to Joseph in a dream to warn of the impending danger.

> When they [the Magi] had gone, an angel of the Lord appeared to Joseph in a dream. 'Get up,' he said, 'take the child and his mother and escape to Egypt. Stay there until I tell you, for Herod is going to search for the child to kill him.[295]

The stark interaction between the Magi's sincere quest and Herod's calculated, self-serving manipulation underscores the themes of light versus darkness—meaning good versus evil—which were concepts introduced by Zoroaster and played out dramatically on the stage of history by Zoroastrians, Jews, and the Manifestation who brought us Christianity. Can there be any more exciting scriptural testimony than this to the linkage between Manifestations of God and the concept of progressive revelation?

---

294 The *Bible*, Matthew 2:11.
295 The *Bible*, Matthew 2:13.

Chapter 17:
Judaic Prophecies

Judaism traces its origins back over three thousand years. It began with the covenantal relationship between God (referred to as Yahweh in Hebrew tradition) and the Hebrew patriarchs, particularly Abraham, Isaac, and Jacob, as described in the Torah, the foundational text of Judaism.

According to the Hebrew Bible, God instructed Abraham—a Manifestation of God—to leave his homeland and promised to make his descendants a great nation. This agreement, called a covenant, marked the beginning of Judaism as a distinct faith centered on monotheism—the belief in one God. Abraham's son Isaac and grandson Jacob (later renamed Israel) continued the covenant. Jacob's twelve sons became the progenitors of the Twelve Tribes of Israel.

Then a major event in Jewish history occurred—the birth of Moses, a Manifestation of God, to Hebrew parents in Egypt. According to classical biblical reckoning, Moses was born on February 26, 1393 BCE. However, the exact date of Moses's birth is hard to determine as it is based on interpretations of the Bible.

Because the governing pharaoh of Egypt was afraid that the exploding Israelite population would become a threat to his rule, he ordered all newborn Hebrew boys to be killed.[296] To save Moses

---

296 The *Bible*, Exodus 1:22.

from certain death, his mother, Jochebed, tucked him into a papyrus basket and set it afloat on the Nile River, trusting that God would protect him. Moses's sister, Miriam, watched from a distance to see what would happen.

Jochebed's act of giving up her baby was a courageous decision to ensure his survival in the face of an oppressive and dangerous situation.

Fortunately, the pharaoh's daughter discovered the basket and took pity on the baby. Miriam quickly approached and offered to find a Hebrew woman to nurse the child, temporarily reuniting Moses with his biological mother, who became his nursemaid. After the infant was weaned, the pharaoh's daughter adopted him and named him Moses. He was raised as an Egyptian prince, and most scholars agree he would have been given a royal education including literacy, leadership, and exposure to Egyptian culture.

Despite being raised as an Egyptian, Moses was aware of his Hebrew heritage. This awareness became evident when he defended a Hebrew slave by killing an Egyptian taskmaster.[297] Anticipating punishment, Moses fled to Midian, where He married a woman named Zipporah, the daughter of Jethro, and then became a shepherd.

The Burning Bush

While tending sheep on Mount Horeb, Moses encountered a burning bush that failed to be consumed by fire. During this encounter, God spoke to Moses, revealing His name (Yahweh) and commanding Moses to return to Egypt to free the Israelites from slavery.

This story, as described in the Bible and the Qur'an—whether fact, myth or a mixture of both—symbolically signifies Moses as a Manifestation of God openly proclaiming his mission to lead the Israelites and convey God's teachings. Moses obeyed God, returning to Egypt with his brother, Aaron, as his spokesperson. Apparently,

---

297 The *Bible*, Exodus 2:11–12.

Moses complained of not being able to speak well.[298] Together, Moses and Aaron confronted the pharaoh and demanded the release of the Israelites. This led to a series of ten plagues intended to soften the stubborn pharaoh's resolve to continue the Israelites bondage and, eventually, resulted in the Exodus.

The Wilderness

In a profound way, the Exodus represents the transition from the patriarchal period of Abraham[299] to the covenant between Moses and God established on Mount Sinai with the revealing of the Ten Commandments.[300] Progressive revelation involves each Manifestation building upon the work of the previous ones:

> The Revelation of each of the Manifestations of God hath been destined to unfold itself, and is subject to a process of gradual disclosure. It is for this reason that, in every age, the signs of God have been revealed gradually unto men.[301]

Leaving Egypt was only the beginning. For forty years, the Israelites wandered through the wilderness seeking the Promised Land. They endured numerous trials and tests that prepared them for their eventual future as a community under the protection of God's covenant.

> The Lord your God has led you these forty years in the wilderness, that He might humble you, testing you to know what was in your heart, whether you would keep His commandments or not.[302]

---

298 The *Bible*, Exodus 4:10–17; 7:1.
299 The *Bible*, Exodus 3:6.
300 The *Bible*, Exodus 19–24.
301 Bahá'u'lláh, *Gleanings from the Writings of Bahá'u'lláh*, pp. 79–80.
302 The *Bible*, Deuteronomy 8:2.

Similarly, progressive revelation encounters challenges that humanity must overcome as it assimilates divine teachings and grows spiritually. The wilderness journey serves as a metaphor for periods of spiritual preparation and growth between major revelations delivered by Divine Educators. After a span of over three millennia, the Bahá'í Faith reinforced this timeless message when Bahá'u'lláh wrote:

> All men have been created to carry forward an ever-advancing civilization.[303]

The giving of the Ten Commandments to Moses was a foundational revelation for the Israelites and underscores how Divine Educators are directed to provide guidance appropriate for the age in which they live. This concept was highlighted in Bahá'í scriptures thousands of years later:

> Every Prophet Whom the Almighty and Peerless Creator hath sent unto the peoples of the earth hath been entrusted with a Message, and charged to act in a manner that would best meet the requirements of the age in which He appeared.[304]

The Israelites' long journey through the wilderness eventually resulted in a measure of unity among the Israelites under God's covenant. This difficult journey is a fitting metaphor that foreshadows the ultimate goal of progressive revelation to unify humanity, a prerequisite for peace and security:

> The well-being of mankind, its peace and security, are unattainable unless and until its unity is firmly established.[305]

---

[303] Bahá'u'lláh, *Gleanings from the Writings of Bahá'u'lláh*, p. 214.
[304] Bahá'u'lláh, *Gleanings from the Writings of Bahá'u'lláh*, pp. 79–80.
[305] Bahá'u'lláh, *Gleanings from the Writings of Bahá'u'lláh*, p. 287

Messianic Prophecies

In the early days of Judaism, the Hebrew word Mashiach ("Messiah") was used for anyone appointed for a sacred purpose, such as kings like Saul[306] and David,[307] priests like Aaron and his descendants,[308] and was sometimes implied for prophets.[309]

Over time, the term began to be used for a concept often referred to as the Messianic hope—a longing for a Manifestation of God, a divinely-appointed deliverer like Moses who had been prevented from entering the Promised Land.[310] This longing grew into an anticipation for a powerful figure who would bring redemption, restore Israel, and restore justice and peace.

Moses's prohibition from entering the Promised Land for an act of "disobedience" can be understood as a symbolic lesson within a sacred narrative. The story demonstrates God's justice, the consequence of actions, and the completion of Moses's divine mission, emphasizing His ultimate spiritual success rather than a human flaw.

The Jews came to envision the Messiah as a king in the line of David who would restore Israel's sovereignty, particularly in times of oppression, as God told the prophet Jeremiah.

> I will raise up for David a righteous Branch, a King who will reign wisely and do what is just and right in the land.[311]

Significantly, Bahá'u'lláh was also a descendant of David through the tribe of Judah, fulfilling the biblical expectation of a messianic figure from David's line. This dual lineage of Bahá'u'lláh—from

---

306 The *Bible*, 1 Samuel 10:1.
307 The *Bible*, 1 Samuel 16:13.
308 The *Bible*, Leviticus 8:12.
309 The *Bible*, 1 Kings 19:16.
310 The *Bible*, Deuteronomy 32: 48–52.
311 The *Bible*, Jeremiah 23:5.

Abraham through Ishmail and Muhammad, and from Abraham through Isaac and King David—symbolically unites the two branches of Abrahamic descent (Isaac and Ishmail) and fulfills the prophetic promises made to both. It is difficult to consider such a complex lineage as coincidental.

The Messiah anticipated by the Jews was expected to establish righteousness, protect the poor, and judge the wicked as explained by the prophet Isaiah.

> **The Spirit of the Lord will rest on him... He will not judge by what he sees with his eyes, or decide by what he hears with his ears; but with righteousness he will judge the needy.**[312]

The Messiah was also expected to renew the covenant between God and the Israelites, as God had promised Jeremiah.

> **I will make a new covenant with the people of Israel and with the people of Judah.**[313]

The Messiah was often associated with the Davidic covenant,[314] where God promised King David that his throne would be established forever. This led to the expectation of a future king who would lead Israel to greatness and fulfill the covenant and was a reason why the New Testament presented two genealogies of Jesus, one of which traced his ancestry through King David.

The Old Testament provides many prophecies of a future Messiah. Perhaps the first one is found in Genesis in which God declares that the seed of the woman will crush the serpent's head, symbolizing victory over evil. Speaking to the serpent, God says:

---

312 The *Bible*, Isaiah 11:2–4.
313 The *Bible*, Jeremiah 31:31.
314 The Bible, 2 Samuel 7:12–16.

> I will put enmity between you and the woman, and between your offspring and hers; he will crush your head, and you will strike his heel.[315]

In the Pentateuch, God tells the Israelites that he will raise up another Jewish prophet like Moses to guide them.

> The Lord your God will raise up for you a prophet like me from among you, from your fellow Israelites. You must listen to him.[316]

A prophecy embedded in the Davidic Covenant promises that a descendant of David will establish an everlasting kingdom.

> When your days are over and you rest with your ancestors, I will raise up your offspring to succeed you, your own flesh and blood, and I will establish his kingdom. He is the one who will build a house for my Name, and I will establish the throne of his kingdom forever.[317]

Another prophecy appears to describe the Messiah's atoning sacrifice in a manner remarkably consistent with the suffering of Jesus.

> He was despised and rejected by mankind, a man of suffering, and familiar with pain... But he was pierced for our transgressions, he was crushed for our iniquities; the punishment that brought us peace was on him, and by his wounds we are healed.[318]

---

315 The *Bible*, Genesis 3:15
316 The *Bible*, Deuteronomy 18:15
317 The *Bible*, 2 Samuel 7:12–13.
318 The *Bible*, Isaiah 53:3–7.

The Virgin Birth

The following prophecy addresses a miraculous birth as a sign of the Messiah.

> **Therefore the Lord himself will give you a sign: The virgin will conceive and give birth to a son, and will call him Immanuel.**[319]

The book of Matthew in the New Testament tells us that Jesus's mother was a virgin and connects this extraordinary event to the Isaiah prophecy:

> **This is how the birth of Jesus the Messiah came about: His mother Mary was pledged to be married to Joseph, but before they came together, she was found to be pregnant through the Holy Spirit... All this took place to fulfill what the Lord had said through the prophet: "The virgin will conceive and give birth to a son, and they will call him Immanuel" (which means "God with us.**[320]

The theme of divine intervention in human conception is a common motif in mythologies and spiritual traditions worldwide. Here are a few examples:

- **Egyptian Mythology—Horus.** In ancient Egyptian texts, such as the *Pyramid Texts* and the *Coffin Texts,* the god Horus, associated with kingship and protection, was conceived after his father Osiris was killed and dismembered. Isis, his mother, miraculously conceived Horus without a sexual union by reassembling Osiris's body and using her divine powers. Consequently, Horus's conception was seen as a symbol of divine authority and the renewal of life.

---

319 The *Bible*, Isaiah 7:14.
320 The *Bible*, Matthew 1:18–23.

- **Greek Mythology—Perseus.** In *Library, Book 2* by Apollodorus, Perseus, who slew Medusa, was born of the virgin Danaë. Zeus, the king of the gods, impregnated Danaë by appearing as a gold shower that entered her locked chamber. The miraculous conception highlighted Perseus's divinity and heroic destiny.

- **Roman Mythology—Romulus and Remus.** In *Ab Urbe Condita, Book 1* by Livy, Romulus and Remus, the legendary founders of Rome, were born to Rhea Silvia, a Vestal Virgin. Mars, the god of war, was said to have fathered them through divine intervention. Their divine parentage reinforced the idea that Rome's origins were divinely ordained.

- **Chinese Mythology—Laozi.** In Taoist legends and folklore, Laozi, the founder of Taoism, is said to have been born of a virgin mother who conceived him after being touched by a shooting star or divine light. He was carried in her womb for decades and was born as an old man with white hair. The miraculous birth reflects Laozi's wisdom and otherworldly origins.

- **Aztec Mythology—Huitzilopochtli.** In Aztec codices and oral traditions, the Aztec god of war, Huitzilopochtli, was born to the goddess Coatlicue, who conceived him after a ball of feathers descended from the sky and touched her. The miraculous conception symbolized divine intervention and the god's role as a protector of the Aztecs.

- **Norse Mythology—Heimdall.** In *Prose Edda* by Snorri Sturluson, Heimdall, the guardian of the Bifrost Bridge, is said to have been born of nine mothers (the nine waves, daughters of Ægir) in a mysterious and miraculous conception. His unique birth highlights his divine and extraordinary nature as a protector of the god.

The "immaculate conception" of Jesus was not the first or only virgin birth to occur in the scriptures of acknowledged Manifestations of God. Two others are mentioned:

- ***Hindu Mythology: Karna.*** In Adi Parva, a hero of the Mahabharata, Karna, was born to the virgin Kunti. She invoked a divine mantra that summoned the sun god, Surya, who blessed her with a son without physical conception. Karna's miraculous birth underscores his divine origin and his role in the epic's moral and spiritual lessons.

- **Hinduism—Krishna**. In the story of Krishna's birth, the god Vishnu, the preserver of the universe, descended into the womb of a woman named Devaki and produced the infants Krishna. Some say that this was not a true "virgin" birth, however, because Devaki had previously given birth to seven children.

- **Zoroastrianism—Zoroaster**. In later traditions, Zoroaster is said to have been born of a virgin. According to these traditions, Zoroaster's mother, Dughdova, conceived him from a shaft of light (God) while remaining a virgin.

- **Buddhist Tradition: Siddhartha Gautama (Buddha)** In Lalitavistara Sūtra, Queen Māyā, the mother of Siddhartha Gautama (the Buddha), conceived him miraculously in a dream in which a white elephant entered her side. This miraculous birth symbolizes the Buddha's divine mission to bring enlightenment to the world.

Post-Christian wisdom traditions founded upon the teachings of Manifestations of God do not explicitly verify or refute the Hindu, Zoroastrian and Buddhist stories that appear above, but Islam and the Bahá'í Faith do explicitly confirm the virgin birth of Jesus (Isa) as a miraculous event.

The following dialogue beautifully explains the miraculous conception of Jesus (*Isa*) and emphasizes Mary's (*Maryam's*) purity, the divine decree of God, and the humanity of Mary as she faces the challenges of giving birth alone. The virgin birth of Jesus is presented as a sign of God's power and His mercy to humanity. Speaking with the angel Gabriel, Mary said:

> "How can I have a boy while no man has touched me and I have not been unchaste?" He [Gabriel] said, 'Thus [it will be]; your Lord says, 'It is easy for Me.'"

Islam emphasizes the miraculous nature of Jesus's birth as a sign of God's power and evidence of His divine will without connecting it to similar stories or validating those in other traditions. This may be an indication that the birth of Jesus was considered a unique event by Muhammad.

The Bahá'í Faith presents the virgin birth as a spiritual truth that transcends material understanding, thus cannot be disproved by science, which has no way of testing its veracity. It signifies the divine origin and mission of Jesus as a Manifestation of God.

> **It is clear and evident that the influence of the Holy Spirit caused the conception of Christ. This is not contrary to science—although it is mysterious and supernatural.**[321]

'Abdu'l-Bahá explains that miraculous events like the virgin birth are consistent with the powers of the Manifestations of God, Who are divinely chosen to perform occasional extraordinary acts as a testament to their spiritual authority.

Because so many previous and colorful stories of virgin births, such as those noted above, were present in the minds of Old Testament prophets and the people of Jesus's time, it may be that

---

321 'Abdu'l-Bahá, *Some Answered Questions*, p. 87.

an actual virgin birth would be the single most obvious proof to humanity that Jesus was in fact the Son of God. The mythologies and prophecies lingering in the consciousness of the public may have provided a context within which the meaning of this compelling "miracle" could be easily understood by most people whatever their backgrounds or beliefs.

> **Every one of the Manifestations is the Word of God, but the appearance of each is specialized to their age and their capacity.**[322]

If not for the memorability and impact of all the preceding virgin births stories, that of Jesus may have gone barely noticed.

Many scholars, of course, see the immaculate conception of Jesus as an example of syncretism, the borrowing of an ancient allegory and applying it to a contemporary event as demonstrated in many mythologies. Admittedly, this is likely true, which would underscore the proposition that previous myths may have been a *prerequisite* for a true virgin birth of Jesus to have impacted the world as it clearly has.

Clearly, the idea of the virgin birth of Jesus sets Him apart from ordinary human beings, affirming his divine origin and unique mission. It also symbolizes Jesus's role as a spiritual being, whose mission would resonate more vibrantly because of His station. The miracle of the virgin birth also served as evidence to help people recognize Jesus's divine status in an era when physical signs were more effective in conveying spiritual truths.

The Resurrection

The Old Testament contains several passages that Christians interpret as prophecies fulfilled by the resurrection of Jesus Christ. They do not explicitly mention the Messiah's resurrection but are understood

---

[322] 'Abdu'l-Bahá, *Paris Talks*, p. 57.

in a prophetic sense as pointing to this event. Other religions interpret these passages differently. The first is from the Psalms.

> I keep my eyes always on the Lord. With him at my right hand, I will not be shaken. Therefore my heart is glad and my tongue rejoices; my body also will rest secure, because you will not abandon me to the realm of the dead, nor will you let your faithful one see decay. You make known to me the path of life...[323]

Christianity generally interprets this as a direct prophecy of Jesus's resurrection, suggesting that God would not allow his "faithful one" (the Messiah) to remain in the grave or experience physical corruption. This view is confirmed by Peter in Acts 2:27 ("For you will not abandon my soul to Hades, or let your Holy One see corruption," and by Paul in Acts 13:35 ("You will not let your holy one see decay.")

Judaism, however, traditionally attributes this Psalm to King David, who is expressing confidence in God's protection and deliverance from danger or death. The words "your faithful one" is interpreted by many Jews as literally referring to King David himself as a righteous individual, not a prophecy of a future Messiah. As a concept, resurrection is usually viewed in Judaism as a future event at the "end of days," in which all righteous individuals will be resurrected, or raised from the dead.

The Qur'an addresses the broader themes of this passage, which are God's protection, care for the righteous, and victory of death in an afterlife.[324] The Bahá'í Faith, our most recent wisdom tradition, reminds us that scriptures are written mostly to communicate spiritual truths.

---

323 The *Bible*, Psalm 8–11 (NIV)
324 Qur'an 41:30.

> All the texts and teachings of the holy Testaments have intrinsic spiritual meanings. They are not to be taken literally.[325]

Also, the Bahá'í Faith teaches that a prophecy may be partially fulfilled by one manifestation and fully realized by another.[326] In fact, each Manifestation can be regarded as the same as all the Others.

> Inasmuch as these Birds of the celestial Throne are all sent down from the heaven of the Will of God, and as they all arise to proclaim His irresistible Faith, they therefore are regarded as one soul and the same person. For they all drink from the one Cup of the love of God, and all partake of the Fruit of the same Tree of Oneness.[327]

The idea of the resurrection of Manifestations of God was clearly unknown to Moses and the writers of the Old Testament. Resurrection took on new meaning during the development of Christianity, indicating the physical return to life of Jesus Christ after his crucifixion. Islam appears to agree with Judaism on this topic, and the Bahá'í Faith steers us into a nonliteral interpretation that focuses on the meaning of the act or the metaphor.

Here are some other prophecies that are interpreted differently by Judaism and Christianity. From the Book of Isaiah:

> Yet it was the Lord's will to crush him and cause him to suffer, and though the Lord makes his life an offering for sin, he will see his offspring and prolong his days, and the will of the Lord will prosper in his hand. After he has suffered, he will see the light of life and be satisfied.[328]

---

325 'Abdu'l-Bahá, *The Promulgation of Universal Peace*, p. 459.
326 Bahá'u'lláh, *Kitáb-i-Íqán*, p. 78–79.
327 Bahá'u'lláh, *Kitáb-i-Íqán*, p. 152–153.
328 The *Bible*, Isaiah 53:10–11 (NIV).

The "Suffering Servant" passage in Isaiah 53 is viewed by Christians as a prophecy about Jesus's death and resurrection. The phrases "prolong his days" and "see the light of life" are seen as references to His resurrection after suffering and dying for humanity's sins.

> After two days he will revive us; on the third day he will restore us, that we may live in his presence.[329]

Though it originally referred to Israel's restoration, as Judaism rightly claims, many Christians interpret this verse also as a foreshadowing of Jesus's resurrection on the third day.

> Now the Lord provided a huge fish to swallow Jonah, and Jonah was in the belly of the fish three days and three nights.[330]

While not a direct prophecy, Jonah's time in the belly of the fish is seen by Christians as a *pre-enactment* or foreshadowing of Jesus's burial and resurrection after three days. Jesus Himself makes this connection in Matthew 12:40: "For as Jonah was three days and three nights in the belly of a huge fish, so the Son of Man will be three days and three nights in the heart of the earth."

The long-suffering Job, who endured many trials and tribulations, wrote:

> I know that my redeemer lives, and that in the end he will stand on the earth. And after my skin has been destroyed, yet in my flesh I will see God; I myself will see him with my own eyes—I, and not another. How my heart yearns within me![331]

---

329 The *Bible*, Hosea 6:2 (NIV).
330 The *Bible*, Jonah 1:17 (NIV)
331 The *Bible*, Job 19:25–27 (NIV).

Christians view this as a personal expression of hope in resurrection and as a messianic prophecy pointing to Jesus's resurrection as the Redeemer. This, despite the fact that Job explicitly says, "I myself will see him with my own eyes—I, and not another." Judaism often interprets this passage, in which Job responds to his friends by expressing confidence and eventual vindication, as meaning "God Himself" when he mentions "redeemer."

Chapter 18:
Christian Prophecies

Many important prophecies that potentially point to Jesus in the Old Testament lend credibility to the concept that all the Manifestations of God were united and participated in God's divine curriculum for humankind through progressive revelation. But within the New Testament, we can find prophecies for future Manifestations, signifying that Jesus was not the last One to appear.

Christianity, through its thousands of different strands of interpretation, are unified in a belief in the "second coming of Christ." Here are ten prominent quotations from the New Testament that most Christians agree point to Jesus's return.

> **Then will appear the sign of the Son of Man in heaven. And then all the peoples of the earth will mourn when they see the Son of Man coming on the clouds of heaven, with power and great glory.**[332]

Christians interpret this verse as a literal prophecy of Jesus's visible and glorious return to earth to judge humanity and establish His kingdom. Some believe Jesus will actually appear on clouds in the sky.

---

332 The *Bible*, Matthew 24:30.

The Bahá'í Writings interpret this passage symbolically, with "coming on the clouds of heaven" representing spiritual renewal and the return of Christ's teachings through another Manifestation of God. Bahá'ís also point out that in scriptures, references to clouds are often used as metaphors for obstacles, in this case, perhaps obstacles of belief that get in the way of recognizing the Manifestation when He appears.

In the book of Acts, the following passage addresses those who were expecting Jesus to literally return after his "ascension" into heaven.

> "Men of Galilee," they said, "why do you stand here looking into the sky? This same Jesus, who has been taken from you into heaven, will come back in the same way you have seen him go into heaven."[333]

This verse is often viewed as a promise of Jesus's bodily and visible return to earth. Again, Bahá'ís generally interpret this symbolically, asserting that the return refers to the reappearance of Christ's spirit and teachings through another Divine Messenger. Another prophecy is often interpreted as forecasting the return of Jesus.

> "Look, he is coming with the clouds," and "every eye will see him, even those who pierced him"; and all peoples on earth "will mourn because of him." So shall it be! Amen.[334]

Christians often see this as a prophecy of Jesus's universal and visible return accompanied by divine judgment, even though a physical return "with the clouds" would only be visible to a small group of people, so every eye would *not* see him. The claim that

---

333 The *Bible*, Acts 1:11.
334 The *Bible*, Revelation 1:7.

"even those who pierced him" would see His return makes little sense today, two thousand years later, when those who nailed Jesus to the cross and pierced his side are long dead. The clues point to symbolism.

Bahá'í Writings explain that "coming with the clouds" indicates the obscurities that usually surround the appearance of a new Manifestation of God, at which time recognition of His station may initially be "clouded" by misunderstandings or veils.

Regarding the timing of Jesus's "second coming," Matthew has this to say:

> But about that day or hour no one knows, not even the angels in heaven, nor the Son, but only the Father.[335]

For Christians, this underscores the unpredictability of Christ's return, which encourages vigilance and readiness among believers. Most Bahá'ís, I think, would generally agree, emphasizing that this is a reminder of the hidden and unforeseen nature of divine revelations, which require spiritual insight for recognition.

Here is another frequently cited prophecy of Christ's return.

> For the Lord himself will come down from heaven, with a loud command, with the voice of the archangel and with the trumpet call of God, and the dead in Christ will rise first. After that, we who are still alive and are left will be caught up together with them in the clouds to meet the Lord in the air.[336]

Many Christians interpret this as a literal description of the resurrection of believers from the dead and their unification with Christ at his return. The Bahá'í writings offer a simpler explanation— that this should be viewed symbolically to represent the spiritual

---
335 The *Bible*, Matthew 24:36.
336 The *Bible*, 1 Thessalonians 4:16-17.

awakening and transformation of humanity through God's new revelation introduced by a coming Manifestation of God.

Christians often see the following verse as Jesus's promise to physically return for His followers, bringing them into eternal fellowship with Him.

> And if I go and prepare a place for you, I will come back and take you to be with me that you also may be where I am.[337]

Many Bahá'í's see in this promise the return of Christ's spirit through a new Manifestation to guide humanity. Referring to the Manifestations including Jesus, the Bahá'í writings say, "They all abide in the same Tabernacle, soar in the same heaven, are seated upon the same throne, utter the same speech, and proclaim the same Faith."[338]

The following verse from 2 Peter speaks to the stealth of Christ's return.

> But the day of the Lord will come like a thief. The heavens will disappear with a roar; the elements will be destroyed by fire, and the earth and everything done in it will be laid bare.[339]

For Christians, this verse is often seen as a description of the end of the world and the final judgment. Many movies with astounding special effects have dramatized the spectacular metaphors used in this passage as if they should be taken literally.

Bahá'ís usually interpret the "day of the Lord" as a transformative era where old systems are metaphorically "destroyed" to make way for a new divine order. Bahá'ís view this as a beautiful metaphor for

---

337 The *Bible*, John 14:3.
338 Bahá'u'lláh, *Gleanings from the Writings of Bahá'u'lláh*, p. 52.
339 The *Bible*, 2 Peter 3:10.

the judgment of humanity's spiritual condition when compared to the teachings of a new Manifestation of God.

Islamic interpretations of these verses often overlap with Christian eschatology in recognizing the return of Jesus as a central figure in the Last Day. Each of these verses is significant for both Christians and Bahá'ís, offering differing yet profound insights into the concept of Christ's return and its spiritual implications. However, we can now see a difference of opinion arising about the continuing chain of progressive revelation.

Time Prophecies about Jesus

There are many time prophecies in the Old Testament that cumulatively build a strong case for progressive revelation. Interpretations are my own unless cited from external references. One of these prophecies, from the book of Daniel, seems perplexing until adding some historical context available only after fulfillment of the prophecy, which is presented in two parts that together accurately foretell the time of Jesus's crucifixion. In the following interpretations, "sevens" means "seven-year periods" according to various Bible passages.

Daniel's Prophecy of 69 Sevens[340]

> Know and understand this: From the time the word goes out to restore and rebuild Jerusalem until the Anointed One, the ruler, comes, there will be seven "sevens," and sixty-two "sevens." It will be rebuilt with streets and a trench, but in times of trouble. After the sixty-two 'sevens,' the Anointed One will be put to death and will have nothing.[e] The people of the ruler who will come will destroy the city and the

---

340 See Some Answered Questions, Chapter 10, paragraphs 13-14 for 'Abdu'l-Bahás interpretation.

> sanctuary. The end will come like a flood: War will continue until the end, and desolations have been decreed.[341]

$$7 + 62 = 69 \text{ weeks}$$
$$69 \times 7 = 483 \text{ years.}$$

As interpreted, the "Anointed One" must refer to Jesus, as the numbers will prove. So, what is the starting point for the 69-year period designated in the first sentence? And why is 69 broken into two separate units—7 and 62—which must be summed to arrive at 69?

In Biblical parlance, seven "sevens", the "sevens" indicates a unit of measure of seven days, or a "week." The phrase sixty-two "sevens" then must mean sixty-two "weeks." If you add seven weeks and sixty-two weeks, you end up with sixty-nine weeks. To find the number of days, we must then multiply sixty-nine weeks times seven (days); thus, we arrive at 483 days in the specified time period in the Daniel quotation.

Bible scholars generally agree that this prophecy starts "from the time the word goes out to restore and rebuild" Jerusalem. The third decree to rebuild was issued to Ezra in 457 BCE and matches this description, as it is the only such decree to be enacted upon. Counting forward 483 years brings us to 26 CE. But when transitioning to the new era, the new calendar started with 1 CE, not 0 CE, which means that we are missing a year between BCE and CE. Therefore, we must add one year to our calculation.

$$457 \text{ BCE} + 26 \text{ CE} + 1 = 27 \text{ CE}$$

The year 27 CE is the approximate beginning of Jesus's final ministry, which lasted about seven years according to many Biblical scholars. Symbolically, then, this points to the beginning of a period of redemption for the Jewish people that coincides with the period of Jesus's active ministry. But all such periods have a termination

---

341 The *Bible*, Daniel 9:25–26 (NIV).

date, which in this case we can expect to be the crucifixion of Jesus. Amazingly, Daniel's prophecy also reveals the year that would occur.

The verse in Daniel prior to the prophecy of 69 days clearly states that the Jewish people must change their ways. This prophetic verse also sets the termination date for their period of redemption—seventy "sevens" (490 years) from the start of the rebuilding of the Jerusalem temple.

What does the other time period in this prophecy mean? It tells us: "until the Anointed One, the ruler, comes, there will be seven "sevens," and sixty-two 'sevens'… After the sixty-two 'sevens,' the Anointed One will be put to death." This must set a date for His crucifixion.

The "seven 'sevens' mentioned in this passage refers to the forty-nine years that it took to reconstruct the temple. This brings us to the year 408 BCE, the year that rebuilding was finished. So now our math looks like this, allowing for transition to the new calendar and the missing year:

$$408 \text{ BCE} + 33 \text{ CE} + 1 = 34 \text{ CE}$$

The year 34 CE is a plausible date for the crucifixion, according to many Bible scholars producing an astonishingly accurate prophecy made hundreds of years earlier.

Daniel's Prophecy of 70 Sevens[342]

> Seventy "sevens" are decreed for your people and your holy city to finish transgression, to put an end to sin, to atone for wickedness, to bring in everlasting righteousness, to seal up vision and prophecy and to anoint the Most Holy Place.[343]

$$70 \times 7 = 490 \text{ years.}$$

---

342 See *Some Answered Questions*, Chapter 10, paragraphs 11-12 for 'Abdu'l-Bahá's interpretation.
343 The *Bible*, Daniel 9:24 (NIV).

What is the difference between the "69 weeks" and the "70 weeks?" The Bahá'í Writings clarify this for us:

> The second [period] begins after the completion of the rebuilding of Jerusalem, which is sixtytwo weeks until the ascension of Christ. The rebuilding of Jerusalem took seven weeks, which is equivalent to fortynine years. Seven weeks added to sixtytwo weeks makes sixtynine weeks, and in the last week the ascension of Christ took place. This completes the seventy weeks, and no contradiction remains.[344]

My understanding, then, is that during the seventieth week (a seven-year period), the ascension of Jesus occurred. This means that to find the number of years in this seventy-week period, we must multiply 70 (weeks) times 70 (the number of days in each week. The result in 490 days, or in Biblical terms, 490 years.

Counting forward, then, from the date of the decree to rebuild Jerusalem, we should find that same date for the crucifixion as we calculated from the prophecies above. Again, we must allow for that missing transitional year between the BCE and CE calendars. The number of years between 457 BCE and 34 CE is exactly 490.

$$457 \text{ BCE} + 1 = 34 \text{ CE}$$

Bahá'í writings confirm that this prophecy refers to Christ.

> Thirty-three added to 457 is 490, which is the time announced by Daniel for the advent of Christ. ... The third edict of Artaxerxes was issued in 457 B.C., and Christ was thirtythree years old at the time of His martyrdom and ascension. Thirtythree added to 457 is 490 years—the time announced by Daniel for the advent of Christ.[345]

---

344 'Abdu'l-Bahá, *Some Answered Questions*, pp. 47-48.
345 'Abdu'l-Bahá, *Some Answered Questions*, Chapter 10, p. 37.

The Hebrew Bible with confirmations from Christianity and the Bahá'í Faith provide convincing evidence of this testament to the concept of progressive revelation.

Judaism's Rejection of Jesus

While Judaism anticipated the coming of a future Messiah, it did not accept Jesus due to a combination of theological, historical, and cultural factors. Traditional Jewish belief envisioned the Messiah as a human leader descended from King David Who would fulfill specific roles including:

- Rebuilding the Temple in Jerusalem.
- Gathering all Jews back to the Land of Israel.
- Ushering in an era of universal peace and the end of war.[346]
- Establishing global recognition of God's sovereignty.[347]
- Restoring the Davidic monarchy and enforcing Torah law.

Jewish authorities in Jesus's time, and rabbis even today, argue that Jesus did not accomplish these messianic tasks. For example, the Roman occupation of Judea continued, the Temple was eventually destroyed in 70 CE, and universal peace was not established.

Also, theologically, Judaism is strictly monotheistic and does not accept the idea of a divine Messiah. The concept of God taking human form is seen as incompatible with Jewish theology (Deuteronomy 6:4: "Hear, O Israel: The Lord our God, the Lord is one.").

Another incompatibility is that Christianity emphasizes Jesus's role as a Savior who atones for humanity's sins. Judaism does not have a doctrine of "original sin" (Adam and Eve sinned so we are all sinners because of them) and teaches that individuals are responsible only for their own actions. Repentance, prayer, and good deeds are seen as the path to forgiveness.

---

346 The *Bible*, Isaiah 2:4.
347 The *Bible*, Zechariah 14:9.

The fact that Jesus challenged some interpretations of Jewish law and presented new teachings must have been a major irritant too. Judaism holds the Torah as eternal and unchanging.[348] Any perceived attempt to alter or replace it would be considered unacceptable.

Historically, many Jews in Jesus's time were hoping for a Messiah who was a political and military leader to liberate them from Roman rule. Jesus's emphasis on spiritual salvation rather than political liberation did not align with these expectations. Also, during and after Jesus's life, there were several other claimants to the title of Messiah. None were accepted as the true Messiah, including Jesus, as they did not fulfill Jewish messianic prophecies.

After the destruction of the Second Temple, Jewish religious life was reorganized around Rabbinic Judaism, which solidified Jewish law (*Halakha*) and theology. The divergence between Judaism and Christianity became more pronounced during this period.

While Christians often point to passages in the Hebrew Bible (e.g., Isaiah, the Psalms, Daniel) as pointing to Jesus as the Messiah, Jewish interpretations differ. And though Christians teach that Jesus will fulfill Messianic prophecies in his Second Coming, Judaism rejects this concept because it expects the Messiah to fulfill all prophecies in a single lifetime.

As Jesus's followers increasingly included Gentiles and moved away from Jewish practices like circumcision and dietary laws, the gap between Judaism and Christianity widened. When the Apostle Paul continued to reinterpret Jewish law and claim Jesus was the fulfillment of the Messianic promise, Jews saw these interpretations as inconsistent with Torah principles.

While Jesus is a central figure in Christianity, in Judaism he is often seen as a teacher or prophet who failed to fulfill the roles of the prophesied Jewish Messiah.

---

348 The *Bible*, Deuteronomy 13:1.

Our most recent wisdom tradition addresses the rejection of Jesus by the Jewish community as part of a broader principle of religious history. This principle highlights the recurring challenges faced by each new Manifestation of God in being accepted by the followers of previous revelations. In explaining this rejection, Bahá'u'lláh emphasized that religious leaders and followers of all faiths often misunderstand or misinterpret the symbolic language of their scriptures. For example, Jews expected the Messiah to fulfill certain literal prophecies, such as restoring the Davidic monarchy.

> The people sought shelter and refuge in the outward and veiled themselves from the inward. ... They that clung to the letter of the law and cast away its spirit are, in the sight of God, the followers of error.[349]

'Abdu'l-Bahá added that clinging to outward forms and traditions often blinds people to the spiritual essence of religion, suggesting that the Jewish leaders were so focused on the letter of the Law that they missed its fulfillment in Jesus.

> They failed to perceive that the purpose of a new Manifestation of God is to breathe a new life into the body of religion and to renew its eternal truths.[350]

As we shall see, these common errors continue to this day.

Christianity's Rejection of Future Manifestations

Just as Jews rejected Jesus as the promised Messiah, both Jews and Christians have failed to perceive the advent of Muhammad, the Báb and Bahaullah because of misinterpretation, attachment to past traditions, and resistance to change. These rejections highlight humanity's challenge in recognizing the divine in new forms. The

---

349 Bahá'u'lláh, *Kitáb-i-Íqán*, pp. 41–42.
350 'Abdu'l-Bahá, *Some Answered Questions*, p. 123.

writings of our latest wisdom tradition, however, emphasize that over time each revelation is eventually embraced and its truths become universally acknowledged.

Jews have difficulty accepting the Báb and Bahá'u'lláh for the same reasons they reject Muhammad and Jesus. Christians have some newly developed beliefs that make it hard to accept Muhammad, the Báb and Bahá'u'lláh. Muslims also find difficulty in accepting the Manifestations who followed Muhammad.

Belief in the Finality of Jesus's Revelation

Many Christians believe that Jesus's mission was the final revelation from God, citing scriptures such as this one, in which Jesus says:

> I am the way and the truth and the life. No one comes to the Father except through me.[351]

This belief in finality created a barrier to recognizing subsequent revelations. Rigidly held beliefs are called paradigms, and most people can't break free from them to navigate a paradigm shift even when logic dictates they should.

Our most recent wisdom tradition emphasized that when a Manifestation of God refers to Himself in spirit, He is referring to all the Manifestations of God, because they are the same in spirit. So, when Jesus said, "No one comes to the Father except through me," He was referring to Himself in the present tense, but also to the Manifestations who would follow Him.

> These sanctified Mirrors... are one and all the Exponents on earth of Him Who is the central Orb of the universe.[352]

---

351 The *Bible*, John 14:6.
352 Bahá'u'lláh, *Gleanings from the Writings of Bahá'u'lláh*, p. 73.

> They are regarded as one soul and the same person, for they all drink from the one Cup of the love of God.[353]

Another Bible verse from Bible is often interpreted by Christians as insisting that no new scriptures, which include the Qur'an and the Bahá'í writings, can be accepted.

> For truly I tell you, until heaven and earth disappear, not the smallest letter, not the least stroke of a pen, will by any means disappear from the Law until everything is accomplished.[354]

The Bahá'í Faith explains that the phrases "until heaven and earth disappear" and "everything is accomplished" refer to the end of one Manifestation's dispensation and the introduction of a new revelation from God delivered by another Manifestation. Just as Jesus reformed the laws of Judaism in many ways without violating those earlier laws and edicts, so to do new Divine Educators expand understanding and affirm new laws for society. God's promise of continuing guidance for humanity would be inconsistent with the notion of an end to new guidance appropriate for a new age.

Misunderstanding of Prophecy

Christians often interpret prophecies in a way that exclude Muhammad. For instance, references to the "Comforter" in the New Testament are interpreted by Christians as the Holy Spirit, while Muslims and Bahá'ís interpret this as a reference to Muhammad or future revelations.

> And I will pray the Father, and he shall give you another Comforter, that he may abide with you for ever;[355]

---

353 Bahá'u'lláh, *Kitáb-i-Íqán*, p. 152.
354 The *Bible*, Matthew 5:18 (NIV).
355 The *Bible*, John 14:16.

Cultural and Religious Differences

Numerous cultural and religious differences have created tensions between Christianity and Islam. Christianity developed primarily within a Greco-Roman cultural framework and used languages such as Greek and Latin. Islam emerged in an Arabic-speaking world, with cultural practices and traditions distinct from those of the Christian West.

Muhammad's message, originating in Arabia and expressed in Arabic, was seen as foreign to the predominantly Greco-Roman world of Christianity. The shift in customs, laws, and practices made Islam appear alien to many Christians. Christians often view Islamic theology as incompatible with their understanding of God, while Muslims see Christian doctrines, such as the Trinity (God the Father, God the Son, and God the Holy Ghost) and the divinity of Jesus, as a departure from monotheism.

While Christians view Jesus as the final incarnation of God, Muslims regard Muhammad as the Seal of the Prophets, the final messenger completing the line of prophecy. These competing claims to finality have historically led to mutual rejection.

Christians regard the Bible as the authoritative and complete Word of God, particularly the New Testament, which fulfills the Old Testament. Muslims believe the Qur'an supersedes previous scriptures, including the Bible, which they believe was altered or misinterpreted over time. For Muslims, the Qur'an is seen as the final and unadulterated revelation.

Historical and Military Hostility

The political and military conflicts between Christian and Muslim societies during the early centuries of Islam reinforced mutual suspicion and rejection. After Muhammad's death, Islam expanded rapidly, often coming into conflict with the Byzantine Christian Empire. These interactions were marked by military campaigns, many Islamic conquests, and later the bloody Crusades. These conflicts fostered an "us vs. them" mindset that reinforced mutual distrust and rejection.

Divergent Practices and Laws

Christianity emphasizes sacraments, such as baptism and the Eucharist, as key rituals of worship. Islam practices the Five Pillars, including daily prayers, fasting during Ramadan, and pilgrimage to Mecca. These distinct practices highlight the differences in religious expression and reinforce the perception of Islam as a fundamentally separate and incompatible faith.

Islamic Sharia law encompasses all aspects of life, including governance and societal rules, which can contrast with Christianity's more ecclesiastical focus. This divergence has created a perception among Christians that Islam was more political and legalistic.

Stereotypes and Misunderstandings

During the Middle Ages, Christian writers often portrayed Muhammad in negative terms, accusing him of heresy or immorality because of practices such as polygamy. These attacks reinforced a deeply rooted cultural aversion to Islam. On the other hand, Islamic critiques of Christianity as having deviated from monotheism were similarly misunderstood or rejected by Christian audiences. Even today, misunderstandings about Islam persist in Christian-majority societies, perpetuating the historical rejection of Muhammad as a prophet.

Terrorism Acts

The perception of Islam as a "terrorist religion" is rooted in a combination of historical events, political circumstances, media portrayals, and misunderstandings of Islamic teachings. This perception is not representative of the faith itself, which emphasizes peace, compassion, and justice.

It is true that groups like Al-Qaeda, ISIS, Boko Haram, and the Taliban have committed acts of terrorism in the name of Islam.

These extremist groups claim to justify their actions using distorted interpretations of Islamic texts, which has led some to associate Islam with violence. Extremists often misinterpret or take Qur'anic verses out of context. For example, verses about self-defense or warfare during specific historical battles are cited as blanket endorsements of violence, ignoring the broader principles of peace and restraint emphasized in the Qur'an, which repeatedly emphasizes peace.

> **If they incline to peace, then incline to it [also] and rely upon Allah.**[356]

Historically, many predominantly Muslim regions experienced colonization and exploitation, leading to resistance movements. Over time, some of these movements adopted violent tactics, which were often framed as religious struggles. In the post-colonial period, geopolitical struggles in the Middle East, South Asia and Africa have contributed to tremendous instability. In many cases, these conflicts were driven by political, ethnic, or economic factors but were framed as religious wars. Later, foreign interventions, such as wars in Iraq and Afghanistan, have fueled resentment in some Muslim communities. Extremists exploit this resentment to recruit members and frame their actions as resistance against oppression.

Many people don't understand that Islam, like other major religions, explicitly condemns the killing of innocent people:

> **Whoever kills a soul unless for a soul or for corruption [done] in the land—it is as if he had slain mankind entirely.**[357]

The term *jihad* is often misunderstood as "holy war." In Islamic theology, it primarily refers to a personal struggle for self-improvement and adherence to faith. Only in specific contexts

---

356 *Quran* 8:61.
357 *Quran* 5:32.

does it include defensive warfare, and even then, with strict ethical guidelines.

Blaming Islam for terrorism is like blaming Christianity for racism. While not officially a Christian organization, the Ku Klux Klan used Christian symbols, rhetoric and imagery while lynching Blacks. The Christian Identity Movement today promotes a white supremacy ideology anchored in a distorted interpretation of Christianity.

It is critical to separate the actions of extremists from the teachings of Islam and the practices of the vast majority of Muslims

Chapter 19: Islamic Prophecies

Islam identifies several prophecies from the Hebrew Bible, the New Testament, Zoroastrian texts, Hindu scriptures, and other traditions as foretelling the coming of Muhammad. These interpretations reflect the Islamic view of Muhammad as the final prophet who fulfills the expectations of various religious traditions, bringing a universal message of monotheism and guidance. While these interpretations are accepted within Islamic theology, they are inevitably subject to debate among scholars of other faiths.

Bible Prophecies about Muhammad

The Spirit of Truth

Islam identifies a few New Testament passages as foretelling the coming of Muhammad within the context of Jesus announcing his successor. Islamic interpretations identify the words "advocate" and "spirit of truth" as a reference to Muhammad.

> And I will ask the Father, and he will give you another advocate to help you and be with you forever—the Spirit of truth.[358]

---

358 The *Bible*, John 14:16 (NIV).

> But when he, the Spirit of truth, comes, he will guide you into all the truth. He will not speak on his own; he will speak only what he hears, and he will tell you what is yet to come.[359]

The Qur'an itself refers to Muhammad as a prophet who speaks only what he hears from God,[360] which is always the truth. Muslims argue that this prophecy aligns with Muhammad's mission to deliver God's final revelation.

I Will Put My Words in His Mouth

Though part of the Old Testament, the following verse from Deuteronomy is often linked with New Testament writings:

> I will raise up for them a prophet like you from among their brothers; I will put my words in his mouth, and he will tell them everything I command him.[361]

This passage is often cited in conjunction with Islamic claims that Jesus's followers should anticipate another prophet. Muslims argue that Muhammad fulfills this prophecy as a Prophet like Moses with a law-bearing mission and direct communication from God.

Many Bahá'í's also interpret the two New Testament verses above as referring to Muhammad, but their interpretation also has a broader context. The "advocate" (or "Comforter" in some Bible translations) and the phrase "Spirit of Truth" can also represent the succession of divine revelations beginning with Muhammad and culminating with Bahá'u'lláh. Bahá'ís emphasize that these passages illustrate the ongoing guidance provided to humanity through successive Manifestations of God.

---

359 The *Bible*, John 16:13 (NIV).
360 *Qur'an* 53:3-4.
361 The *Bible*, Deuteronomy 18:18 (NIV).

Other Sheep

Another New Testament passage also refers to Muhammad when Jesus said:

> I have other sheep that are not of this sheep pen. I must bring them also. They too will listen to my voice, and there shall be one flock and one shepherd.[362]

I interpret this as Jesus acknowledging the universality of divine guidance, which extends beyond His immediate audience, and Muhammad can be seen as one of these divine figures sent to unite humanity under God's guidance. The words "other sheep" could include followers of other religious traditions such as Zoroastrians, Hindus, Buddhists, those awaiting further revelation after Jesus's time, and the followers of future Divine Educators.

The "sheep pen" can be interpreted as the immediate circle of Jesus's followers during his ministry—those who accepted His message and became part of His community. But in a broader sense, "sheep pen" could also represent any specific religious community or tradition that has been guided by a Manifestation of God. While these communities provide initial spiritual nurturing, Bahá'í writings emphasize that they are not meant to remain isolated or exclusive.

> God's purpose is to weld all peoples into one.[363]

The phrase "there shall be one shepherd" represents the singular divine source that guides all humanity. While different Manifestations of God appear at various times, they all reflect the will of the same God.

---

362 The *Bible*, John 10:16 (NIV).
363 Bahá'u'lláh, *Gleanings from the Writings of Bahá'u'lláh*, p. 203.

> These sanctified Mirrors... are one and all the Exponents on earth of Him Who is the central Orb of the universe.[364]

The "shepherd" can also symbolize the successive Manifestations of God Who guide humanity in different religious eras. According to the Bahá'í writings, Bahá'u'lláh fulfills this prophecy by calling all humanity into a unified spiritual and social order. Within the concept of progressive revelation, each successive Manifestation of God brings teachings suitable for humanity's needs at the time. But the ultimate purpose of these revelations is to lead humanity to unity and maturity.

He Is Altogether Lovely

From the Hebrew Bible, some Muslims see Muhammad referred to in this verse:

> His mouth is most sweet, and he is altogether lovely. This is my beloved, and this is my friend, O daughters of Jerusalem.[365]

In the original Hebrew text, the phrase "he is altogether lovely" includes the word "Machmad" (מַחְמָד), which some Muslims interpret as a reference to Muhammad. While this is debated among scholars, Muslims see this as a possible mention of the Prophet's name.

Mount Paran

From Habakkuk in the Hebrew Bible, Muslims often see Muhammad implied in this verse:

> God came from Teman, the Holy One from Mount Paran. His glory covered the heavens, and his praise filled the earth.[366]

---

364 Bahá'u'lláh, *Gleanings from the Writings of Bahá'u'lláh*, p. 74.
365 The *Bible*, Song of Solomon 5:16.
366 The *Bible*, Habakkuk 3:3.

"Mount Paran" is identified by many Muslims with the wilderness of Paran, linked to Ishmael and his descendants in Genesis 21:21. They interpret this as a reference to the revelation of Muhammad, Whose message began in the region of Paran (modern-day Mecca) and Whose praise is spread worldwide through the Qur'an.

As for Ishmael

> As for Ishmael, I have heard you: I will surely bless him; I will make him fruitful and will greatly increase his numbers. He will be the father of twelve rulers, and I will make him into a great nation.[367]

Muslims view this verse from Genesis as a prophecy about Ishmael's descendants, culminating in the emergence of Muhammad. The "great nation" is seen as a reference to the Muslim *ummah* (community), which began with Muhammad and spread globally.

Other Prophecies about Muhammad

Hindu Scriptures

> A malechha [foreigner] spiritual teacher will appear with his companions. His name will be Mahamad. Raja (Bhoj) after giving this Mahadev Arab a bath in the Panchgavya and the Ganges water, offered him the presents of his sincere devotion and showing him all reverence, said: 'I make obeisance to you.[368]

This prophecy is thought by some Muslims to describe Muhammad, referred to as *"Mahamad,"* coming with his companions (*Sahabah*) to spread monotheism. This interpretation is debated by some scholars, but it is often cited in comparative religious discussions.

---

367 The *Bible*, Genesis 17:20.
368 Bhavishya Purana.

Buddhist Scriptures

> A Buddha named Maitreya, the Buddha of universal fellowship, will come... to preach his holy religion.[369]

Some Muslims interpret Maitreya as a reference to Muhammad. They emphasize his role in bringing a message of universal fellowship and guidance for humanity. The Bahá'í Faith generally regards Maitreya as a reference to Bahá'u'lláh, though it could apply to all Manifestations that follow Buddha.[370]

Samaritan Expectations

The Samaritans believed in a future Prophet like Moses called the *Taheb*. Muhammad is seen by Muslims as fulfilling the role of this Prophet by bringing a universal law.

Islamic Validation

The Quran itself asserts that previous scriptures foretold Muhammad's coming.

> Those who follow the Messenger, the unlettered Prophet, whom they find written in what they have of the Torah and the Gospel..." (Quran 7:157)

This verse indicates that prophecies about Muhammad's coming can be found in earlier scriptures, though interpretations of these prophecies vary between religious traditions.

Bahá'í Faith Confirmation of Muhammad

Although most Muslims reject the Bahá'í Faith and its Founders, Bahá'í writings affirm Muhammad as a Manifestation of God, emphasizing His pivotal role in the spiritual evolution of humanity.

---

369 Bhavishya Purana.
370 Shoghi Effendi, *God Passes By*, p. 94.

His revelation is regarded as a cornerstone in the divine process of progressive revelation, preparing the way for subsequent Manifestations, including the Báb and Bahá'u'lláh. Muhammad is honored as a source of divine guidance and a unifier of humanity, embodying the principles of justice, mercy and monotheism. Here are a few passages from Bahá'í tablets.

The Báb

> "He Who hath revealed verses unto Muhammad, the Apostle of God, hath likewise revealed verses unto 'Alí-Muhammad [the Báb]. For who else but God can reveal to a man such clear and manifest verses as overpower all the learned?" [371]

This statement affirms that Muhammad is an Apostle of God, a Manifestation Who has received verses from God [known as the Qu'ran]. The Báb here is recognizing Muhammad's spiritual precedence—an important declaration given the Shi'a context of the Báb's time.

Bahá'u'lláh

> Thus hath Muhammad, the Point of the Qur'án, revealed: 'I am all the Prophets.' Likewise, He saith: 'I am the first Adam, Noah, Moses, and Jesus.' ... In like manner, in every subsequent Revelation, the return of the former Revelation is a fact....[372]

In these words, Bahá'u'lláh, affirms the divine station of Muhammad and links him directly to the chain of progressive revelation.

---

371 The Báb, *Selections from the Writings of the Báb.*
372 Bahá'u'lláh, *Gleanings from the Writings of Bahá'u'lláh.*

> What could have been the evidence produced by the Pharisees and the idolatrous priests to justify their denial of Muhammad, the Apostle of God when He came unto them with a Book that judged between truth and falsehood…?[373]

This statement recognizes Muhammad as the Apostle of God.

'Abdu'l-Bahá

> Consider how… the sacred power of His Holiness Muḥammad became the means of uniting and harmonizing the contentious tribes and the different clans of Peninsular Arabia—to such an extent that one thousand tribes were welded into one tribe; strife and discord were done away with; all of them unitedly and with one accord strove in advancing the cause of culture and civilization, and thus were freed from the lowest degree of degradation, soaring toward the height of everlasting glory![374]

'Abdu'l-Bahá emphasizes Muhammad's role in unifying disparate groups under the spiritual and moral power of divine revelation.

Shoghi Effendi

> To Him [Bahá'u'lláh] Muḥammad, the Apostle of God, had alluded in His Book as the 'Great Announcement'…[375]

Shoghi Effendi clearly identifies Muhammad as a predecessor of Bahá'u'lláh in the chain of divine revelation referred to as the Great Announcement.

---

373 Bahá'u'lláh, *Epistle to the Son of the Wolf*, p. 81
374 'Abdu'l-Bahá, *Tablets of the Divine Plan*.
375 Shoghi Effendi, *God Passes By*, p. 104.

Chapter 20:
Bahá'í Prophecies

A Hindu Prophecy

Hindus are awaiting the coming of the Kalki Avatar at the end of this present age called Kalki Yuga (Dark or Iron Age). Baha'is believe that the Kalki Yuga age has already ended and, as promised in the Bhagavad Gita, the Lord has again manifested Himself to humanity. The following Hindu prophecy describes the appearance of a new Avatar or "Manifestation" to be born of a wealthy family at a time when "the institutes of law have nearly ceased" to renew religion and restore righteousness to the hearts of men. The Bahá'í Faith asserts that this is a prophecy fulfilled by Bahá'u'lláh.[376]

> **When the practices taught by the Vedas and the institutes of law shall nearly have ceased, and the close of the Kali age shall be nigh... He will be born as Kalki in the family of an eminent brahmin... He will then re-establish righteousness upon earth; and the minds of those who live at the end of the Kali age shall be awakened, and shall be as pellucid as crystal.**[377]

---

376 Shoghi Effendi, *God Passes By*, p. 94-95.
377 *Vishnu Purana* 4.24.

A Buddhist Prophecy

A prophecy regarding Maitreya, the "Fifth Buddha" and prophesied successor to Siddhartha Buddha, is detailed in several Buddhist texts from the Theravada and Mahayana traditions. A significant reference from the Theravada tradition mentions Maitreya, referred to in Pali as Metteyya:

> In that era, there will arise in the world an Exalted One named Metteyya, Fully Awakened, abounding in wisdom and goodness, happy, with knowledge of the worlds, unsurpassed as a guide to mortals willing to be led, a teacher for gods and men, an Exalted One, a Buddha, even as I am now. He, by himself, will thoroughly know and see, as it were face to face, this universe, with Its worlds of the spirits… [378]

As discussed throughout this book, all of the conditions for the appearance of Meitreya (*Metteyya*) have been fulfilled in Bahá'u'lláh.

Bible Prophecies about the Báb and Bahá'u'lláh

There are many Bible prophecies that the Bahá'í Faith claims refer specifically to the Báb and Bahá'u'lláh. Here are a few:

The Messenger of the Covenant

In this verse from the Hebrew Bible, the Báb is seen as the "messenger" who prepares the way for Bahá'u'lláh.

> Behold, I will send my messenger, and he shall prepare the way before me: and the Lord, whom ye seek, shall suddenly come to his temple, even the messenger of the covenant, whom ye delight in: behold, he shall come, saith the Lord of hosts.[379]

---

378 *Digha Nikaya*, 26.
379 The *Bible*, Malachi 3:1 (KJV).

The Báb's role as the forerunner and herald of Bahá'u'lláh aligns with this prophecy, as He announced the imminent appearance of "He Whom God shall make manifest" (referring to Bahá'u'lláh).

The Seven Seals

In the following prophecy from the book of Revelation, the Báb and Bahá'u'lláh are seen by many Bahá'ís as the Ones who open the scrolls and reveal divine mysteries. The Báb's revelation can be seen as unlocking the spiritual seals and preparing humanity for Bahá'u'lláh.

> Then I saw in the right hand of him who sat on the throne a scroll with writing on both sides and sealed with seven seals. And I saw a mighty angel proclaiming in a loud voice, "Who is worthy to break the seals and open the scroll?" But no one in heaven or on earth or under the earth could open the scroll or even look inside it. I wept and wept because no one was found who was worthy to open the scroll or look inside. Then one of the elders said to me, "Do not weep! See, the Lion of the tribe of Judah, the Root of David, has triumphed. He is able to open the scroll and its seven seals."[380]

Christians often identify the "Lion of the tribe of Judah" and the Root of David" as Jesus because these are references to His Messianic lineage. Our newest wisdom tradition clarifies this symbolism by affirming that the Lion symbolizes Bahá'u'lláh, whose lineage also traces back to David and Abraham. Bahá'u'lláh is seen as fulfilling the Messianic prophecies of various religions including Judaism, Christianity and Islam, by inaugurating a new spiritual era.

---

380 The *Bible*, Revelation 5:1–5.

> The Revelation which, from time immemorial, hath been acclaimed as the Purpose and Promise of all the Prophets of God, and the most cherished desire of His Messengers, hath now, by virtue of the pervasive Will of the Almighty and at His irresistible bidding, been revealed unto men.[381]

The scroll represents divine knowledge, truth, and the eternal will of God. The scroll is "sealed," signifying that humanity had been unable to access or comprehend the deeper spiritual truths necessary for the new stage in its development. Thus, the scroll can be seen as the new covenant of God, which is revealed progressively through His next Manifestations. The Báb and Bahá'u'lláh "unseal" previously hidden mysteries and bring humanity closer to understanding God's plan.

The "seven seals" represent the layers of spiritual mysteries, veils of misunderstanding, and barriers that prevent humanity from fully understanding divine truth. The number seven signifies completeness and perfection in biblical symbolism, emphasizing the comprehensive nature of these barriers. The Báb and Bahá'u'lláh are seen as the figures who unseal these mysteries. The Báb prepared humanity by unlocking spiritual truths, and Bahá'u'lláh brought the full revelation that establishes global unity and the spiritual maturity of humanity.

The Mountain of the Lord

> In the last days the mountain of the Lord's temple will be established as the highest of the mountains; it will be exalted above the hills, and all nations will stream to it. Many peoples will come and say, 'Come, let us go up to the mountain of the Lord, to the temple of the God of Jacob. He will teach us his ways, so that we

---

381 Bahá'u'lláh, *Gleanings from the Writings of Bahá'u'lláh*, p. 5.

> may walk in his paths.' The law will go out from Zion, the word of the Lord from Jerusalem. He will judge between the nations and will settle disputes for many peoples. They will beat their swords into plowshares and their spears into pruning hooks. Nation will not take up sword against nation, nor will they train for war anymore.[382]

Bahá'u'lláh fulfills this prophecy by calling for global unity, the abolition of war, and the establishment of universal peace. His teachings emphasize justice, reconciliation, and the spiritual renewal of humanity as in the following passage by Bahá'u'lláh.

> That all nations should become one in faith and all men as brothers; that the bonds of affection and unity between the sons of men should be strengthened; that diversity of religion should cease, and differences of race be annulled – what harm is there in this?[383]

As a side note, I was privileged to attend the opening of the nineteen terraces on Mount Carmel, known as the Mountain of the Lord in the Old Testament. I believe the western slope of Mount Carmel matches the description of the "mountain of the Lord's temple" and is now the home of the Bahá'í World Center and the Shrine in which the remains of the Báb are kept. During the opening of the beautiful terraces, over five thousand individuals in their native garb from around the world ascended the terraces in a celebration of Bahá'u'lláh's vision for global unity.

---

[382] The *Bible*, Isaiah 2:2–4.
[383] Bahá'í.org. Available at https://www.bahai.org/library/authoritative-texts/compilations/peace/2#185433425.

The Bahai World Center lower terraces on Mount Carmel in Haifa, Israel. The Shrine of the Báb is at the top.

> Every age hath its own problem, and every soul its particular aspiration. The remedy the world needeth in its present-day afflictions can never be the same as that which a subsequent age may require.[384]

The Three "Woes"

The Bible foretells the future appearance of two Manifestations of God. The second One appearing shortly after the first. The Bible refers to the appearance of these new Manifestations as the "Day of the Lord," meaning that time when God's Kingdom will be established and "His Will" shall be done on earth as it is in heaven. But the appearance of a Manifestation is also depicted as a day of "woe" because it is also a "woeful" time of reckoning and suffering for those who do not recognize the new Manifestation. The Qur'an describes that day as the "Day of God," the "Last Day," the "Day of Judgment," or the "Day of Reckoning."

---

[384] Bahá'u'lláh, *Gleanings from the Writings of Bahá'u'lláh*, p. 213.

The Old Testament prophet Ezekiel defined this day in his prophecy about the coming of the Messiah, Jesus, which would end the dispensation of Moses and begin a new dispensation under the teachings of Jesus. While outwardly speaking about God's judgment of Egypt, Christians point to this passage as clearly prophesying the coming of a time when Jesus will return to judge the heathen nations.

> **The word of the Lord came again unto me, saying, Son of man, prophesy and say, Thus saith the Lord God; Howl ye, Woe worth the day! For the day is near, even the day of the Lord is near, a cloudy day; it shall be the time of the heathen.**[385]

Several centuries later, quoting Jesus, John wrote in the Book of Revelation:

> **The first woe has passed; behold, two woes are still to come.**[386]

Following the Christian interpretation of the first "woe" as a time when the Christian dispensation begins with the appearance of Jesus, this verse from Revelation appears to address a time when the dispensation of Jesus has "passed. This would mean, of course, that another Manifestation would have appeared. This would be the advent of Muhammad, Who chronologically followed Jesus.

This passage also tells us that two additional Manifestations after Muhammad will appear to renew God's revelation ("two woes are still to come.") In other words, two more Manifestations of God will appear after Muhammad. The Book of Revelation prophesies that these two "woes" will come close together, just as the Báb preceded Bahá'u'lláh by just nine years.

---

385 The *Bible*, Ezekiel 30:1–3.
386 The *Bible*, Revelation 9:12

> The second woe is past; and behold, the third woe is coming quickly.[387]

With adequate historical knowledge about the Báb, who heralded the coming of Bahá'u'lláh in the mid-1800s, these obscure prophecies become clear.

By the Numbers

In principle, almost all measurable aspects of the physical universe can be described mathematically because they obey consistent patterns or laws. These patterns can often be expressed using equations, algorithms, or statistical models. Some systems, however, especially those involving chaotic or highly complex behaviors, are difficult to describe fully in mathematical terms.

Weather systems and fluid dynamics involve chaotic processes that are sensitive to initial conditions, making precise predictions difficult. Biological systems and ecosystems are often so complex that while they can be modeled mathematically, such models are simplifications. Some phenomena, like consciousness or human behavior, may not yet be fully reducible to mathematical descriptions. They involve layers of complexity and emergent properties that are challenging to quantify.

Imagine, then, reducing the prophecies regarding the appearance of Manifestations of God to math, as in elapsed time between events or a calculated year in a specific type of calendar. And yet, we can find prophecies that precisely state the timing of specific events numerically so that in hindsight we can fix our gaze on the target and determine the correctness of the prophecy.

William Miller, Pastor and Mathematician

Many people have tried to determine the date of the Second Coming of Jesus based on scriptural clues. One of them was William

---

387 The *Bible*, Revelation 11:14.

Miller (1782–1849), an American Baptist preacher and farmer who became the central figure in a religious revival movement known as the Millerite Movement. Originally a skeptic, Miller experienced a religious conversion in 1816 and became a devout Christian. He began a deep study of the Bible, focusing on a particular prophecy in Daniel:

> Unto two thousand and three hundred days; then shall the sanctuary be cleansed.[388]

Miller interpreted these 2,300 "days" as 2,300 "years," following the statement recorded by the prophet Ezekiel ("I have appointed thee each day for a year.")[389] He concluded that the "cleansing of the sanctuary" referred to the Second Coming of Christ. Based on his calculations, Miller determined that Christ would return between March 21, 1843, and March 21, 1844.

This belief gained traction, and Miller began preaching publicly in 1831, attracting thousands of followers called Millerites. The movement grew rapidly, spreading across the United States. It drew support from a range of Christian denominations and was marked by fervent expectation of the imminent return of Christ.

When Christ did not visibly return within the expected timeframe, the movement faced a crisis. A recalculation set the date for October 22, 1844, as the definitive date of Christ's return. When Christ again failed to materialize, the event became known as the Great Disappointment.

Many followers left the movement, but others sought new interpretations of the prophecy. Some Millerites concluded that October 22, 1844, marked the beginning of Christ's *heavenly* ministry rather than His *physical* return. These reinterpretations eventually led to the formation of new religious movements, most notably the Seventh-day Adventist Church.

---

388 The *Bible*, Daniel 8:14.
389 The *Bible*, Ezekiel 4:6.

May 22, 1844

Could it be that Miller simply misinterpreted the return of Jesus as a physical event and was looking in the wrong place?

On the evening of May 22, 1844, the Manifestation of God Who heralded Bahá'u'lláh and the Bahá'í Faith, declared His mission. This date, unknown in America for some time, aligns closely with the period in which Miller was anticipating the culmination of prophetic fulfillment. This is seen by Bahá'ís as a significant spiritual event that began a new religious era, even if Miller's understanding of the prophecy was different.

Bahá'ís believe that the "return of Christ" is symbolic, referring to the return of the same spiritual reality and mission through another Manifestation of God as implied by Jesus:

> **The one who is victorious I will make a pillar in the temple of my God. Never again will they leave it. I will write on them the name of my God and the name of the city of my God, the new Jerusalem, which is coming down out of heaven from my God; and I will also write on them my new name.**[390]

Bahá'ís interpret this prophecy as symbolically referring to the coming of a new Manifestation of God. The "new Jerusalem" symbolizes the establishment of a new spiritual and social order brought by a new Manifestation's teachings. The "new name" represents the new station and human identity of the Manifestation who fulfills the prophecies of Christ's return. This New Testament passage is viewed as part of the larger biblical theme of progressive revelation, in which each Manifestation of God assumes a new identity and renews divine teachings for the age in which they appear.

Ultimately, Bahá'ís regard Bahá'u'lláh as the fulfillment of the Christian expectation of Christ's return, but the Báb as herald began

---

390 The *Bible*, Revelation 3:12 (NIV).

the process of ushering in the new spiritual age. Miller may have gotten his math right, though his faulty expectations were unmet.

Daniel's Time Prophecies about the Báb and Bahá'u'lláh

Time prophecies have a big advantage over other prophecies because of their precision. Numbers constitute clear or fixed entities that are least subject to misjudgment or disagreement. A prophecy that in the last days "evil shall abound" simply points to the character of the age, so it cannot be conclusive proof. Evil rises and falls on a curve, sometimes almost imperceptibly. Skeptics can argue there has always been evil in the world and always will be. Once a certain prophesied date has passed, however, an unfulfilled prophecy for that date will always remain unfulfilled.

Every prophecy requires two things. First, that the person hearing or reading the prophecy understands what is promised. Second, that person must know if that promise has been fulfilled. If it was *not* fulfilled, there are two alternatives to consider—either the promise was fulfilled but undetected, or the promise was misunderstood or broken. In the case of William Miller in the section above, both alternatives apply—Miller misunderstood the promise *and* the promise was fulfilled but undetected.

The Old Testament prophet Daniel made prophecies that not only revealed the exact time of the first advent of Jesus, but that of the second advent as well. He is the only biblical prophet to predict the precise year of the coming of both the Báb and Bahá'u'lláh. And he is the only prophet to reveal the time of the second advent in relation to two other great wisdom traditions—Christianity and Islam.

In evaluating the following prophecy, we will consider a companion prophecy to the Daniel prophecies we studied earlier when calculating the year of Jesus's final year of ministry and His crucifixion. It is astonishing that this companion Daniel prophecy predicts the appearance of the Bab, as you shall see.

Gary Lindberg

The Prophecy of 2300 Days

> Then I heard a holy one speaking, and another holy one said to him, "How long will it take for the vision to be fulfilled—the vision concerning the daily sacrifice, the rebellion that causes desolation, the surrender of the sanctuary and the trampling underfoot of the Lord's people?" He said to me, "It will take 2,300 evenings and mornings; then the sanctuary will be reconsecrated."[391]

First, let's consider the symbolism used in this passage. The "daily sacrifice" refers to religious rituals and practices associated with spiritual devotion that had ceased when the Jerusalem temple was desecrated. The cessation of these practices more broadly symbolizes a time of spiritual decline during which divine truth was obscured and the purity of religious practices diminished. This aligns with a spiritual decline in the time before the revelation of the Báb.

The "rebellion" or "transgression" signifies a period of corruption, materialism, and neglect of true spiritual values, leading to desolation in the religious and moral fabric of society. This refers universally to the spiritual condition of humanity and the state of religion during the centuries prior to the Báb's revelation. It represents the darkness and disunity that necessitated divine renewal.

The "sanctuary" symbolizes the heart of true faith and divine revelation. Its desecration and the oppression of "the Lord's people" reflect a time when religious institutions and spiritual truths were corrupted or persecuted. This points to the persecution of religious reformers and the obscuring of spiritual truths by dogmatism and sectarianism, culminating in the need for a new Manifestation of God.

---

[391] The *Bible*, Daniel:13–14 (NIV).

In prophetic language, a "day," sometimes translated as "evening and morning," often represents a year.[392] Thus, "2,300 evenings and mornings" represent 2,300 years.

The starting point of this time prophecy made by Daniel begins with the decree by Artaxerxes I in 457 BCE to rebuild Jerusalem.[393] This particular decree marked a pivotal moment in Jewish history and is often used as a starting point for other biblical prophecies. Adding 2,300 years to 457 BCE—which requires us to add the missing year between the BCE and CE calendars—brings us to the year 1844 CE, the year that the Báb declared his mission. (To calculate, subtract 457 from 2300 to determine the number of years on the CE calendar (1386).

$$457 \text{ BCE} + 1386 + 1 = 1844 \text{ CE}$$

In 1844, the Báb proclaimed that He was the promised Qa'im (the expected one in Shi'a Islam) and the forerunner of "He Whom God shall make manifest" (Bahá'u'lláh). This declaration marked the beginning of the Bahá'í Era and the reconsecration of spiritual truth symbolized by the "sanctuary." The reconsecration of the sanctuary is also a metaphor for the purification of human hearts and the establishment of a universal faith

The Prophecy of 1260 Days

The Revelation of John in the New Testament was revealed to prepare people, especially Christians, for the Object of their desire, the Redeemer of their age. It begins with these words:

> **The revelation of Jesus Christ, which God gave him to show his servants what must soon take place… Blessed is the one who reads the words of this prophecy, and blessed are those who hear it and take to heart what is written…[394]**

---

392 The *Bible*, Ezekiel 4:6.
393 The *Bible*, Ezra 7:12–26.
394 The *Bible*, Revelation 1:1–3.

The prophecies of Revelation, like those of the book of Daniel, are revealed to John in a vision. Like all visions, these wear the veil of symbolism. At first glance, we may have difficulty understanding the underlying meanings of these symbols, but once the veil is lifted, the meanings become so apparent and so interrelated with all the other segments of the prophetic profile that we would have difficulty *not* recognizing them.

Book of Revelation twice includes a prophecy of "1,260 days," which we have noted earlier means 1,260 *years* in the language of biblical prophecy, a significant period of time. The first prophecy is this:

> **And I will appoint my two witnesses, and they will prophesy for 1,260 days, clothed in sackcloth.**[395]

There are two mysterious symbols in this simple statement. One wonders—who are the "two witnesses," to what does "prophesy for 1,260 days" refer, and what is the meaning of "clothed in sackcloth?"

Some Jewish scholars speculate that these two individuals must be prophets from the Hebrew Bible such as Elijah and Enoch, or Moses and Aaron. But Revelation is a book of prophecy, thus forward-looking. The personification of the two witnesses is so vivid that according to theologian William Barclay, the passage seems to refer to specific persons.[396]

Many Muslims identify these "twin witnesses" as a prophecy of the coming of Muhammad and his successor in Shi'a Islam, 'Ali. This is given more credibility by the writings of the Bahá'í Faith.

> **By these two witnesses are intended Muhammad the Messenger of God and 'Alí the son of Abú-Tálib.**[397]

---

395 The *Bible*, Revelation 11:3 (NIV).
396 *William* Barclay. *The Revelation of John* (3rd ed. fully rev. and updated. ed.) 2004. Louisville, Ky.: Westminster John Knox Press, p. 60.
397 'Abdu'l-Bahá, *Some Answered Questions*, p. 49

Seeing God in Many Mirrors

This perspective aligns with the Baháʼí view of the continuity of divine revelation by recognizing both Muhammad and ʻAlí as pivotal figures in the spiritual history of humanity.

In Islam, "sackcloth" often represents humility, suffering, and the rejection of materialism. In Islamic thought, true prophets and divine figures such as Muhammad and ʻAli often face opposition and hardship as they deliver God's message, emphasizing their detachment from worldly power. The Baháʼí writings clarify by telling us that the phrase "clothed in sackcloth" means that...

They are clothed in sackcloth, meaning that they, apparently, were to be clothed in old raiment, not in new raiment; in other words, in the beginning they would possess no splendor in the eyes of the people, nor would their Cause appear new...[398] The phrase "1.260 days," meaning 1,260 *years*, is intriguing because the New Testament author would have used the Julian calendar in everyday life. Since Islam had not yet appeared, there could have been no Islamic calendar yet invented. And yet, John the Revelator, appears to have understood the Islamic calendar in this prophecy, which was declared about 540 years before the second caliph of Islam, Umar I, instituted it in 639 CE.

Muslims count their Islamic calendar according to a lunar year that starts from the migration of Muhammad from Mecca to Medina (the *Hijrah*) in 622 CE. The abbreviation used to identify Islamic dates is "AH" for the latin "anno Hegirae," meaning "in the year of the Hijrah").

Let's do the math using the Islamic calendar. Starting with 0 AH, the year in which Islam officially began, and adding to it the prophetic number 1,260, we arrive at 1260 AH. If we convert the Islamic lunar calendar to our current Gregorian solar calendar, the surprising result is the year 1844 CE—the year in which the Báb declared His mission and a new religion was begun.

Unless this is an astounding coincidence, John revealed the exact year in which a new religious dispensation would occur, one

---

398 ʻAbduʼl-Bahá, *Some Answered Questions*, Part 24.

initiated by the declaration of the Báb. Islam was not replaced at that time, but a new revelation had begun. Previous revelations (religions) always continue on after a new revelation is inaugurated. Christianity continued throughout the Islamic revelation, and both Christianity and Islam continue well into the Bahá'í revelation. Zoroastrianism is still with us, though in significantly reduced numbers of followers. Hinduism and Buddhism are still popular and potent sources of spiritual inspiration.

The Prophecy of 1290 Days

The Old Testament book of Daniel, like the book of Revelation, provides numerous fulfilled prophecies, including this mysterious verse:

> **From the time that the daily sacrifice is abolished and the abomination that causes desolation is set up, there will be 1,290 days.**[399]

More than 500 years later, Jesus quoted from this verse, demonstrating that he found the prophecy highly significant. In the book of Matthew, we learn that Jesus's disciples wanted to know when Jesus would return.

> **As Jesus was sitting on the Mount of Olives, the disciples came to him privately. "Tell us," they said, "when will this happen, and what will be the sign of your coming and of the end of the age?"**[400]

After explaining the signs of His return in veiled terms, Jesus finally referred to the *time itself*.

---

399 The *Bible*, Daniel 12:11 (NIV).
400 The *Bible*, Matthew 24:3 (NIV).

> So when you see standing in the holy place "the abomination that causes desolation," spoken of through the prophet Daniel, stand in the holy place—let the reader understand—[401]

Clearly, Jesus has referred specifically to the prophecy we are now examining, asserting that it refers to the time of His return. But how should we interpret the two symbols contained in this verse from Daniel: "the daily sacrifice is abolished" and "the abomination that causes desolation."

In Bible prophecies, according to most scholars, a reference to the abolishment of the daily sacrifice symbolically refers to the beginning of a new religious age or dispensation. As we learned previously, this same symbol is used in Daniel 9:27 to signal the beginning of the public ministry of Jesus.[402] The context surrounding this symbol is that less than forty years after the crucifixion of Jesus, Titus caused the daily sacrifice of the Jews to cease. Five years after Muhammad died, 'Umar did the same thing for Muslims.

Titus and 'Umar both stopped the sacrifices, and in cruel acts performed hundreds of years apart, they pushed the Jews out of their beloved Jerusalem and dispersed them among other nations. Each of these atrocities was truly an "abomination" that caused the "desolation" of the Jewish people. Each was also an outward expression of a spiritual desolation that always occurs when followers of previous religions deny a new Manifestation of God.

---

401 The *Bible*, Matthew 24:15 (NIV).

402 This verse reads as follows: "He will confirm a covenant with many for one 'seven.' In the middle of the 'seven' he will put an end to sacrifice and offering. And at the temple he will set up an abomination that causes desolation, until the end that is decreed is poured out on him." The term "seven" refers to seven years, or the final week of Jesus's life, the beginning of which marks the start of Jesus's public ministry. During this week, he modified or abolished some Jewish laws including social laws such as ways of worship, daily sacrifice, marriage, divorce, dietary restrictions, holy days, et cetera.

Muhammad inaugurated his public ministry ten years before the Islamic calendar was instituted, so the start of His ministry was -10 AH. Bahá'u'lláh inaugurated his public ministry in 1280 AH. Thus, Bahá'u'lláh ushered in a new religious age, as referred to in Daniel's prophecy, 1,290 years after Muhammad opened the Islamic age.

$$10 + 1280 \text{ (AH)} = 1290 \text{ years (1280 CE)}$$

Jesus told us that this specific prophecy from Daniel referred to the timing of his return. The language of the prophecy supports this. According to Judaism and Christianity, then, the return of Jesus was fulfilled by Bahá'u'lláh in 1280 CE.

Chapter 21:
Shared Spiritual Principles

Recognizing common spiritual principles shared across the world's major religions is vital for fostering understanding, unity, and harmony among diverse communities. These universal values—such as love, justice, humility and service—form the foundation of humanity's spiritual heritage and demonstrate the shared aspirations of all peoples, regardless of faith or culture.

This perspective is central to the concept of progressive revelation, which suggests that divine truths are revealed progressively through time, each building upon previous teachings while addressing the needs of evolving societies. By identifying these shared principles, we can appreciate the continuity of spiritual guidance and recognize the interconnectedness of humanity's sacred traditions and their followers.

In this chapter, we will identify and study spiritual principles common to all the world's great wisdom traditions. Each wisdom tradition expresses this principle differently as appropriate for its specific culture and historic era and based on previous teachings. We will present a concise glimpse of how each religion views the principle from the oldest wisdom tradition to the newest. Following this, we will address the issue of evolving social laws and rituals.

Unity and Oneness

This principle affirms the reality of the interconnectedness of all life and, often, a divine source of knowledge or ultimate reality.

Hinduism

Hinduism acknowledges the unity of all creation as emanating from a single divine source, often referred to as *Brahman*, the ultimate reality [God] that underlies all existence.

> Only the Infinite must be sought after. The Infinite is Brahman and is Supreme.[403]

> I am the Self, O Gudakesha, seated in the hearts of all creatures. I am the beginning, the middle, and the end of all beings.[404]

Zoroastrianism

Zoroastrianism teaches the unity of Ahura Mazda [God], the one supreme God, and emphasizes the harmony of creation, encouraging followers to align their actions with divine will.

> I recognize Thee, O [Ahura] Mazda, as the holy, the bestower of rewards, the creator of existence.[405]

> All good things proceed from Thee, O Ahura Mazda [God], and depend on Thy will.[406]

---

403 *Chandogya Upanishad* 7.23.1.
404 *Bhagavad Gita* 10:20.
405 *Yasna* 31:7.
406 *Yasna* 43:4.

Judaism

Judaism emphasizes the oneness of God (monotheism) and the unity of creation under this divine sovereignty. The Shema prayer, central to Jewish belief, declares this oneness.

> Hear, O Israel: The Lord our God, the Lord is one.[407]

> Have we not all one Father? Did not one God create us?[408]

Buddhism

In his teachings, the Buddha emphasized the Dharma (the "law" or "truth") as a universal, eternal principle guiding the cosmos. Some view this as a conceptual parallel to an ultimate truth or reality. In other words, a Supreme Reality such as God.

> All living beings are but parts of one body; one should perceive all existence in oneself and oneself in all existence.[409]

> He who sees the Dharma sees me; he who sees me sees the Dharma.[410]

Christianity

Christianity teaches the unity of God through the Trinity (Father, Son, and Holy Spirit) and the oneness of humanity through Christ. Believers are called to live in harmony as one body in Christ.

---

407 *The Bible*, Deuteronomy 6:4.
408 *The Bible*, Malachi 2:10.
409 *Avatamsaka Sutra*.
410 *Samyutta Nikaya* 22.87.

> There is one body and one Spirit... one God and Father of all, who is over all and through all and in all.[411]

> For there is one God and one mediator between God and mankind, the man Christ Jesus.[412]

Islam

Islam stresses the oneness of God (*Tawhid*) and the unity of humanity under God's guidance, transcending divisions of race and culture.

> Say, He is Allah [God], [Who is] One, Allah, the Eternal Refuge.[413]

> Indeed this, your religion, is one religion, and I am your Lord, so worship Me.[414]

Bahá'í Faith

The Bahá'í Faith highlights the oneness of God, the unity of all religions as part of a single divine plan, and the unity of humanity as one global family.

> The one true God, exalted be His glory, hath ever been, and shall forever continue to be, sanctified above the attributes of human beings and comprehended by the understanding of all that dwell on earth and in the heavens.[415]

---

411 *The Bible*, Ephesians 4:4–6.
412 *The Bible*, 1 Timothy 2:5.
413 *Quran* 112:1–2.
414 *Quran* 21:92.
415 Bahá'u'lláh, *Gleanings from the Writings of Bahá'u'lláh*, Section 19.

> The earth is but one country, and mankind its citizens.[416]

> Ye are the fruits of one tree, and the leaves of one branch.[417]

Compassion and Love

This spiritual principle emphasizes the importance of kindness, empathy, and love for others.

Hinduism

Hinduism emphasizes compassion (*daya*) and love as essential virtues for achieving spiritual progress and maintaining harmony in the world. Compassion and empathy are rooted in the understanding of the unity of all beings.

> **One who sees all living beings as identical with their own self, and who considers the pleasure and pain of others as their own, truly sees.**[418]

> **May all beings look at me with a friendly eye. May I do likewise, and may we all look on each other with the eyes of a friend.**[419]

Zoroastrianism

In Zoroastrianism, compassion and love are expressed through good thoughts, good words, and good deeds, reflecting the divine will of God.

---

416 Bahá'u'lláh, *Gleanings from the Writings of Bahá'u'lláh*.
417 *Bahá'u'lláh, Epistle to the Son of the Wolf.*
418 *Bhagavad Gita* 6:32.
419 *Yajurveda* 36.18.

> **Bring love and unity among all. Be kind to others and create a loving world.**[420]

> **May we be among those who make the world grow with acts of love.**[421]

Judaism

Judaism emphasizes *chesed* (loving-kindness) and compassion as central to its ethical teachings. God's love for humanity serves as a model for human relationships.

> **This is what the Lord Almighty said: Administer true justice; show mercy and compassion to one another.**[422]

> **You shall not oppress a stranger, for you know the soul of the stranger, since you were strangers in the land of Egypt.**[423]

Buddhism

Buddhism teaches *metta* (loving-kindness) and *karuna* (compassion) as core practices, extending to all sentient beings as a means to alleviate suffering.

> **Just as a mother would protect her only child with her life, even so let one cultivate boundless love towards all beings.**[424]

---

420 Avesta, *Yasna* 43.1.
421 Avesta, *Yasna* 60.5.
422 The *Bible*, Zechariah 7:9.
423 The *Bible*, Exodus 23:9.
424 *Metta Sutta*, Khuddakapatha.

> If you want others to be happy, practice compassion. If you want to be happy, practice compassion.[425]

Christianity

Christianity emphasizes love and compassion as the central tenets of Jesus's teachings, calling for selflessness and care for others, including one's enemies.

> Love your enemies and pray for those who persecute you, that you may be children of your Father in heaven.[426]

> A new command I give you: Love one another. As I have loved you, so you must love one another.[427]

Islam

Islam emphasizes *rahma* (mercy and compassion) as one of God's primary attributes, and believers are encouraged to emulate this in their relationships with others.

> The believers, in their mutual love, mercy, and compassion, are like one body: if one limb aches, the whole body responds with sleeplessness and fever.[428]

> The Most Merciful (Allah) has mercy on those who show mercy to others. Be merciful to those on the earth, and the One above the heavens will have mercy upon you.[429]

---

425 Dalai Lama, referencing the Buddha's teachings.
426 The *Bible*, Matthew 5:44-45.
427 The *Bible*, John 13:34.
428 Sahih al-Bukhari and Sahih Muslim.
429 *Sunan al-Tirmidhi*, Hadith 1924.

Bahá'í Faith

The Bahá'í Faith emphasizes universal love, empathy and compassion, teaching that humanity is one family and urging individuals to act with kindness and care toward all.

> Let your heart burn with loving-kindness for all who may cross your path.[430]

> Be generous in prosperity, and thankful in adversity. Be a treasure to the poor, an admonisher to the rich, an answerer of the cry of the needy.[431]

Rioghteousness (Justice and Morality)

The spiritual principle of justice and morality upholds also the virtues of fairness, ethical behavior and righteousness.

Hinduism

Hinduism teaches that justice and morality are inherent in *Dharma*, the universal law governing righteousness and ethical living. Adhering to *Dharma* ensures harmony in society and spiritual growth.

> When justice is destroyed, the family perishes, and when the family perishes, the eternal laws of morality are destroyed.[432]

> By following righteousness, one attains heaven. By unrighteousness, one attains hell. Therefore, righteousness is to be followed, for it leads to eternal happiness.[433]

---

430 Bahá'u'lláh, *Gleanings from the Writings of Bahá'u'lláh*, Section 8.
431 Bahá'u'lláh, *Tablets of Bahá'u'lláh*, p. 137.
432 *Bhagavad Gita* 1:39.
433 *Mahabharata*, Shanti Parva 262.5.

Zoroastrianism

Zoroastrianism emphasizes justice and morality through the principles of *asha* (truth and order) and the practice of good thoughts, good words, and good deeds. Justice is seen as aligning human actions with divine truth.

> Speak the truth, O Zarathustra, and practice righteousness to bring about the reign of Ahura Mazda [God].[434]

> A righteous person is one who upholds truth and acts justly toward others.[435]

Judaism

Judaism emphasizes justice (*tzedek*) and morality as divine mandates. Followers are commanded to pursue righteousness and fairness, particularly in their treatment of others.

> Justice, justice you shall pursue, so that you may live and possess the land the Lord your God is giving you.[436]

> He [God] mocks proud mockers but shows favor to the humble and oppressed.[437]

Buddhism

Buddhism teaches justice and morality as inherent in the Eightfold Path, particularly in *Right Action* and *Right Livelihood*. Justice is about avoiding harm and promoting fairness and compassion.

---

434 *Yasna* 31.19.
435 *Yasna* 43.4.
436 The *Bible*, Deuteronomy 16:20.
437 The *Bible*, Proverbs 3:34.

> **The just man is one who does not deviate from the truth, is impartial, and does what is fair. He is not swayed by preference, bias, or selfish motives.**[438]

> **Do not harm living beings. Speak always in kindness and act in justice.**[439]

Christianity

Christianity promotes justice and morality through the teachings of Jesus and the commands of God, urging believers to act righteously and love their neighbors.

> **But seek first his kingdom and his righteousness, and all these things will be given to you as well.**[440]

> **Blessed are those who hunger and thirst for righteousness, for they will be filled.**[441]

Islam

Islam emphasizes justice (*'adl*) as a fundamental divine principle, urging believers to act fairly and uphold moral values in all dealings.

> **O you who have believed, be persistently standing firm in justice, witnesses for Allah, even if it be against yourselves or parents and relatives.**[442]

---

438 *Dhammapada* 256-257.
439 *Dhammapada* 10.2.
440 The *Bible*, Matthew 6:33.
441 The *Bible*, Matthew 5:6.
442 *Quran* 4:135.

> Indeed, Allah commands you to render trusts to whom they are due and when you judge between people to judge with justice.[443]

Bahá'í Faith

The Bahá'í Faith views justice as a cornerstone for individual and societal well-being. It emphasizes fairness and moral conduct as necessary for peace and unity.

> The best beloved of all things in My sight is Justice; turn not away therefrom if thou desirest Me, and neglect it not that I may confide in thee.[444]

> O Son of Spirit! The light of men is Justice. Quench it not with the contrary winds of oppression and tyranny.[445]

Service to Others

This spiritual principle encourages selflessness and helping those in need.

Hinduism

Hinduism regards service to others (*seva*) as an expression of *Dharma* (righteous duty) and a pathway to spiritual growth. Serving others selflessly is seen as serving God, as divinity resides in all beings.

> [446]The best way to find yourself is to lose yourself in the service of others.

---

443 *Quran* 4:58.
444 Bahá'u'lláh, *Hidden Words*, Arabic 2.
445 Bahá'u'lláh, *Hidden Words*, Arabic 1.
446 *Bhagavad Gita* 3:20.

> **Strive constantly to serve the welfare of the world; by devotion to selfless work, one attains the supreme goal of life.**[447]

Zoroastrianism

In Zoroastrianism, service to others reflects the principle of good deeds and is central to living a righteous life in alignment with the divine order (*asha*).

> **He who sows goodness reaps goodness; he who sows evil reaps evil. Do acts of service to humankind.**[448]

> **Help the poor and needy with a charitable spirit and a generous hand.**[449]

Judaism

Judaism emphasizes service to others as an act of loving-kindness (*chesed*) and fulfilling God's commandments. It is central to building a just and compassionate society.

> **You shall open wide your hand to your brother, to the needy and to the poor, in your land.**[450]

> **Defend the weak and the fatherless; uphold the cause of the poor and the oppressed.**[451]

---

447 *Bhagavad Gita* 3:19.
448 *Yasna* 31.1.
449 *Avesta, Vendidad* 4.1
450 The *Bible*, Deuteronomy 15:11.
451 The *Bible*, Psalm 82:3.

Buddhism

Service to others is intrinsic to the Buddhist practice of *karuna* (compassion). Helping others is seen as a means of reducing suffering and cultivating spiritual growth.

> Teach this triple truth to all: A generous heart, kind speech, and a life of service and compassion are the things which renew humanity.[452]

> If you light a lamp for someone, it will also brighten your path.[453]

Christianity

Christianity teaches that service to others is an act of love and obedience to God, reflecting the example of Jesus, who served humanity selflessly.

> The greatest among you will be your servant.[454]

> For even the Son of Man did not come to be served, but to serve, and to give his life as a ransom for many.[455]

Islam

Islam emphasizes service to others as a duty to God, highlighting acts of charity and kindness as essential expressions of faith.

---

452 *Dhammapada* 224.
453 *Sutta Nipata* 1.8.
454 The *Bible*, Matthew 23:11.
455 The *Bible*, Mark 10:45.

> The best of people are those who bring the most benefit to others.[456]

> And they give food in spite of love for it to the needy, the orphan, and the captive.[457]

Bahá'í Faith

The Bahá'í Faith views service to others as the highest form of worship and a means of contributing to the betterment of humanity.

> Service to humanity is service to God.[458]

> All effort and exertion put forth by man from the fullness of his heart is worship, if it is prompted by the highest motives and the will to do service to humanity.[459]

Humility and Surrender

This spiritual principle requires one to acknowledge something greater than oneself and to cultivate humility.

Hinduism

Hinduism emphasizes humility and surrender as essential qualities for spiritual progress. Surrendering to *Ishvara* (God) and letting go of ego are core practices in Bhakti Yoga (the path of devotion).

---

456 *Sunan al-Kubra*, Hadith 10609.
457 *Quran* 76:8.
458 Abdu'l-Bahá, *Paris Talks*.
459 Abdu'l-Bahá, *Paris Talks*, p. 176.

> Those who surrender themselves completely to Me, seeking My protection alone, shall attain peace and liberation from the cycle of birth and death.[460]

> The wise one who sees the same Lord present everywhere does not exalt himself or degrade others.[461]

Zoroastrianism

In Zoroastrianism, humility is reflected in aligning one's will with the divine order (*asha*). Surrender involves obedience to Ahura Mazda's [God's] commandments and striving for righteousness.

> Let the wise and humble bow before the Divine Law and serve Ahura Mazda with faith and reverence.[462]

> Let us be humble in thought, word, and deed, and give thanks to Ahura Mazda [God] for His blessings.[463]

Judaism

Judaism emphasizes humility as a key virtue and surrendering to God's will as the path to righteousness. Humility is seen in recognizing God's greatness and relying on Him for guidance.

> What does the Lord require of you? To act justly and to love mercy and to walk humbly with your God.[464]

---

460 *Bhagavad Gita* 18:66.
461 *Bhagavad Gita* 5:18.
462 *Yasna* 33.11.
463 *Yasna* 12.8.
464 The *Bible*, Micah *6:8*.

> The fear of the Lord is instruction in wisdom, and humility comes before honor.[465]

Buddhism

Buddhism views humility as essential for letting go of ego and achieving enlightenment. Surrender is about releasing attachment to self and desires to follow the Eightfold Path.

> One is not lowly because of birth, nor high because of birth. One is lowly if their actions are lowly, and one is noble if their deeds are noble.[466]

> The wise who are free from pride and selfishness, who are calm and meditative, attain the highest wisdom.[467]

Christianity

Christianity teaches humility and surrender as central virtues, reflecting submission to God's will and selflessness in serving others, modeled by Jesus Christ.

> Humble yourselves before the Lord, and he will lift you up.[468]

> Not my will, but yours be done.[469]

---

465 The *Bible*, Proverbs 15:33
466 *Dhammapada* 393.
467 *Dhammapada* 94.
468 The *Bible*, James 4:10.
469 The *Bible*, Luke 22:42.

Islam

Islam means "submission," reflecting the essence of humility and surrender to God (*Allah*). Believers are called to accept God's will with humility and gratitude.

> And they were commanded not but that they should worship Allah, and worship none but Him alone, and perform prayer and give charity. That is the right religion.[470]

> Indeed, those who humble themselves in prayer will inherit Paradise.[471]

Bahá'í Faith

The Bahá'í Faith teaches humility as essential for spiritual growth and stresses surrender to God's will to live a life of service and harmony.

> O Son of Man! Humble thyself before Me, that I may graciously visit thee. Arise for the triumph of My cause, that thou mayest attain the glory of My kingdom.[472]

> Be generous in prosperity, and thankful in adversity. Be worthy of the trust of thy neighbor, and humble before God.[473]

---

470 *Quran* 98:5.
471 *Quran* 23:1-2.
472 Bahá'u'lláh, *Hidden Words*, Arabic 42.
473 Bahá'u'lláh, *Gleanings from the Writings of Bahá'u'lláh*, Section 153.

The Golden Rule

This universal spiritual principle calls us to treat others as we wish to be treated.

Hinduism

In Hinduism, the principle of reciprocity is expressed as a foundation of *Dharma* (righteous living), emphasizing treating others as one wishes to be treated.

> This is the sum of duty: Do not do to others what would cause pain if done to you.[474]

> By self-control and by making Dharma (righteousness) your focus, treat others as you treat yourself.[475]

Zoroastrianism

Zoroastrianism presents the Golden Rule as part of the ethical framework of good thoughts, good words, and good deeds.

> That nature alone is good which refrains from doing unto another whatsoever is not good for itself.[476]

> Do not do unto others whatever is injurious to yourself.[477]

Judaism

Judaism emphasizes treating others with fairness and kindness, reflecting the Golden Rule as central to its ethical teachings.

---

474 *Mahabharata*, Anusasana Parva 113.8.
475 *Mahabharata*, Shanti Parva 167.9.
476 *Dadistan-i-Dinik* 94:5.
477 *Shayast-na-Shayast* 13.29.

> You shall love your neighbor as yourself.[478]

> What is hateful to you, do not do to your neighbor. That is the whole Torah; the rest is the explanation; go and learn.[479]

Buddhism

Buddhism teaches compassion and reciprocity through *Metta* (loving-kindness) and emphasizes avoiding harm to others as one would wish to avoid harm to oneself.

> Hurt not others in ways that you yourself would find hurtful.[480]

> Consider others as yourself.[481]

Christianity

In Christianity, the Golden Rule is explicitly stated as a summary of the ethical teachings of Jesus.

> So in everything, do to others what you would have them do to you, for this sums up the Law and the Prophets.[482]

> Love your neighbor as yourself.[483]

---

478 The *Bible*, Leviticus 19:18.
479 *Talmud, Shabbat* 31a.
480 *Udana-Varga* 5:18.
481 *Dhammapada* 10.1.
482 The *Bible*, Matthew 7:12.
483 The *Bible*, Mark 12:31.

Islam

Islam promotes the Golden Rule as a principle of justice and compassion, encouraging believers to treat others as they would like to be treated.

> None of you [truly] believes until he wishes for his brother what he wishes for himself.[484]

> Worship Allah and associate nothing with Him, and do good to parents, relatives, orphans, the needy, the near neighbor, the neighbor farther away, the companion at your side, the traveler, and those whom your right hands possess.[485]

Bahá'í Faith

The Bahá'í Faith stesses the unity of humanity and encourages treating others with the same respect one desires for oneself.

> Lay not on any soul a load that you would not wish to be laid upon you, and desire not for anyone the things you would not desire for yourself.[486]

> Blessed is he who preferreth his brother before himself.[487]

Detachment

This spiritual principle of detachment asks each person to cancel their desires for material things and focus on what is spiritual.

---

484 *Sahih al-Bukhari* and *Sahih Muslim*.
485 *Quran* 4:36.
486 Bahá'u'lláh, *Gleanings from the Writings of Bahá'u'lláh*, Section 66.
487 Bahá'u'lláh, *Tablets of Bahá'u'lláh*, p. 71.

Hinduism

In Hinduism, detachment (*vairagya*) is considered essential for spiritual liberation (*moksha*). It involves renouncing attachment to material possessions and desires while performing one's duties selflessly.

> One who remains unattached to the material world, free from desires, attains peace.[488]

> You have the right to perform your duty, but you are not entitled to the fruits of your actions. Let not the fruits of action be your motive, nor let your attachment be to inaction.[489]

Zoroastrianism

In Zoroastrianism, detachment is associated with living a life of moderation, focusing on spiritual growth rather than excessive material accumulation.

> Be moderate in your desires and let not greed or worldly possessions sway your mind from the path of righteousness.[490]

> He who is contented with what is enough and does not crave more walks in harmony with the divine order.[491]

---

[488] *Bhagavad Gita* 2:71.
[489] *Bhagavad Gita* 2:47.
[490] *Yasna* 31.19.
[491] *Yasht* 10.3.

Judaism

Judaism values detachment from material things as part of living a righteous and God-centered life. The focus is on using wealth responsibly and not letting it dominate one's heart.

> Do not wear yourself out to get rich; have the wisdom to show restraint.[492]

> Whoever loves money never has enough; whoever loves wealth is never satisfied with their income. This too is meaningless.[493]

Buddhism

Buddhism teaches detachment from material things as a core practice to overcome suffering, emphasizing the impermanence of all worldly possessions and desires.

> Attachment is the root of suffering. Therefore, abandon attachment to worldly possessions and desires.[494]

> The wise do not cling to sensual pleasures or material things, knowing them to be fleeting and the source of sorrow.[495]

Christianity

Christianity encourages detachment from material things as a way to focus on spiritual treasures and reliance on God. Jesus frequently taught about the dangers of wealth and attachment.

---

492 The *Bible*, Proverbs 23:4.
493 The *Bible*, Ecclesiastes 5:10.
494 *Dhammapada* 213.
495 *Dhammapada* 83.

> Do not store up for yourselves treasures on earth, where moths and vermin destroy, and where thieves break in and steal. But store up for yourselves treasures in heaven.[496]

> What good will it be for someone to gain the whole world, yet forfeit their soul?[497]

Islam

Islam teaches that material wealth is a test of character, and that detachment is essential to avoid greed and misuse of wealth. Believers are reminded to prioritize spiritual goals over material gain.

> And do not let your eyes extend toward what We have given certain classes of them to enjoy [as a trial]—the splendor of worldly life by which We test them. But the provision of your Lord is better and more enduring.[498]

> Wealth and children are [but] adornment of the worldly life, but the enduring good deeds are better to your Lord for reward and better for [one's] hope.[499]

Bahá'í Faith

The Bahá'í Faith teaches that detachment from material things is essential for spiritual progress and alignment with God's will. Material possessions are not inherently bad but should be used wisely and without attachment.

---

[496] The *Bible*, Matthew 6:19-20.
[497] The *Bible*, Matthew 16:26.
[498] *Quran* 20:131.
[499] *Quran* 18:46.

> O Son of Man! Thou dost wish for gold and I desire thy freedom from it. Thou dost reckon the gold, while I prize thy freedom therefrom. By My life! This is My knowledge, and that is thy fancy; how can My way accord with thine?[500]

> Be not content with the ease of a passing day, and deprive not thyself of everlasting rest. Barter not the garden of eternal delight for the dust-heap of a mortal world.[501]

Independent and Rational Thinking

This spiritual principle of detachment asks each person to cancel their desires for material things and focus on what is spiritual.

Hinduism

Hinduism values rational thinking as a means to discern truth and achieve spiritual knowledge. The path of *Jnana Yoga* (the yoga of knowledge) encourages seekers to use reasoning to explore the nature of reality and self.

> The mind is restless, turbulent, strong, and unyielding, but it can be controlled by practice and detachment.[502]

> By the intellect alone can truth be realized, and by right thinking and discernment can one attain liberation.[503]

---

500 Bahá'u'lláh, *Hidden Words*, Arabic 56.
501 Bahá'u'lláh, *Gleanings from the Writings of Bahá'u'lláh*, Section 152.
502 *Bhagavad Gita* 6:35.
503 *Katha Upanishad* 1.3.12.

Zoroastrianism

Zoroastrianism emphasizes the importance of using good thoughts and wisdom (*Vohu Manah*) to make moral choices and discern the divine will.

> **Man must use his reason to recognize truth, reject falsehood, and choose the path of righteousness.**[504]

> **Hear with your ears the best things; reflect with a clear mind.**[505]

Judaism

Judaism encourages rational inquiry and independent thinking to understand God's laws and apply them to life. Study and interpretation of scripture are central to Jewish tradition.

> **Come now, and let us reason together, says the Lord.**[506]

> **Teach me good judgment and knowledge, for I believe in your commandments.**[507]

Buddhism

Buddhism advocates independent reasoning and critical thinking, encouraging individuals to seek truth through personal experience and reflection rather than blind faith.

---

504 *Yasna* 31.11.
505 *Yasna* 30.2.
506 The *Bible*, Isaiah 1:18.
507 The *Bible*, Psalm 119:66.

> Do not believe in anything simply because you have heard it. Examine it and see if it leads to the good, the welfare, and the happiness of all. Only then accept it.[508]

> The wise man examines the truth and does not blindly accept what others say.[509]

Christianity

Christianity values rational thought in the pursuit of truth, emphasizing that faith and reason are complementary paths to understanding God.

> Test all things; hold fast to that which is good.[510]

> You shall love the Lord your God with all your heart, with all your soul, and with all your mind.[511]

Islam

Islam places great emphasis on rational thinking and reflection, urging believers to use their intellect to understand the signs of God in creation and scripture.

> Indeed, in the creation of the heavens and the earth, and the alternation of the night and the day, are signs for those of understanding.[512]

---

508 *Kalama Sutta.*
509 *Dhammapada* 276.
510 The *Bible*, 1 Thessalonians 5:21.
511 The *Bible*, Matthew 22:37.
512 *Quran* 3:190.

> Do they not reflect upon the Quran? If it had been from other than Allah, they would have found within it much contradiction.[513]

Bahá'í Faith

The Bahá'í Faith teaches that independent investigation of truth and the use of reason are essential for spiritual growth. Blind imitation of tradition is discouraged.

> Man must independently investigate truth, that he may find by himself the reality of God.[514]

> The first teaching of Bahá'u'lláh is the investigation of reality. Man must seek reality himself, forsaking imitation and adhering to that which is true. The responsibility rests upon the intellect and reason to determine the truth.[515]

Spiritual Principles Added or Expanded by Successive Revelations

The fundamental spiritual principles of each of the major wisdom traditions are essentially the same with minor variances due to prior histories, cultural factors, points of emphasis and the effects of syncretism and traditions. And yet the process of progressive revelation has caused successive revelations to expand humanity's knowledge of certain principles and introduce new ones as they became necessary over time. Here is a summary of principles that have been added or expanded by later revelations.

---

513 *Quran* 4:82.
514 'Abdu'l-Bahá, *Paris Talks*, p. 136.
515 'Abdu'l-Bahá, *The Promulgation of Universal Peace*, p. 62.

Progressive Revelation

Judaism → Christianity → Islam → Bahá'í Faith

- **Judaism** introduced the idea of a covenant between God and humanity, establishing a relationship where divine guidance would unfold through prophets.
- **Christianity** expanded the concept with Jesus Christ as the fulfillment of Jewish prophecy, emphasizing love, grace, and salvation as part of God's evolving plan.
- **Islam** reinforced progressive revelation by recognizing earlier prophets (e.g., Moses, Jesus) and positioning Muhammad as the final prophet delivering the comprehensive message of Islam.
- **Bahá'í Faith** formalized the concept of progressive revelation as a divine mechanism, asserting that all major religions are part of a unified process and that Bahá'u'lláh is the latest Manifestation.

Global Unity

Christianity → Islam → Bahá'í Faith

- **Christianity** introduced a universal message, inviting all people (Jews and Gentiles alike) to accept God's kingdom and emphasizing the oneness of humanity under Christ.
- **Islam** emphasized the global unity of humanity under one God, transcending tribal, racial, and cultural boundaries with the concept of the *Ummah* (community of believers).
- **Bahá'í Faith** elevated global unity as a central principle, advocating for the oneness of humanity and the establishment of global peace through universal cooperation and justice.

Equality

Christianity → Islam → Bahá'í Faith

- **Christianity** taught the spiritual equality of all believers, including marginalized groups such as women, the poor, and outcasts, through the teachings of Jesus.
- **Islam** affirmed the equality of all believers before God regardless of race or class, and granted significant rights to women and orphans, advancing social justice.
- **Bahá'í Faith** took equality further by advocating for the complete equality of men and women, the oneness of all people, and by emphasizing racial, social, and economic justice as prerequisites for peace.

Adaptation to Modernity

Islam → Bahá'í Faith

- **Islam** introduced practical legal frameworks and social reforms suited to the seventh-century Arabian context, addressing issues like inheritance, trade, and governance with lasting relevance.
- **Bahá'í Faith** directly addressed modernity by integrating spiritual principles with contemporary issues such as gender equality, universal education, and the harmony of science and religion.

Specific Rituals and Practices

Hinduism → Judaism → Islam → Bahá'í Faith

- **Hinduism** developed a rich tradition of rituals, from Vedic sacrifices to temple worship, designed to align human actions with cosmic order.

- **Judaism** introduced specific rituals, including dietary laws, Sabbath observance, and annual festivals, as markers of covenantal faithfulness.
- **Christianity** introduced specific sacraments or holy ordinances, including baptism, eucharist (holy communion), confession and reconciliation, marriage as a sacred covenant, confirmation, anointing of the sick (healing), and ordination.
- **Islam s**implified and universalized rituals such as daily prayer (*Salat*), fasting (*Sawm*), and pilgrimage (*Hajj*), making them accessible to all believers.
- **Bahá'í Faith r**efined and simplified religious practices, the abolishment of clergy, and a calendar suited to global observance, to align with the principle of unity and a rapidly advancing world.

Added by Successive Revelations

1. **Progressive Revelation**: The idea that religious truth unfolds over time through successive messengers or scriptures.

2. **Global Unity**: Later traditions emphasize the unity of humanity and the world as a single community.

3. **Equality**: Expanding notions of equality, including gender, race, and class, in modern revelations.

4. **Adaptation to Modernity**: Addressing contemporary societal, scientific, and global challenges.

5. **Specific Rituals and Practices**: Unique methods of worship, prayer, or meditation tailored to the culture and era of the revelation.

Chapter 22:
The Oneness of Religion

The concept of progressive revelation establishes the fundamental truth that religions are one in origin. The oneness of religion is a profound theological and philosophical assertion that suggests a fundamental unity in the spiritual and moral guidance provided by different religions throughout human history. This final chapter explores the meaning of the oneness of religion, reviews the forces that can corrupt or obscure religious teachings over time, summarizes the significance of these ideas for modern society, and analyzes how our most recent wisdom tradition articulates and values the concept of progressive revelation.

Understanding the Oneness of Religion and Progressive Revelation

At its core, the oneness of religion is the belief that all major religious traditions share a common spiritual source and aim. They are different chapters of the same book, written across various ages and cultures by the Divine to guide humanity. Progressive revelation explains how expanded and updated religious teachings are provided successively to humanity by a series of Divine Educators, each of Whom brings teachings appropriate for the time and place of Their appearance but consistent in its essence with the teachings of previous Educators. This is analogous to a school curriculum, where lessons are tailored to the evolving capacity of students as they gain knowledge and critical thinking skills.

Corruption and Outdating of Religious Teachings

Despite the divine origin of religious teachings, over time they can become corrupted or outdated due to several factors. Human interpretations and the institutionalization of religion can lead to distortions of the original messages. Political, cultural, and social influences can also corrupt teachings and practices, making them more rigid and dogmatic. As humanity progresses, some of the laws and practices prescribed by older revelations may no longer be suitable for modern conditions, requiring new guidance.

Proofs of Progressive Revelation

Mutual Recognition Among Manifestations

One of the significant proofs of progressive revelation is the mutual recognition and affirmation found among the Manifestations of God. Throughout religious texts, there are instances where later prophets acknowledge and affirm the missions and teachings of Those who came before Them. For example, Jesus Christ in the Christian tradition acknowledged the laws of Moses and built upon them, while Muhammad in Islam recognized both Moses and Jesus as preceding Prophets. This continuity supports the idea that each Manifestation is part of a divine plan, advancing a coherent message through successive revelations.

Prophecies Fulfilled

Another strong indicator of progressive revelation is the fulfillment of prophecies across various religions. Many religious scriptures contain prophecies that future Manifestations fulfill. For instance, numerous prophecies in the Hebrew Bible are considered by

Christians to be fulfilled in the life and mission of Jesus. Similarly, Bahá'í writings interpret certain Islamic prophecies as foretelling the coming of Bahá'u'lláh. These fulfillments link religions together, suggesting a divine architecture at place throughout history.

Similarity of Spiritual Principles

Despite inevitable differences in rituals and doctrines, there is a profound similarity in the core spiritual principles advocated by all major religions. Principles such as the Golden Rule (the imperative to love one's neighbor,) justice, mercy, humility, and the pursuit of truth are universal. This consistency across diverse cultures and epochs suggests that these principles have a common source and are essential to the spiritual evolution of humanity.

Perennial Appearance of Manifestations of God

History shows that Manifestations of God have appeared in every age and culture, providing spiritual and practical guidance delivered by a divine faculty adhering to a common curriculum tailored to the needs and capacities of the people at that time. This pattern supports the concept of progressive revelation.

Manifestations of God Beyond Known Figures

Divine Guidance is a Universal and Ongoing Process

This divine guidance is not restricted to a few historical figures known in the Aryan or Abrahamic religious traditions but is a universal phenomenon. The Bahá'í teachings assert that divine guidance is an ongoing process, and that God has never left humanity without guidance. This implies that many Manifestations, possibly known only within Their own cultures or forgotten in the annals of history and pre-history have also appeared. The principle of progressive revelation suggests that as humanity grows and evolves, Manifestations will arise to provide the necessary guidance for each new age.

Future Manifestations

In addition to recognizing past Manifestations, progressive revelation also asserts that future Manifestations of God will be necessary. Bahá'u'lláh, the founder of the Bahá'í Faith, confirmed that he would not be the final Manifestation, and that as humanity progresses and the conditions of society evolve, new Divine Educators will appear to lead humanity closer to its collective maturity and spiritual destiny.

Global and Inclusive Revelation

The idea that divine guidance has been delivered and will continue to appear globally reinforces the oneness of religion and humanity itself. It suggests that no single culture or historical period has a monopoly on spiritual truth. Instead, divine wisdom is accessible to all people across different times and places, emphasizing the unity and interdependence of the human family.

The Value of Understanding the Oneness of Religion

Understanding the oneness of religion through progressive revelation holds immense value for individuals and society in general. It promotes religious harmony by highlighting the shared roots and objectives of different faiths, reducing religious intolerance and conflict. It also encourages spiritual and moral growth by providing a broader and more inclusive perspective on religious truth, urging individuals to recognize the value of all religious traditions. This understanding can foster a more unified and peaceful global community.

Guidance for a Modern Society

In modern society, where change is rapid and communities are increasingly diverse and divided, the concept of progressive revelation is especially relevant. It provides a framework for understanding and appreciating both continuity and change in religious thought, affirming that divine guidance is ongoing and responsive to human needs and conditions. This idea can help modern societies navigate challenges posed by globalization, technological advancements, and complex modern social issues by advocating for principles such as unity, justice, and equality.

A Modern Example of Progressive Revelation

The Bahá'í Faith, founded by Bahá'u'lláh in the nineteenth century, offers a clear example of how the value and meaning of progressive revelation are expressed. Bahá'u'lláh taught that He was the latest in a line of prophets or Manifestations of God, which includes figures such as Abraham, Moses, Buddha, Jesus, and Muhammad, and that He also fulfilled the prophecies of Hinduism, Zoroastrianism and Buddhism. The Bahá'í teachings emphasize that while the social teachings of each religion may differ according to the needs of their time and place, the spiritual principles remain unchanging, though they may become better understood. The Bahá'í Faith advocates for the unity of all people, the elimination of prejudice, and the establishment of a global civilization that reflects the essential oneness of humanity.

Conclusion

Realized through progressive revelation, the oneness of religion offers a hopeful vision for the future, one that embraces diversity while recognizing the unity of all human endeavors in the search for truth and meaning. By understanding this concept, individuals and societies can better appreciate the contributions of all religions and work toward a more peaceful, unified world.

The Bahá'í Faith, through its teachings on progressive revelation, provides a practical demonstration that this vision can be realized, asserting that religion, when understood in its truest form, continues to be a vital force for good in the modern world. This perspective not only enriches individual lives but also has the potential to guide humanity toward greater harmony and understanding. Therefore, our most recent wisdom tradition, the Bahá'í Faith is...

> far from aiming at the overthrow of the spiritual foundation of the world's religious systems. Its avowed, unalterable purposes is to broaden their basis, to to restate their fundamentals, to reconcile their aims, to readjust their teachings, to reinvigorate their life, to demonstrate their oneness, to restore the pristine purity of their teachings, to coordinate their functions and to assist in the realization of their highest aspirations.[516]

---

[516] Shoghi Effendi, *The World Order of Bahá'u'lláh*, p. 114.

APPENDICES

Aryan Religious Texts

W

Appendix A: Hindu Texts

Scriptures and God in Hinduism

In Hinduism, the concept of one Supreme Being coexists with the worship of many gods and goddesses, which can seem paradoxical at first glance. However, the apparent multiplicity of deities serves a specific philosophical, theological, and cultural purpose within Hinduism, reflecting its inclusive and diverse approach to spirituality. Here is an explanation of why there are many gods in Hinduism despite the teaching of one Supreme Being:

Multiplicity as Manifestations of One Reality:

- **Brahman as the Ultimate Reality**: Hinduism teaches that all gods and goddesses are manifestations of the one ultimate reality, Brahman. Brahman is beyond human comprehension and attributes, so it is often expressed through various forms that make the divine more accessible to human understanding and worship. Each god or goddess represents a different aspect of the supreme, allowing devotees to connect with the divine in ways that are meaningful to them.

- **Different Aspects of the Divine:** The gods and goddesses in Hinduism symbolize different qualities and functions of the one Supreme Being:
    - **Vishnu** represents preservation and protection.
    - **Shiva** symbolizes destruction and transformation, which is necessary for creation.
    - **Devi** (the Goddess) embodies the nurturing and creative power of the universe.
    - **Ganesha** is the remover of obstacles and represents wisdom.
    - **Lakshmi** represents wealth and prosperity.

  This allows individuals to focus on particular attributes of the divine that resonate with their needs, roles, or desires at any given time.

- **Personalization of the Divine**: Hinduism acknowledges that individuals have different temperaments, inclinations, and spiritual needs. The worship of various deities allows for personal connection with the divine. For example, a person seeking strength may worship Durga, while another seeking wisdom may worship Saraswati. It is believed that this personalization fosters a deeper, more intimate relationship with God.

- **Cultural and Regional Diversity:** Hinduism is not a monolithic religion but a vast, pluralistic tradition that evolved over thousands of years across different regions of India. As a result, different communities developed their own forms of worship, with local deities often incorporated into the broader Hindu framework. This cultural diversity contributes to the rich tapestry of gods and goddesses within Hinduism.

- **Symbolism and Allegory:** Many Hindu deities are symbolic and represent profound philosophical and moral teachings. For instance, Krishna symbolizes divine love and joy, Hanuman represents devotion and selfless service, and Kali embodies the destruction of ignorance and ego. These deities serve as allegorical figures that teach important life lessons and spiritual truths.

- **Polytheism and Henotheism**: Hinduism is often described as henotheistic, meaning that it acknowledges the existence of multiple deities but considers them all as manifestations of one supreme reality. This approach allows Hindus to worship many gods without contradicting the idea of a single divine source.

- **Philosophical Flexibility:** Hinduism is inherently flexible and does not demand a single approach to understanding or worshiping the divine. This inclusivity allows believers to see unity in diversity—viewing all gods and goddesses as various paths leading to the same ultimate goal.

The many gods and goddesses in Hinduism do not contradict the belief in one Supreme Being but rather enrich it, providing a multitude of ways to understand, experience, and connect with the divine. This diversity reflects the broad, inclusive nature of Hinduism, which celebrates different forms and paths while ultimately pointing to a single, all-encompassing truth.

Krishna as the Eighth Avatar

In Hinduism, Lord Krishna is considered the eighth Avatar, Who is responsible for the preservation and protection of the universe. The concept of Avatars is particularly emphasized in Vaishnavism, a tradition within Hinduism that worships Vishnu as the supreme

God.

The ten principal Avatars of Vishnu, known as the DashAvatara, are listed in various texts, with slight variations in some sources. The most commonly accepted list, especially as mentioned in texts like the Bhagavata Purana, includes the following seven Avatars preceding Krishna:

1. **Matsya (The Fish):** Matsya is described as a divine fish who saved Manu, the progenitor of mankind, from a great deluge that destroyed the world. This Avatar is analogous to the flood myths found in various cultures, including the story of Noah's Ark in the Abrahamic traditions.

2. **Kurma (The Tortoise):** As Kurma, Vishnu took the form of a giant tortoise to support the churning of the Ocean of Milk, a cosmic ocean, to obtain Amrit (the nectar of immortality). The churning of the ocean is a foundational myth in Hindu cosmology that explains the origin of several celestial beings and objects.

3. **Varaha (The Boar):** In the Varaha Avatar, Vishnu took the form of a boar to rescue the Earth (personified as the goddess Bhudevi) from the demon Hiranyaksha who had dragged it to the bottom of the cosmic ocean.

4. **Narasimha (The Man-Lion):** Narasimha, a half-man, half-lion Avatar, was taken to slay the demon king Hiranyakashipu, who could not be killed by man or beast, inside or outside, day or night. Narasimha killed him at twilight on the threshold of his courtyard, thereby circumventing the boon of invincibility granted to Hiranyakashipu by Brahma.

5. **Vamana (The Dwarf):** Vamana appeared in the form of a dwarf brahmin to subdue King Bali, a generous but

ambitious king who had gained dominion over the three worlds. Vamana asked for three paces of land and covered the entire universe in two steps, subduing Bali with the third.

6. **Parashurama (Rama with the Axe):** Parashurama is the fierce warrior-priest who appeared to check the tyranny of warrior castes (Kshatriyas) who were oppressing the priestly castes (Brahmins) and other social orders. He is known for his anger and also as the mentor to various other legendary figures in Hindu epics.

7. **Rama (The Prince of Ayodhya)** Perhaps one of the most celebrated Avatars, Rama is the protagonist of the Ramayana, an epic that narrates his life, his ideal kingship, and his victory over the demon king Ravana.

Determining the historical dates for these Avatars is inherently challenging as Hindu texts tend to view time cyclically and mythologically. The events described in these stories are considered to occur in a mythical framework of Yugas (ages), each spanning thousands or even millions of years according to Hindu cosmology. Assigning specific dates to these Avatars is seldom attempted by serous scholars who typically regard these stories as theological and moral narratives rather than historical.

Primary Hindu Texts

Hinduism is one of the world's oldest religions and its scriptures span thousands of years. These texts provide profound insights into the spiritual, philosophical, and cultural heritage of ancient India. Within the vast body of Hindu literature, some texts are considered the most ancient and least altered by later influences, preserving the core teachings of early Hindu thought. Below is an exploration of these ancient scriptures with approximate dates and citations.

The Vedas (c. 1500–500 BCE)

The Vedas are the oldest and most authoritative scriptures of Hinduism, comprising a collection of hymns, mantras, and rituals. They are regarded as *śruti* (that which is heard), meaning they were directly revealed to ancient sages (*rishis*) through divine inspiration rather than human authorship. The Vedas are divided into four main collections:

- **Rigveda (c. 1500 BCE)**: The Rigveda is the oldest of the Vedas and consists of 1,028 hymns dedicated to various deities like Agni (fire), Indra (king of gods), and Soma (a ritual drink). It emphasizes the worship of natural forces and the performance of sacrifices. The hymns reflect a nomadic, pastoral society and focus on the relationship between humans and the divine. Being one of the earliest known religious texts in the world, the Rigveda remains largely unaltered since its composition.

- **Samaveda (c. 1200 BCE)**: The Samaveda primarily consists of hymns from the Rigveda, rearranged for liturgical purposes, particularly for chanting during rituals. Its focus is on musical recitation and the power of sound, contributing significantly to the development of Indian classical music.

- **Yajurveda (c. 1100 BCE):** The Yajurveda is a compilation of sacrificial formulas and mantras used during rituals. It is divided into two parts: the White (*Shukla*) and Black (*Krishna*) Yajurveda. It serves as a guide for priests performing *yajnas* (sacrificial rituals), emphasizing the proper conduct of rituals rather than philosophical teachings.

- **Atharvaveda (c. 1000 BCE):** The Atharvaveda differs from the other Vedas by focusing on everyday life rather than purely ritualistic practices. It contains hymns, incantations, and spells for healing, protection, and prosperity. Its content reveals a more personal and domestic aspect of Vedic religion, reflecting the concerns of ordinary people.

Brahmanas (c. 1000–800 BCE)

The Brahmanas are prose texts that serve as commentaries on the Vedas, providing explanations of rituals, ceremonies and sacrifices. They offer insights into the early religious practices of Vedic society and expand on the cosmology and symbolism of Vedic rituals. Notable Brahmanas include:

- **Shatapatha Brahmana (c. 800 BCE):** Associated with the White Yajurveda, this text is one of the most detailed Brahmanas, exploring the intricacies of ritualistic practices and philosophical ideas. It also provides early references to concepts such as karma and dharma, laying the groundwork for later Hindu thought.

Aranyakas (c. 800–600 BCE)

Aranyakas, or "forest treatises," serve as a bridge between the ritualistic Brahmanas and the philosophical Upanishads. They were intended for ascetics who withdrew to the forest to meditate on the deeper meanings of the rituals and emphasize internal reflection over external ceremonies.

- **Taittiriya Aranyaka (c. 700 BCE):** Linked with the Yajurveda, this text explores the significance of rituals and introduces early meditative and contemplative practices. It represents a shift from external ritual to internal spirituality, laying a foundation for the philosophical developments found in the Upanishads.

Upanishads (c. 800–500 BCE)

The Upanishads are considered the philosophical culmination of the Vedas, focusing on spiritual knowledge, metaphysics, and the nature of the self (*Atman*) and the ultimate reality (*Brahman*). Unlike the ritualistic nature of the earlier texts, the Upanishads stress introspection and the pursuit of knowledge. Key Upanishads include:

- **Brihadaranyaka Upanishad (c. 700 BCE):** As one of the earliest and most profound Upanishads, this one explores the nature of reality, the self, and the interconnectedness of all existence. It introduces the concept of Brahman as the ultimate reality and Atman as the individual soul, suggesting that self-realization is the path to liberation.

- **Chandogya Upanishad (c. 600 BCE):** Associated with the Samaveda, this text explores meditative practices, the power of sound (*Om*), and the unity of the individual soul with Brahman. It contains the famous Mahavakya (great saying) "Tat Tvam Asi" ("That Thou Art"), highlighting the oneness of the self and the divine.

- **Isha Upanishad (c. 600 BCE):** A short but significant text, it emphasizes the balance between material life and spiritual wisdom, advocating for a life of detachment and understanding of the divine presence in all things.

Authenticity and Preservation of Hindu Texts

The Vedas, Brahmanas, Aranyakas and Upanishads collectively represent the most ancient and foundational texts of Hinduism, each layer reflecting a different stage in the evolution of Hindu thought. These texts have remained remarkably consistent over millennia, preserving the core teachings and philosophies of early Hindu spirituality. Their emphasis on rituals, meditation, and metaphysical inquiry continues to influence Hindu belief and practice, offering timeless wisdom that has shaped the spiritual landscape of India and the world.

Appendix B:
Zoroastrian Texts

Scripture in Zoroastrianism

The scriptures of Zoroastrianism represent a remarkable body of spiritual and cultural heritage. Despite historical challenges, including the loss of original manuscripts and the fragmentation of texts, the Avesta and later writings have survived through a combination of oral and written traditions. The Gathas, which tradition tells us were written by Zoroaster Himself, remain the centerpiece of Zoroastrian theology, reflecting the profound spiritual vision of Zoroaster, one of humanity's earliest known Prophets.

Primary Zoroastrian Texts

No original transcripts of the orally transmitted Avesta or other Zoroastrian scriptures exist today. The texts were first written down in Avestan script during the Achaemenid era (559–321 BCE), but much was lost during Alexander the Great's conquest and subsequent invasions. What remains is a reconstruction based on surviving fragments and oral traditions.

The Avestan alphabet was specifically developed for the Avestan language, a branch of the Indo-Iranian family of languages and derived from Pahlavi scripts, which in turn were derived from Aramaic, the language spoken by Jesus.

The core scriptures of Zoroastrianism are collectively known as the Avesta, a compilation of liturgical and religious texts that serve as the foundation of Zoroastrian worship and doctrine. The Avesta can be divided into the following main sections:

- **Yasna**: The Yasna is the primary liturgical text of the Avesta used during Zoroastrian ceremonies. Within the Yasna lies the Gathas—hymns attributed to Zoroaster (also known as Zarathustra). The Gathas are considered the most sacred and ancient portion of the Avesta and are believed to date back to approximately 1500 BCE, making them some of the oldest religious compositions in the world.

- **Visperad**: This text is an extension of the Yasna, containing additional invocations and offerings. It is often recited during specific high rituals.

- **Vendidad**: The Vendidad, or "law against the demons," is a compilation of myths, religious laws, and detailed purification rituals likely composed between 1000 and 500 BCE.

- **Yashts**: These are hymns dedicated to various Zoroastrian divinities, known as Yazatas. The Yashts often contain mythological narratives and were likely composed between 1000 and 500 BCE.

- **Khordeh Avesta**: Also called the "Little Avesta," this is a collection of shorter prayers and hymns for everyday use by lay practitioners.

Beyond the Avesta, there are significant texts composed later in the Pahlavi (Middle Persian) language. These texts, written in Middle Persian, were composed during the Sasanian era and after the Islamic conquest of Persia, which was between the third and tenth centuries CE. These texts include:

- **Bundahishn**: A cosmological and mythological text describing the creation and the nature of the universe.
- **Denkard**: A comprehensive theological and philosophical compendium of Zoroastrian teachings.
- **Arda Viraf Namag**: The narrative of a visionary journey through the afterlife.
- **Zatspram**: Another important theological and mythological text.
- **Selections from Zadspram** and the **Pahlavi Rivayats**: Commentaries and collections of religious practices.

Authenticity and Preservation of Zoroastrian Texts

The Gathas and other texts were meticulously preserved through oral transmission by priests (*Mobeds*). This tradition, known as "*kathavibhuva*," ensured the accurate memorization and recitation of texts. The earliest surviving written manuscripts of the Avesta date to the thirteenth century CE. While these are not original manuscripts, they are based on earlier textual traditions.

Scholars have analyzed the archaic language of the Gathas, confirming their antiquity and authenticity. The Younger Avesta reflects a later stage of the Avestan language, consistent with its hypothesized timeline. Inscriptions from Achaemenid kings (sixth through the fourth century BCE), such as Darius I, mention Ahura Mazda—the supreme deity of Zoroastrianism—and reflect Zoroastrian influence, providing indirect support to the authenticity of the scriptures.

Appendix C: Buddhist Texts

Scripture in Buddhism

Buddhism emerged as a distinct religious tradition in ancient India around the fifth century BCE. It developed from the prevailing religious culture recognized as Hinduism.

Siddhartha Gautama, who later became known as the Buddha ("the Enlightened One"), is traditionally believed to have been born in Lumbini (now in modern-day Nepal) around the fifth century BCE. He was a prince of the Shakya clan but renounced his worldly life at the age of twenty-nine after witnessing the suffering inherent in human existence.

Buddhism developed as a reform movement within the Sramana tradition, which was itself a reaction against the ritualistic Brahmanic Vedic religion, a type of Hinduism. The Sramana movements emphasized ascetic practices and direct personal spiritual experience over ritual sacrifices and mediated religious activities. Siddhartha Gautama, after His enlightenment, formulated a Middle Way between severe asceticism and sensual indulgence. His teachings emphasized the "Four Noble Truths" and the "Eightfold Path" as means to attain Nirvana—the cessation of suffering and the cycle of rebirth (samsara).

Unlike the Vedic Hindu religion, which focused on rituals and the intercession of priests (*Brahmins*), Buddhism focused on personal practice and insight. It rejected the authority of the Vedas and the caste system, emphasizing individual spiritual liberation as accessible to all, regardless of social status.

Succession of Buddhas

In Buddhist tradition, Gautama Buddha is seen as one of many Buddhas (enlightened ones) who have appeared throughout history. According to texts like the Buddhavamsa and Mahayana sutras, there were three past Buddhas before Siddhartha Gautama, making him the fourth Buddha. Future Buddhas are prophesied. The most commonly mentioned Buddhas preceding Gautama are Kakusandha Buddha, Konagamana Buddha, and Kassapa Buddha. The next expected Buddha to appear is referred to as Maitreya Buddha. He is prophesied to arrive when the teachings of the current Buddha have been forgotten.

Primary Buddhist Texts

Buddhist scriptures are mainly divided between the two major Buddhist traditions—Theravada and Mahayana.

Theravada Scriptures

Known as the "Pali Canon" or "Tipitaka" (Three Baskets), these texts are written in Pali and include:

- **Vinaya Pitaka**: The code of monastic discipline.
- **Sutta Pitaka**: Discourses of the Buddha and his close disciples, including the Dhammapada, a collection of sayings.
- **Abhidhamma Pitaka**: Philosophical and doctrinal analyses and summaries.

Mahayana Scriptures

These texts were written in Sanskrit and later translated into other languages like Tibetan and Chinese. They include:

- **Prajnaparamita Sutras**: These focus on the perfection of wisdom and include texts like the Heart Sutra and the Diamond Sutra.
- **Lotus Sutra**: Tis text emphasizes the universal potential for Buddhahood and the importance of compassion.
- **Pure Land Sutras**: These describe the creation of idealized Buddhalands.

The Pali Canon texts were orally transmitted for several centuries before being written down during the first century BCE in Sri Lanka. The Mahayana sutras were composed between the first century BCE and the second century CE, a timeline surrounding the birth and ministry of Jesus and the writing of the Gospels of the New Testament.

Authenticity and Preservation of Buddhist Texts

The authentication of Buddhist scriptures is based largely on textual analysis, historical consistency, and the preservation practices of monastic communities. These texts have been scrutinized in terms of their doctrinal consistency, linguistic style, and the congruity of their historical references with archaeological findings. Monastic traditions have played a crucial role in preserving, copying, and transmitting these texts through well-established and rigorous practices, ensuring their fidelity over centuries. Buddhist scriptures represent a vast body of literature preserved and revered within different traditions of Buddhism, reflecting both continuity and diversity in Buddhist thought and practice.

APPENDICES

Abrahamic Religious Texts

Appendix D: Abrahamic and Judaic Texts

Scripture in the Abrahamic Religion

No written records have been found representing the pre-Judaic religious beliefs of Abraham. What we know of Him is derived mainly from the Hebrew Bible. Some of that information may have been passed down orally, but archaeological evidence is lacking.

Abraham is said to have originated from Ur in Mesopotamia, a region rich in diverse religious practices that were predominantly polytheistic. Gods associated with cities, natural phenomena, and ancestral spirits were commonly worshiped. While cuneiform writing was in wide use in Abraham's time, there is no evidence from the Bible about Abraham's literacy or use of cuneiform tablets.

As a Manifestation of God with divine knowledge, however, the rendering of Abraham in the Bible seems on point. The Book of Genesis portrays Him as a key figure in the development of monotheism. He could also be considered a henotheist (one who worships a single god without rejecting the existence of others). The Genesis and Qur'anic accounts do not show him overtly rejecting other gods except for inanimate idols that cannot speak or guide. For this reason, he may have represented the concept of progressive revelation—the gradual expansion of divine knowledge over time as appropriate. The Bahá'í Faith identifies him with the emergence of monotheism.

In the Qur'an, Abraham vehemently rejected idolatry and even debated the issue with His father, who was an idol maker.[517] This partial rejection of polytheism shows Abraham as a transitional Manifestation, which is part of the job description of Them all.

Primary Judaic Texts

The primary scripture of Judaica is the Hebrew Bible, or Tanakh, which also has significant influence in Christianity and Islam. The text spans centuries and contains a blend of religious laws, historical and mythical accounts, poetry, and prophetic writings. The Hebrew Bible is traditionally divided into three parts: the Torah (Law), the Nevi'im (Prophets), and the Ketuvim (Writings).

The teachings of the Old Testament, like those of other scriptures, were perfectly suited to the social conditions and the capacities of the people at the time they were revealed. For instance, the laws given in the Torah through Moses addressed both the spiritual needs and the social circumstances of the Israelites. Progressive revelation implies that religious truth is not absolute but relative to the needs and capacities of humanity at any given time. Therefore, while the Old Testament contains eternal spiritual truths, some of its social laws and practices were meant for a specific previous era.

The composition of the Hebrew Bible occurred over a vast period, likely from the twelfth century BCE to the second century BCE. It is the result of a complex process of oral traditions and written sources conflated over time. The exact history of the compilation of texts is a topic of scholarly debate, but the Tanakh was likely canonized (declared authoritative) around the second century CE. Each section of the Tanakh contributes to the rich tapestry of

---

517 *Qur'an*, Surah 6:74-79; see also Surah 21:51-70

Jewish history, law, theology and ethics, and together the texts form the canonical scripture of Judaism.

The Torah (Law)

The Torah, also known as the Pentateuch, includes the first five books of the Bible. These books are foundational and contain the laws given to Moses by God as well as narratives that range from the creation of the world to the death of Moses. The books in the Torah are:

- **Genesis (*Bereishit*)** covers the creation of the world, the early stories of humanity, and the patriarchs of the Israelite people.
- **Exodus (*Shemot*)** describes the enslavement of the Israelites in Egypt, their liberation under Moses, the receiving of the Torah at Mount Sinai, and the wanderings in the desert.
- **Leviticus (*Vayikra*)** focuses on religious rituals, moral and ceremonial laws, and the duties of the priesthood.
- **Numbers (*Bamidbar*)** continues the story of the Israelites in the desert, including various censuses, laws and episodes of rebellion.
- **Deuteronomy (*Devarim*)** consists mostly of Moses's speeches reiterating and expanding the laws given earlier as the Israelites prepared to enter the Promised Land.

Prophets (Nevi'im)

The Nevi'im is divided into two sub-sections: the Former Prophets, which are historical accounts that include significant amounts of prophetic interpretation, and the Latter Prophets, which consist primarily of writings attributed to specific prophets.

Former Prophets

- **Joshua** describes the conquest of Canaan.

- **Judges** covers the time from the death of Joshua to the rise of the monarchy, featuring cycles of apostasy and deliverance.

- **Samuel (1 and 2 Samuel)** chronicles the establishment of the monarchy, including the reigns of Saul and David.

- **Kings (1 and 2 Kings)** continues the narrative from the death of David through the division of the kingdom into Israel and Judah, ending with the Babylonian exile.

Latter (Minor) Prophets

The following books, each attributed to a different minor prophet, address a variety of themes from judgment to hope and restoration. They comprise a single book in the Hebrew Bible. The minor prophets are: Hosea, Joel, Amos, Obadiah, Jonah, Micah, Nahum, Habakkuk, Zephaniah, Haggai, Zechariah, and Malachi.

Writings (Ketuvim)

The Ketuvim includes a diverse collection of poetic writings, wisdom literature and other types of texts.

- **Psalms**: A collection of religious poems and songs.

- **Proverbs**: Aphorisms attributed primarily to Solomon.

- **Job**: A poetic dialogue on suffering and divine justice.

- **Song of Songs**: A series of lyrical poems that celebrate love.

- **Ruth**: A short narrative about loyalty and divine providence.

- **Lamentations**: Poems mourning the destruction of Jerusalem.

- **Ecclesiastes (Kohelet)**: Philosophical reflections on life's meaning.
- **Esther**: The story of a Jewish woman who becomes queen of Persia and saves her people.
- **Daniel**: Stories and visions of Daniel, a Jew in exile in Babylon.
- **Ezra-Nehemiah**: A chronicle of the return of these exiles from Babylon and the rebuilding of the Temple.
- **Chronicles (1 and 2 Chronicles)**: Retold events from Genesis to the return from exile focusing on the Davidic line and temple worship.

Authenticity and Preservation of Judaic Texts

Many scholars believe that the stories of Abraham and the other patriarchs were initially passed down orally and only written down much later. This oral tradition would have been the primary method of preserving and conveying cultural and religious heritage during that time. This method helped preserve the linguistic style and the integrity of the religious teachings, although it may also have allowed for variations and differing interpretations over time.

The core Judaic scripture is the Torah (the Five Books of Moses), which is part of the broader Tanakh or Hebrew Bible. The Torah is traditionally believed to have been given to Moses by God at Mount Sinai. While the oral tradition (later written down as the Talmud and other texts) plays a crucial role in Judaism, especially in interpreting and expanding upon the written law (Torah), the written texts of the Torah and the Prophets were not in place until the late first millennium BCE.

The authenticity of the Hebrew Bible as a document reflecting the principles of Judaism is supported by a combination of textual fidelity, historical plausibility, archaeological evidence, and religious tradition. However, "authenticity" in a religious text also involves accepting that the text functions both as a spiritual guide and a historical document, each aspect evaluated differently based on scholarly methods and religious belief.

Textual Criticism

Textual criticism involves examining the various copies and fragments of biblical manuscripts to trace their development and identify their most authentic form. The discovery of the Dead Sea Scrolls in the mid-twentieth century was particularly significant, providing manuscripts that predated previous copies by about a thousand years. These scrolls affirmed the considerable consistency of the biblical text over centuries, although there were also variations that helped scholars understand the occasionally unreliable processes of textual transmission and development.

Historical Analysis

Scholars use historical analysis to compare biblical accounts with external historical data from archaeology and contemporaneous texts from surrounding cultures. For example, events like the existence of the kingdoms of Israel and Judah are supported by archaeological evidence and external records such as the Moabite Stone and Assyrian texts. However, not all biblical narratives have been definitively corroborated by archaeology, leading to ongoing debates about the historical accuracy of certain biblical events.

Archaeological Evidence

Archaeological discoveries have provided contexts that align with many geographical, cultural, and historical references in the Hebrew Bible, offering a backdrop that supports some of the narratives. Artifacts and site excavations contribute to understanding the material culture, practices, and geopolitical realities of the periods described in the texts.

Comparative Studies

Comparing biblical texts with other ancient Near Eastern texts can highlight similarities and differences in religious thoughts, laws and narratives. For example, laws in the Torah show parallels with those in the Code of Hammurabi, a Babylonian legal text from about 1750 BCE. Such comparisons not only help in understanding the uniqueness of Israelite religion but also how it interacted with and differed from other contemporary religions.

Religious Tradition and Transmission

From a faith perspective, the authenticity of the Hebrew Bible is often viewed in terms of its divine inspiration and the careful process of transmission by religious scholars and scribes. Jewish tradition holds that the Torah was divinely revealed to Moses and that subsequent texts were written by prophets and leaders under divine guidance. The meticulous methods used by Jewish scribes to preserve the text through generations underscore its religious significance and the care taken to maintain its integrity.

Scholarly Consensus

While there is a broad consensus that the Hebrew Bible reflects core religious beliefs and historical aspects of ancient Judaism, scholars acknowledge that the texts were written and compiled by multiple authors over centuries. The Documentary Hypothesis, for example, suggests that the Torah was composed from several source texts. This perspective helps explain variations and developments in the text, which reflects the evolving religious and social landscapes of the Israelite people.

Does God Change?

In the Hebrew Bible, God is often portrayed as having close, direct interactions with His chosen people of Israel. This includes direct communication with figures such as Moses, Abraham, and the prophets. God's partisanship for Israel, His punitive actions against their enemies or in response to Israel's own sins, and His direct interventions reflect a particular stage in the unfolding of God's relationship with humanity. This portrayal also reflects the context of a tribal, nomadic, and later monarchical society where survival often depended on decisive and visible leadership. In the biblical context, this was provided by a directly involved deity.

By contrast, the portrayal of God in the New Testament, especially through the teachings of Jesus, emphasizes universal love, forgiveness, and redemption. Jesus presents God more as a loving Father to all humanity, not just to Israel. The direct divine communications of the Old Testament are replaced by the teachings of Jesus and the guidance of the Holy Spirit, reflecting a shift toward understanding how to establish a more spiritual and less nationalistic relationship with God.

From a post-Judaic perspective, the differences between the Old and New Testament portrayals of God can be seen as reflecting different stages in the divine pedagogy—a teaching method that adapts to the evolving spiritual and moral capacity of humanity, culminating in the teachings of later Manifestations and the ongoing guidance of the Holy Spirit. This progressive revelation is fundamental to understanding the continuity and development concepts within the Christian scriptural tradition and the Bahá'í Faith.

In other words, the nature of God is unchanging, but our understanding of Him continues to develop as we move as a global society through the divine curriculum. And there is so much more to be revealed to us. When all scripture is viewed as a unified but developing narrative, the continuity and brilliance of the overall message shines through.

Remember, $2 + 2$ does not always equal 4.

Appendix E:
Christian Texts

Scripture in Christianity

The primary Christian scriptures are the Old Testament, which is shared with Judaism, and the New Testament, unique to Christianity. For a fuller description of Old Testament texts (the Hebrew Bible) see Appendix D: Abrahamic and Judaic Texts.

Primary Christian Texts

The Old Testament (Hebrew Bible)

The Old Testament consists of texts including the Torah (Pentateuch), historical books, wisdom literature, and the works of various prophets. These books were written by different authors and traditionally attributed to figures such as Moses for the Torah and David for many of the Psalms. Modern scholarship, however, suggests a complex authorship composed from as early as the twelfth century BCE to the second century BCE. The texts included in the Old Testament were originally written in Hebrew with some portions in Aramaic.

The New Testament

The New Testament comprises the Gospels, Acts of the Apostles, Epistles (Letters), and the Book of Revelation written by various early Christian figures. The Gospels are attributed to Matthew, Mark, Luke, and John; Acts and several epistles were apparently written by Luke and Paul, respectively; and Revelation has been attributed to John of Patmos. These texts were composed after the death of Jesus during a period roughly between 50 CE and 110 CE. They originally were written in Koine Greek, the lingua franca of the Eastern Mediterranean at the time.

Shortly after these books and epistles were written and made available, those of apostolic origin and works that were widely used in worship and consistent in doctrine became generally accepted as authoritative.

By the late second century CE, key texts, such as the four Gospels and the majority of Paul's epistles, were being recognized in Christian communities. The canon was not formally recognized, however, until the Synod of Carthage in 397 CE, which ratified the New Testament as it is known today.

Gospels

There are four Gospels in the New Testament:

- **Matthew** presents Jesus as the fulfillment of Old Testament prophecies, emphasizing his role as the Messiah. This book includes the Sermon on the Mount and a collection of Jesus's teachings.

- **Mark** is the shortest gospel, focusing on the ministry of Jesus. It emphasizes the deeds of Jesus more than his teachings and introduces the concept of the suffering Messiah.

- **Luke** offers a detailed and orderly account of Jesus's life, his journey toward Jerusalem, and his teachings, death and resurrection. It highlights Jesus's compassion for Gentiles, the poor, and the outcast.

- **John** focuses on the spiritual identity of Jesus as the

Son of God and "the Word made flesh," with a deeper consideration of Jesus's nature and work. It contains discourses not found in Matthew, Mark and Luke, called the "synoptic" gospels because they share many of the same stories in the same order and with similar wording.

Paul's Epistles (Letters)

Paul, also named Saul of Tarsus, is better known as Paul the Apostle and St. Paul. He was a Christian apostle (from about 5 CE to about 65 CE) and spread the teachings of Jesus in the first-century world through his travels and correspondence. Many of his letters, called epistles, are incorporated into the New Testament, including:

- **Romans** is a theological treatise on the righteousness from God, justification by faith, and the role of Christ in salvation.

- **1 Corinthians** addresses issues in the Corinthian church including divisions, immorality, and questions on spiritual gifts and the resurrection.

- **2 Corinthians** is a personal letter expressing Paul's relief and joy that the Corinthians had received his earlier letter with a positive response.

- **Galatians** defends the gospel's independence from the Law of Moses and stresses justification by faith, not by works.

- **Ephesians** focuses on the cosmic role of Christ and the church as the fullness of Christ who fills all in all.

- **Philippians** is a thank you letter for support, reflecting on joy in Christ despite suffering.

- **Colossians** combats heretical teachings and emphasizes the supremacy of Christ.

- **1 Thessalonians** encourages a young congregation to stand firm in the face of persecution.
- **2 Thessalonians** clarifies misunderstandings about the Second Coming of Christ.
- **1 Timothy, 2 Timothy, Titus** are pastoral epistles that provide guidance on church leadership and pastoral care.
- **Philemon** is a personal letter requesting the manumission of a slave.

General Epistles by Assorted Writers

- **Hebrews**, written by Paul, argues for Christ's superiority over all Old Testament constructs, emphasizing His role as high priest.
- **James** is thought to be written by James, the half-brother of Jesus. It emphasizes practical Christian living and the importance of both faith and works.
- **1 Peter** was written by the Apostle Peter. It offers encouragement to suffering Christians.
- **2 Peter**. Also written by the Apostle, warns against false teachers and stresses the certainty of Christ's return.
- **1 John**, written by the Apostle John, focuses on love as proof of knowing God and the assurance of salvation.
- **2 John**, another epistle written by the Apostle, warns against deceivers who deny Jesus Christ's coming in the flesh.
- **3 John**, also written by the Apostle, deals with church hospitality and conflicts.

- **Jude**, possibly written by Jude, another half-brother of Jesus, urges believers to contend for the faith against false teachings.

Other

- **Acts of the Apostles:** Written by the author of Luke, Acts describes the early church from Jesus's ascension to Paul's journey to Rome, emphasizing the spread of the Gospel through the work of the Holy Spirit amidst persecution.
- **Revelation** was written by John of Patmos while exiled as a result of Roman anti-Christian persecution. Christian tradition says he is the same person as John the Apostle. This is a prophetic and apocalyptic book that contains visions of the future events leading up to the Second Coming of Christ, the final judgment, and the establishment of a new heaven and new earth.

Books Excluded from the New Testament

The canonization process of the Christian New Testament led to the exclusion of some extant texts that were consulted by some early Christian communities but ultimately excluded from the canonical Bible. These books are often referred to as "apocryphal" or "non-canonical" texts. The reasons for their exclusion vary, but they generally include concerns over authorship, doctrinal content, and their use in liturgical settings.

- **The Gospel of Thomas** is a collection of 114 sayings attributed to Jesus but excluded because it lacked narrative content and was considered "Gnostic" in its orientation—a theology soundly rejected by the Church.
- **The Gospel of Judas** presents Judas Iscariot not as a traitor but as acting at Jesus's request. Its Gnostic

themes and theological perspective diverged significantly from the canonical Gospels causing it to be rejected.

- **The Gospel of Mary** focuses on Mary Magdalene and her role as a visionary and leader among the early disciples. It was not included because of its advocacy for a view of spiritual authority that conflicted with the emerging church hierarchy, and because it contained Gnostic elements.

- **The Shepherd of Hermas** is a Christian literary work consisting of five visions, twelve mandates, and ten parables that was very popular in early Christianity. Though it was once considered scriptural by many early Christians, it was eventually seen as too late in composition and lacking apostolic authorship.

- **The Epistle of Barnabas** was a treatise that covered topics like the interpretation of the Old Testament, the Jewish practices, and ethical teachings. Non-apostolic authorship and its doctrine that the Christian Church had superseded the Jewish people made it too controversial to include.

- **The Gospel of Peter** contains an account of Jesus's death and resurrection. Because it implied that Jesus did not suffer physically, it was rejected by mainstream Christianity.

The process of canonization was not merely about selecting religious texts but was also a means of defining orthodoxy and consolidating doctrinal unity within the early Church. This process reflected both theological motivations and the practical needs of early Christian communities to have a standard set of texts for teaching and worship. The books that were excluded often continued to be read and valued in some Christian sects but did not achieve a status as Scripture within the broader Christian canon.

Authenticity and Preservation of Christian Texts

The texts of the New Testament were copied and recopied by hand through the centuries. The discovery of the Dead Sea Scrolls and, later, more manuscripts like the *Codex Sinaiticus* and *Codex Vaticanus*, have provided critical insights into the historical transmission of the texts and variants. Modern biblical scholarship, employing methods from historical-critical methodologies to more recent literary and sociological approaches, continues to explore the origins, authorship, and context of the biblical texts. The process of canonization, which was guided by an unusual mix of spiritual discernment, historical circumstance and political expediency, reflects the Catholic Church's attempt to preserve what it holds as sacred and authoritative.

Appendix F:
Islamic Texts

Scripture in Islam

Islam's scriptures, like those of other world religions, can be viewed as both fulfilling the needs of their time and laying foundational insights and principles that prepare for subsequent revelations such as the Bahá'í Faith. This approach highlights the unity and continuity within religious diversity, emphasizing the complementary nature of divine messages across ages.

Continuity of Revelation

Islam and its scriptures can be seen as part of God's progressive revelation, which is seen as a continuous and evolving dialogue between the divine and humanity. Each religious dispensation, such as Islam, builds upon the previous ones and prepares for the next, progressively revealing God's will and purpose for humanity.

Just as the Qur'an respects the biblical prophets and affirms the scriptures that came before it (e.g., the Torah and the Gospels), it also introduces new teachings and laws suited to the conditions of its time. This reflects the view that each religious revelation renews fundamental spiritual truths and adapts social laws to the needs of the age. The Qur'an's introduction of concepts like the oneness of humanity and the unity of all prophets is seen as pivotal in this ongoing spiritual evolution.

Primary Islamic Texts

The Quran

The Qur'an is the holy book of Islam, believed by Muslims to be the literal word of God (Allah) as revealed to the Prophet Muhammad. Muslims believe that the Qur'an was verbally revealed by God to Muhammad through the Angel Gabriel over approximately twenty-three years beginning in 610 CE in Mecca and concluding in 632 CE in Medina. The Qur'an is considered a comprehensive guide for humanity's moral, spiritual and societal needs. It covers law, theology, worship and ethics, among other topics.

The Qur'an can be divided into various themes and sections, each dealing with different aspects of faith, life, and the universe:

Theological Foundations

- **Monotheism (*Tawhid*)**: The Qur'an emphasizes the oneness of God, Who is all-powerful, all-knowing and merciful. This is a central theme that recurs throughout the text.

- **Prophethood (*Nubuwwah*)**: The Qur'an discusses the roles of various prophets, including Adam, Noah, Abraham, Moses, Jesus and Muhammad, Who is regarded as the final prophet. These sections link Islam with the broader Abrahamic religious tradition.

Cosmology and the Afterlife:

- **Creation and the Natural World**: Various *surahs* (chapters or sections) describe God's creation of the heavens and the earth, natural phenomena, and the purpose of life.

- **Eschatology**: The Qur'an provides detailed accounts of the Day of Judgment, resurrection, heaven (Paradise), and hell (Hellfire), offering vivid descriptions of the afterlife to guide believers' actions.

Legal and Social Codes:

- **Law (*Sharia*)**: The Qur'an sets out guidelines for personal behavior, family life, inheritance, marriage and criminal justice. These laws are supplemented by the Hadith—sayings and actions of Muhammad—which help interpret the Qur'anic text.

- **Moral and Ethical Guidelines**: Beyond formal laws, the Qur'an emphasizes virtues such as honesty, humility, charity, and patience.

Guidance on Personal Conduct:

- **Prayer and Worship**: The Qur'an provides guidance on how to pray, the importance of regular prayer, and other forms of worship.

- **Fasting, Charity, and Pilgrimage**: The Qur'an mandates fasting during the month of Ramadan, giving to the needy, and making the pilgrimage to Mecca, known as Hajj, if one is able.

Stories and Parables:

- The Qur'an contains narratives that serve as moral and spiritual lessons. These stories often involve earlier prophets and communities, and they address themes of faith, obedience, rebellion, and redemption.

Gary Lindberg

Community and Society:

- **Community (*Ummah*)**: The concept of the Muslim community as a unified body is a recurring theme. The Qur'an provides guidance on social justice, community relations, and the responsibilities of individuals towards others.

Each Surah has a unique name, usually derived from a keyword or an important theme discussed within the chapter. For example, "Surah Al-Fatiha" (The Opening) is named after its position as the opening chapter of the Qur'an, and "Surah Al-Baqarah" (The Cow) is named after a story about a cow discussed within the chapter. The length of Surahs varies significantly. The longest Surah, "Al-Baqarah," has 286 *ayahs* (verses), while the shortest, Al-Kawthar, has only three *ayahs*.[518]

Each *ayah* carries a meaning that can stand alone but also contributes to the context of the *surah* (chapter) it is part of. This dual characteristic allows the Qur'anic verses to be recited individually or as part of a longer passage. *Ayahs* are considered the literal words of God, eternal and unchanged.

Memorizing the entire Qur'an is a practice known as *Hifz*, and it is highly esteemed within the Muslim community. Many Muslims memorize significant portions of the Qur'an at a young age.

Surahs are categorized based on whether they were revealed in Mecca or Medina before and after the *Hijra* (migration of Prophet Muhammad from Mecca to Medina, respectively). Meccan *surahs* generally focus on theology, the oneness of God, and the afterlife, while Medinan *surahs* contain more legal instructions and address the social and moral organization of the Muslim community.

---

518 The word "ayah" literally means "sign" or "evidence" in Arabic, reflecting the belief that each verse is a sign from God about His will, commands, or the nature of the universe. The Qur'an is made up of approximately 6,236 ayahs, though the exact number can vary slightly depending on the method of textual division used.

Except for one ("Surah At-Tawbah," the ninth chapter), every surah starts with the phrase *"Bismillah al-Rahman al-Rahim"* ("In the name of God, the Most Gracious, the Most Merciful.") This phrase sets a tone of reverence and submission to God at the beginning of each surah.

The Hadith

The Hadith collections are records of the sayings, actions, and approvals of the Prophet Muhammad, which provide practical examples of the implementation of the Qur'anic teachings. Unlike the Qur'an, the Hadith were compiled by various scholars and are based on oral traditions traced back to those who were close to Muhammad. Key compilers include Sahih Bukhari, Sahih Muslim, Sunan Abu Dawood, and others. The Hadith serve to clarify and explicate the Qur'anic text and offer guidance on religious practices, daily life and spiritual matters.

The compilation of hadiths began orally during the life of Muhammad and continued after his death in 632 CE. The formal, systematic compilation of hadiths into written collections started around the mid-eighth century CE and continued through the ninth century CE. This period saw the creation of the major hadith collections that Muslims use today.

While the Qur'an is considered the literal word of God and holds the highest authority in Islamic doctrine, hadiths play a crucial role in interpreting and understanding the Qur'an. They provide context and detail not available in the Qur'an alone and are used extensively in Islamic jurisprudence (*fiqh*) to resolve matters not explicitly covered by the Qur'an. They also offer Muslims insights into Muhammad's character, making him a model for behavior.

The exact number of hadiths is difficult to determine because there are thousands spread across various collections with significant overlap and repetition among them. Individual collections can contain anywhere from a few hundred to many thousands.

Hadiths are typically organized in collections known as "Hadith books." These collections are not organized by topic but rather by the chain of narration, although within individual books, hadiths may be grouped into chapters or books based on themes such as prayer, fasting, or business transactions.

The primary collections of hadith for Sunni Muslims are known as the "Six Canonical Hadith Collections," which include:

- **Sahih Bukhari** compiled by Imam Bukhari.
- **Sahih Muslim** compiled by Muslim ibn al-Hajjaj.
- **Sunan Abu Dawood** compiled by Abu Dawood.
- **Sunan al-Tirmidhi** compiled by al-Tirmidhi.
- **Sunan al-Nasa'i** compiled by al-Nasa'i.
- **Sunan Ibn Majah** compiled by Ibn Majah.

Shia Muslims have their own collections, with the four most revered books being:

- **Kitab al-Kafi** compiled by Muhammad ibn Ya'qub al-Kulayni.
- **Man la yahduruhu al-Faqih** compiled by al-Shaykh al-Saduq.
- **Tahdhib al-Ahkam**, compiled by al-Tusi.
- **Al-Istibsar**, also compiled by al-Tusi.

Authenticity and Preservation of Islamic Texts

The Qur'an

After Muhammad's death, the Qur'an was compiled into a single book under the caliphate of Abu Bakr and later standardized under Uthman ibn Affan around 650 CE to resolve variations in recitation. The *Uthmanic Codex* was adopted as the standard copy, and all other versions were ordered to be burned, ensuring a uniform text. This version is considered by Muslims to be the definitive and preserved script.

The Hadith

The Hadith were initially transmitted orally but were written down in book form starting in the eighth century CE for fear of losing them. Hadith compilers used rigorous criteria to authenticate reports, including examining the chain of transmission (*isnad*) and the reliability of the narrators. Two kinds of classification are used to identify authenticity:

- **Isnad** (chain of narrators): Each hadith is transmitted with a chain of narrators going back to the Prophet Muhammad. The reliability of a hadith is assessed based on the trustworthiness and accuracy of its narrators.
- **Matn** (text): The actual text of the hadith is evaluated for consistency with established Islamic teachings and other known hadiths.

Four separate levels of authenticity have been approved for ranking the authenticity of individual hadiths:

- ***Sahih*** (authentic), the highest level of authenticity.
- ***Hasan*** (good), considered reliable with a slightly weaker *isnad*.
- ***Da'if*** (weak), considered not reliable for deriving Islamic law but can be used for virtuous actions.
- ***Mawdu*** (fabricated), considered false and not acceptable in Islamic practice.

Hadiths are an indispensable part of Islamic tradition, providing insights into the Prophet's life and elaborations on Qur'anic verses. They help Muslims navigate their personal lives and community matters with religious and ethical guidance.

Appendix G: Bahá'í Texts

Scripture in the Bahá'í Faith

The Bahá'í Faith stands unique among world religions in possessing an extensive corpus of scriptures written directly by its Founders. This appendix aims to explore the profound implications of having such authentic texts, which not only provide unequivocal guidance to adherents but also offer a direct window into the doctrinal and ethical framework of the religion as intended by its Prophets. Central to the Bahá'í scriptural tradition are the writings of the Báb, Bahá'u'lláh, 'Abdu'l-Bahá, Shoghi Effendi, and the continuing guidance provided by the Universal House of Justice.

The inception of the Bahá'í Faith's revelatory period begins with the Báb, who declared His mission in 1844 in Shiraz, Persia. He is considered the Herald of the Bahá'í Faith and foretold a soon-to-come second Messenger, Bahá'u'lláh. The Báb's writings, including numerous letters, prayers, and the foundational text of the *Bayán*, are estimated to number over two thousand separate works, though many have been lost or are yet to be fully authenticated and published.[519]

---

519 *A Twofold Mission*, Bahá'í World Centre Publication.

Bahá'u'lláh, the founder of the Bahá'í Faith, announced His prophetic claim in 1863, marking the commencement of a prolific period of scriptural revelation that lasted until His passing in 1892. His writings, which elaborate on the spiritual and administrative principles for a new world order, include more than 15,000 tablets and letters. These texts address a vast array of topics from the mystical and ethical to the societal and organizational.[520]

Following Bahá'u'lláh, His eldest son 'Abdu'l-Bahá took on the mantle of leadership as the appointed Interpreter of His teachings and the Exemplar of the Faith. 'Abdu'l-Bahá's role was crucial in explaining the profound doctrines of the Bahá'í Faith, and he contributed significantly to its literature through thousands of tablets, letters, and talks, which further expanded upon the foundational texts written by His father.[521]

After 'Abdu'l-Bahá's death, the stewardship of the Bahá'í Faith was passed to Shoghi Effendi who was designated the Guardian of the Faith. Shoghi Effendi's role involved significant translation work, interpretation, and the authorship of a considerable body of letters and texts that guided the expansion and consolidation of the Bahá'í community worldwide.

Lastly, the Universal House of Justice, established in 1963 as the supreme governing body of the Bahá'í Faith as directed by Bahá'u'lláh, continues the process of authoritative contribution through its messages and letters—which provide guidance on a range of issues facing the global Bahá'í community—and the implementation of Bahá'í laws and teachings.

This appendix will explore these sources of scriptures and guidance, focusing on their authenticity, thematic richness, and their role in shaping the Bahá'í identity and administrative order. The discussion will highlight how the direct writings from the Bahá'í Faith's founders, authorized interpreters and the Universal House of

---

520 *SevenYear Plan 1979–1986 Statistical Report*, Ridván 1983.
521 *Bahá'í Encyclopedia Project* (entry on 'Abdu'lBahá).

Justice have uniquely positioned the religion to maintain doctrinal integrity and adapt to the evolving needs of a global community.

Primary Bahai Texts

The Báb

The Báb, whose title means "the Gate" in Arabic, was the precursor to Bahá'u'lláh, the Founder of the Bahá'í Faith. He heralded a new religious dispensation and provided the initial impetus for the development of the Bahá'í Faith through His writings, which laid foundational theological concepts and introduced revolutionary spiritual and social teachings. His writings are extensive, characterized by complex symbolism and metaphysical themes, and were primarily composed during His ministry from 1844 until His martyrdom in 1850. Key texts written by the Báb include:

Commentary on the Súrih of Joseph (Qayyúmu'l-Asmá')

This is one of the earliest works of the Báb, revealed overnight in response to a request from Mulla Husayn to provide a commentary on the Sura of Joseph from the Qur'an. The text dramatically reinterprets the story as a metaphor for spiritual awakening and renewal, setting the tone for the Báb's mission.

The Persian Bayán

Perhaps the Báb's most significant doctrinal work, the *Persian Bayán* expounds the laws, teachings, and principles of the Báb's religion. It is intended as a holy book in its own right, though the Báb stated that its laws were to be superseded by the one He referred to as "Him Whom God shall make manifest" (Bahá'u'lláh).

The Arabic Bayán

Complementary to the *Persian Bayán*, this text delves deeper into theological and philosophical concepts. The *Arabic Bayán* further elaborates on the Báb's innovative religious laws and ethical teachings.

Dalá'il-i-Sab'ih (The Seven Proofs)

The Seven Proofs is a theological treatise that provides arguments in defense of His claim to be the Mahdi or Qá'im long awaited by the Shi'a Muslims. It directly addresses doubts and objections raised by the religious establishment.

Sahífiy-i-Baynúbiyyih (The Book of the Five Grades)

This compilation of writings by the Báb comprises prayers, meditations and homilies, and showcases the devotional and mystical aspects of the Báb's writings.

Various Prayers and Meditations

This collection includes numerous individual prayers, many of which are recited by Bahá'ís today. These prayers emphasize devotion, submission to God's will, and preparation for the coming of Bahá'u'lláh.

★ ★ ★

The writings of the Báb are noted for their intense mysticism and profound symbolism, often focusing on themes of renewal, the day of judgment, and the coming of a new era. They challenge existing religious doctrines and social practices, calling for radical transformation both spiritually and materially.

The Báb's style is marked by a unique use of language, often restructuring classical literary forms to convey his revolutionary message. The Báb's writings not only set the stage for the later unfoldment of the Bahá'í Faith but also contributed to a broader movement of religious and social upheaval in Persia, influencing countless followers and leading to significant social and political repercussions in his homeland.

The texts of the Báb provide essential context for understanding the subsequent revelations of Bahá'u'lláh and the theological foundation of the Bahá'í Faith. His works are considered scriptural texts within the Bahá'í canon, revered for their spiritual depth and their role in transitioning from Islamic traditions to the new religious identity established by Bahá'u'lláh.

Bahá'u'lláh

Bahá'u'lláh, the founder of the Bahá'í Faith, produced a vast body of writings that elaborate on the spiritual and administrative principles of the religion. His works encompass a wide range of literary styles, including theological treatises, mystical writings, laws and ordinances, ethical guidelines, and letters to leaders of society, communities, and individuals. These texts were written over the four decades of His ministry from 1852 until His passing in 1892. Key texts written by Bahá'u'lláh include:

Kitáb-i-Aqdas (The Most Holy Book)

This is Bahá'u'lláh's book of laws, serving as the charter for the worldwide Bahá'í community. It outlines the essential laws and principles for individual conduct and the governance of the Bahá'í community, including laws on marriage, prayer, fasting, and community administration.

Kitáb-i-Íqán (The Book of Certitude)

This theological work provides a profound exposition on the nature of religion. It explains the roles of the Messengers of God in different religious traditions, the concept of progressive revelation, and the spiritual and symbolic interpretation of religious texts. The *Kitáb-*

i-Íqán is essential for understanding Bahá'í perspectives on the continuity of revelation and the unity of all religions.

Hidden Words

A collection of short, aphoristic statements, the *Hidden Words* is described by Bahá'u'lláh as the essence of divine guidance, distilled into brief passages that touch on spiritual and ethical themes. These writings are intended to inspire contemplation and meditation.

The Seven Valleys and The Four Valleys

These two mystical texts describe the stages of the soul's journey toward God. *The Seven Valleys* follows the path of the seeker through the stages of search, love, knowledge, unity, contentment, wonderment, and true poverty and absolute nothingness.

Tablets to the Kings and Rulers

Bahá'u'lláh wrote a series of letters to the leaders of His time, including monarchs and religious authorities, proclaiming His prophetic mission and calling for peace, justice and the unity of humankind. These letters were bold proclamations of His vision for a global civilization characterized by moral and spiritual principles.

Gleanings from the Writings of Bahá'u'lláh

This compilation features selections from various tablets that cover a wide range of topics, including the nature of God, the purpose of human life, the soul, and the development of spiritual qualities.

★ ★ ★

Bahá'u'lláh's writings are central to the Bahá'í Faith, providing guidance on both spiritual and administrative matters. His texts are characterized by a profound depth of philosophical insight and a compelling call for moral reform and spiritual advancement. The language ranges from highly allegorical and mystical to direct and legislative, offering a comprehensive guide for personal development and the construction of a global society. Originally written predominantly in Arabic and Persian, Bahá'u'lláh's writings have been translated into many languages.

His epistles to the rulers of the time underscored a revolutionary aspect of His mission as he engaged directly with the powers of His day in an unprecedented manner. Through these tablets, Bahá'u'lláh not only challenged each leader to reflect on their responsibilities and moral duties but also laid down the principles for a new world order based on justice, equity and unity.

Bahá'u'lláh's writings continue to be a source of inspiration and guidance for millions around the world. They address the most profound questions of human existence and offer a blueprint for a united, peaceful world. His proclamation of the oneness of humanity and the unity of all religions remains a powerful call for global unity and cooperation in an age of fragmentation and conflict.

'Abdu'l-Bahá

'Abdu'l-Bahá, the eldest son of Bahá'u'lláh and His appointed successor, holds a unique position in the Bahá'í Faith. Known as the Centre of the Covenant, he was charged with interpreting and exemplifying his father's teachings and ensuring the unity of the Bahá'í community. His writings are considered scriptural sacred text. They provide essential and authoritative guidance for understanding and applying Bahá'í principles. Key texts written by 'Abdu'l-Bahá include:

Some Answered Questions

This book is an illuminating collection of transcribed conversations between Abdu'l-Bahá and Laura Clifford Barney, an American Bahá'í, in which Abdu'l-Bahá explained many of the philosophical and religious aspects of the Bahá'í teachings. The topics range from the nature of God and prophethood to the interpretation of Christian and Islamic scriptures, and the harmony of science and religion.

The Secret of Divine Civilization

A treatise written before his father's death, this book is addressed to the people of Iran, advocating for progressive reforms in governance and society, the advancement of education, and the application of scientific methods and principles. This work is considered a major contribution to the literature on social and ethical development.

Paris Talks

This is a compilation of talks given by 'Abdu'l-Bahá during his visits to Paris in 1911 and 1912. These presentations cover a wide range of topics including spirituality, the teachings of Bahá'u'lláh, and the principles needed for the advancement of society.

Tablets of the Divine Plan

This collection of fourteen tablets written during World War I outlines a vision for the spiritual conquest of the planet through the spread of the Bahá'í Faith across the Americas, Europe, Asia and beyond. These letters played a pivotal role in expanding the Bahá'í Faith internationally. As of this writing, the Bahá'í Faith is the second most geographically widespread religion in the world with Bahá'í communities in more than 188 sovereign nations and territories, and elected national administrations in 182 countries.[522]

Tablets to The Hague

Addressing the Central Organization for a Durable Peace at The Hague, this book outlines 'Abdu'l-Bahá's proposals on behalf of the Bahá'í Faith for the establishment of a permanent and universal peace predating the formation of the League of Nations.

---

[522] David Barrett, *World Christian Encyclopedia* (Oxford University Press).

It sets forth principles later reflected in international peacekeeping bodies.

★ ★ ★

'Abdu'l-Bahá's writings and talks are extensive, encompassing a broad array of subjects such as ethics, social justice, gender equality, economic development and interfaith harmony. They are characterized by their practicality, clarity, and the deep spirituality that underscores his explanations of Bahá'í teachings.

'Abdu'l-Bahá's style is accessible and direct, aimed at explaining and elaborating the spiritual and social teachings of the Bahá'í Faith to a diverse audience. His writings are less formal and less laden with the mystical symbolism that often permeates the writings of Bahá'u'lláh, making them particularly approachable for new learners of the Bahá'í teachings.

Like the writings of Bahá'u'lláh, 'Abdu'l-Bahá's works have been translated into numerous languages and serve as foundational texts for understanding the practical applications of Bahá'í principles. They are used extensively in Bahá'í study circles, devotional gatherings, and in individual study.

'Abdu'l-Bahá's contributions through his writings and talks were pivotal in articulating the Bahá'í vision to a global audience, especially during his travels to the West. His emphasis on service to humanity, unity among all peoples, and the importance of consultation in all affairs continues to influence the development of the Bahá'í community and its approach to global challenges. His legacy is not only in the written word but also in the example of his life, which remains a model of Bahá'í service and dedication.

Shoghi Effendi

Shoghi Effendi, the great-grandson of Bahá'u'lláh and appointed Guardian of the Bahá'í Faith, played a pivotal role in interpreting the teachings of the Bahá'í Faith and in guiding its administrative development and global expansion. While he did not produce scripture in the manner of Bahá'u'lláh, the Báb and 'Abdu'l-Bahá, his writings are considered authoritative and remain central to understanding the Bahá'í administrative order and the Faith's objectives and strategies at a global level. Key writings of Shoghi Effendi include:

God Passes By

This work is a narrative history of the first Bahá'í century, providing a detailed account of the development of the Bábí and Bahá'í Faiths from 1844 to 1944. Shoghi Effendi outlines major events, figures, and themes, offering interpretation and insight into their significance within the Bahá'í context.

The World Order of Bahá'u'lláh

This work is a collection of letters and essays written to the Bahá'í community that elaborates on the administrative principles, the future world civilization, and the spiritual and organizational requisites for the establishment of the Bahá'í Administrative Order. It is a critical source for understanding Bahá'í governance.

The Advent of Divine Justice

In this letter, Shoghi Effendi provides guidance to the American Bahá'í community, emphasizing the spiritual prerequisites for success in teaching and administration. He discusses the issues of racial unity, the rectitude of conduct, and the need for a chaste and holy life, among other moral prerequisites for the progress of the American Bahá'í community.

Messages to the Bahá'í World

This volume compiles various communications from Shoghi Effendi to the global Bahá'í community, providing direction and encouragement for the spread of the Bahá'í Faith worldwide and the development of the Bahá'í World Center in Haifa, Israel.

★ ★ ★

Shoghi Effendi's writings are characterized by their comprehensive analysis and systematic approach. They address both the spiritual objectives and administrative requirements of the Bahá'í Faith, ensuring that its teachings were correctly understood and effectively applied as the Faith transitioned from the East to the West and became a global religion.

Shoghi Effendi's style is notable for its clarity, precision and depth. His command of English, demonstrated in his translations of Bahá'í texts and his own writings, played a crucial role in making the teachings of the Bahá'í Faith accessible to a Western audience. He effectively used his writings to articulate the integration of spiritual principles with practical administrative guidelines, a hallmark of Bahá'í organizational structure.

Shoghi Effendi's works have been translated into multiple languages and are studied by Bahá'ís around the world. They serve as key texts for understanding the Faith's doctrinal and administrative aspects and continue to guide the Bahá'í community's development.

Through his writings, Shoghi Effendi shaped the Bahá'í Faith's administrative structure and enriched its doctrinal foundation. His insights into the dynamic interplay between spiritual principles and practical governance mechanisms have helped define the Bahá'í approach to building a unified global community. His tenure as Guardian not only consolidated the achievements of the early Bahá'í community but also laid a robust framework for its future expansion and the realization of Bahá'u'lláh's vision for humanity.

The Universal House of Justice

The Universal House of Justice is the supreme governing institution of the Bahá'í Faith, established to guide and administer the global Bahá'í community. According to Bahá'í scripture, it is the institution specifically ordained by Bahá'u'lláh in His writings and further elaborated upon by 'Abdu'l-Bahá in His Will and Testament, which outlines its functions and powers. The Universal House of Justice has been in operation since its first election in 1963, coinciding with the end of the 100-year Bahá'í prophetic cycle that began in 1863 with Bahá'u'lláh's public declaration.

The Universal House of Justice has the exclusive authority to legislate on matters not explicitly revealed in the Bahá'í scriptures. Its decisions, considered infallible, are binding for the Bahá'í community. It administers the affairs of the Bahá'í community globally, ensuring the unity and coordination of national and local Bahá'í institutions. It also provides ongoing spiritual and administrative guidance to the worldwide Bahá'í community, addressing challenges and setting directions for its development. The Universal House of Justice communicates with the global Bahá'í community through a variety of texts such as:

- **Messages and Letters**: Regular communications address the needs of the Bahá'í community and offer guidance on a wide range of issues from spiritual development to community organization and social action.

- **Plans and Appeals**: The Universal House of Justice issues global plans that guide the activities of the Bahá'í community. These plans often focus on themes such as the growth and consolidation of the Bahá'í community, the development of local and national institutions, and the community's engagement in social, humanitarian, and educational activities.

- **Statements and Commentaries**: The Universal House of Justice also releases statements on broader social, ethical and spiritual issues, contributing to global discourse on peace, governance, and human rights.

★ ★ ★

The writings and directives of the Universal House of Justice are characterized by a practical approach to applying Bahá'í principles to the needs of a rapidly evolving world. Messages from the Universal House of Justice are translated into multiple languages and distributed via National Spiritual Assemblies to Bahá'ís around the world. This ensures that all members of the Bahá'í community, regardless of location or background, have access to its guidance.

The Universal House of Justice plays a critical role in fulfilling the administrative order envisioned by Bahá'u'lláh and 'Abdu'l-Bahá. Its writings not only guide the spiritual and administrative life of the Bahá'í community but also offer a model for global governance based on principles of consultation, equity, and universal participation.

Authenticity and Preservation of Bahá'í Texts

The Bahá'í Faith emphasizes the authenticity and accuracy of its sacred texts and their translations. The process of authentication and translation is rigorous given the importance attached to the exactness of the words revealed by its Founders, The Báb and Bahá'u'lláh, and authoritative texts by 'Abdu'l-Bahá. This process ensures that the teachings are preserved accurately and conveyed correctly across different languages and cultures.

Authentication of Writings

The primary method for authenticating Bahá'í texts involves referencing the original manuscripts written by The Báb, Bahá'u'lláh, and 'Abdu'l-Bahá. Many of these original texts are preserved and used as primary sources for verification. In cases where original manuscripts are not available, authorized transcriptions made during the lifetime of the authors or shortly thereafter by trusted secretaries are used. These documents are compared and cross-referenced with other authenticated texts to ensure their accuracy. Understanding the historical context in which a text was revealed is also crucial. This includes knowing to whom and why a particular tablet was revealed, as these factors can influence the interpretation and relevance of the text.

Translation Process

First translations are initially carried out by individuals proficient in both the source language (usually Arabic or Persian) and the target language. These initial translations strive to be as literal as possible while maintaining the readability and spirit of the original text.

These translations are then reviewed and revised by committees or individuals appointed by Bahá'í institutions, ensuring they align with the theological concepts and terminology consistent across Bahá'í literature.

The final step involves the approval of translations by the Universal House of Justice, the supreme governing body of the Bahá'í Faith, which ensures doctrinal consistency and accuracy across all translations.[523]

The Center for the Study of the Texts

The Center for the Study of the Texts is an institution located at the Bahá'í World Centre in Haifa, Israel. It plays a pivotal role in the authentication and translation of Bahá'í texts including:

- **Research and Scholarship**: The Center conducts in-depth research into the writings of the Bahá'í Faith, examining their meanings, contexts and applications. This research is essential for producing authoritative translations and commentaries.

- **Preservation**: The Center is also involved in the preservation of the original writings and transcriptions, ensuring that these priceless resources are maintained for future generations.

---

523 Universal House of Justice, 1999 policies on authorized and provisional translations; also, Craig Alan Volker, *Translating the Bahá'í Writings*.

- **Consultation**: The Center serves as a consultative body for the Universal House of Justice on matters related to Bahá'í texts, providing scholarly insight and guidance on issues of interpretation and application.
- **Educational Programs**: The Center may also develop educational programs and materials to aid individuals and institutions in understanding the Bahá'í writings more deeply.

The authentication and translation of Bahá'í writings are carried out with great care to preserve the integrity and accuracy of the Faith's sacred texts. The Center for the Study of the Texts embodies this commitment, ensuring that Bahá'í teachings are accessible and faithfully represented to a global audience, thus supporting the unity and coherence of the Bahá'í community worldwide.

Research and Study Sources

For those who want to consult the Bahá'í Writings and the sacred Writings of other wisdom traditions discussed in this book, we recommend the following sources:

Bahá'í Reference Library

The authoritative online source of Bahá'í writings. It contains selected works of Bahá'u'lláh, the Báb, 'Abdu'lBahá, Shoghi Effendi, and the Universal House of Justice, as well as other Bahá'í texts.

https://www.bahai.org/library/

Uplifting Words (Online)

An online list of Bahá'í-only texts in multiple formats for reading or download.

https://www.upliftingwords.org/post/baha-i-sacred-texts

Ocean 2.0 Interfaith Reader

An immersive library of the world's sacred literature. Read or listen to texts from these religions: Hindu, Judaism, Confucian, Tao, Islam, Zoroastrianism, Jainism, Buddhist, Christian, Bahai Faith.

https://sacred-traditions.org/ocean/

The Bahá'í Faith Websites

To learn more about The Bahá'í Faith in the United States, visit:

http://www.bahai.us

To learn more about The Bahá'í Faith worldwide, visit:

https://www.bahai.org/

About the Author

Before starting his career in writing and publishing books, Gary Lindberg was an award-winning filmmaker with over a hundred national and international awards. He produced and co-wrote the Paramount feature film *That Was Then, This Is Now* starring Emilio Estevez and Morgan Freeman. Since then, he has authored four #1 bestselling novels and many nonfiction titles. He lives in Minnesota where he has published books for over 150 authors with his partner at Calumet Editions, Ian Graham Leask.

Index

Aaron 122, 189, 248, 249, 251, 302
Abdu'l-Bahá 2, 8, 22, 36, 46, 51, 61, 62, 95, 113, 114, 120, 126, 135, 137, 139, 143, 155, 156, 161, 163, 165, 166, 167, 168, 175, 176, 178, 179, 186, 197, 198, 199, 257, 258, 260, 269, 270, 273, 288, 302, 303, 320, 333, 389, 390, 395, 396, 397, 398, 400, 401
Abdul Muttalib 235
Abhidhamma Pitaka 360
Abjad 101
Aboriginal 98
Abraham v, vi, 23, 28, 29, 78, 91, 97, 113, 115, 121, 124, 130, 134, 144, 146, 153, 157, 167, 183, 184, 185, 186, 187, 231, 232, 233, 234, 235, 236, 237, 239, 247, 249, 252, 291, 339, 341, 348, 363, 365, 366, 369, 371, 373, 382
Abram 184, 185, 187, 231
Achaemenid era 355
Achyuta 215, 219
Acoma Pueblo 98
Acre, penal colony 174
Adam 51, 52, 59, 60, 80, 117, 118, 192, 197, 202, 271, 287, 382
Adi Parva 256
Adnan 235
advent 270
Adventist 297
Afghanistan 278
Africa 26, 58, 63, 65, 67, 68, 72, 278
Agni 131
Agnosticism 144
Ahura Mazda 115, 144, 147, 148, 157, 219, 220, 221, 241, 243, 308, 315, 321, 357
Akhenaten 77

Al-Bashir 117
Alexander the Great 239, 355
Al-Istibsar 386
Allah 153, 154, 191, 192, 194, 197, 198, 199, 200, 278, 310, 313, 316, 317, 323, 326, 333, 382
al-Nabiyyin 158
Alpha 195
Al-Qaeda 277
al-Shaykh al-Saduq 386
al-Tirmidhi 386
al-Tusi 386
Amaterasu 153
Amazon 50
Americas 50, 58, 65, 81, 97, 396
Amos 368
Amrit 348
Amun-Ra 77, 152
Angra Mainyu 144, 148, 219
Anis 173
Anishinaabe (Ojobway) 98
Anunnaki 107
Apollo-11 cave 55, 63
Apollodorus 255
Apostle 35, 272, 287, 288, 373, 375, 376, 377
Arab 8, 9, 34, 58, 101, 157, 158, 168, 172, 197, 201, 204, 205, 211, 234, 276, 285, 288, 317, 323, 330, 384, 391, 392, 395, 402
Aranyaka 351, 352
Arda Viraf Namag 357
Arikara 98
Aristotle 127
Arizona 99
Arjuna 19, 215, 218
Ark (Noah's) 119, 120, 150, 348
Artaxerxes 270, 301
Aryan religious traditions 23, 28, 29,

47, 146, 213, 339, 343
Asia 47, 65, 81, 239, 278, 396
Assyrian 370
Aten 77
Atharvaveda 350
Atheism 145
Atman 352
At-Tawbah 385
Augur, George 95
Augustine 25
Australia 58, 63, 81, 97, 98
Avalokiteshvara 152
Avatar 45, 51, 114, 117, 151, 213, 225, 289, 347, 348, 349
Avesta 46, 132, 219, 220, 221, 225, 312, 318, 355, 356, 357, 409, 415
Ayodhya 349
Aztec 81, 82, 83, 86, 87, 255

B

Báb 22, 32, 35, 36, 43, 52, 94, 95, 99, 113, 118, 125, 126, 130, 137, 158, 169, 172, 173, 174, 177, 190, 195, 200, 201, 202, 203, 204, 207, 208, 209, 210, 235, 236, 240, 241, 273, 274, 287, 290, 291, 292, 293, 294, 295, 296, 298, 299, 300, 301, 303, 304, 389, 391, 392, 393, 398, 401, 405
Babel 150
Babel, Tower of 150
Bábí 24, 43, 52, 124, 125, 126, 173, 204, 398
Babylon 243, 369
Babylonian 243, 368, 371
Badasht 173
Baghdad 174, 204
Bahá'í vi
Bahá'ís 29, 30, 43, 91, 96, 103, 154, 173, 174, 175, 177, 189, 190, 192, 193, 194, 195, 196, 199, 201, 203, 209, 211, 212, 213, 264, 265, 266, 267, 275, 282, 291, 298, 392, 399,
401
Bahá'u'lláh iv, 1, 5, 6, 18, 22, 32, 33, 35, 36, 45, 46, 48, 50, 52, 81, 82, 91, 97, 103, 113, 118, 126, 127, 130, 135, 136, 137, 138, 139, 143, 154, 158, 159, 162, 163, 164, 165, 166, 167, 168, 169, 170, 172, 173, 174, 175, 176, 177, 179, 185, 186, 187, 189, 190, 195, 196, 197, 198, 199, 200, 201, 202, 203, 204, 205, 206, 207, 208, 209, 210, 211, 212, 213, 216, 235, 236, 240, 241, 249, 250, 251, 252, 260, 266, 273, 274, 275, 282, 283, 284, 286, 287, 288, 289, 290, 291, 292, 293, 294, 296, 298, 299, 301, 306, 307, 310, 311, 314, 317, 323, 326, 330, 333, 334, 339, 340, 341, 342, 389, 390, 391, 392, 393, 394, 395, 396, 397, 398, 399, 400, 401, 405
Bahrain 60
Bamidbar 367
Barnabas 378
Bayan 172
Bethlehem 242, 244, 245, 246
Bhagavad Gita 19, 131, 213, 214, 215, 216, 218, 225, 289, 308, 311, 314, 317, 318, 321, 327, 330
Bhagavata Purana 51, 214, 217, 218, 348
Bhakti Yoga 320
Bhavishya Purana 285, 286
Bishárát-i-Kutub-i-ásmání 240
Bitahni 99
Bochica 98
Bodhisattva 115
Book of Revelation 195, 204, 295, 302, 373
Brahman 114, 144, 146, 147, 149, 151, 308, 345, 352
Breathmaker 98
Brihadaranyaka 352
Buck 91, 92, 99

Buck, Christopher 91
Buddhas 45
Buddhism 5, 23, 24, 29, 45, 46, 115, 128, 130, 132, 145, 146, 148, 149, 151, 152, 157, 168, 239, 304, 309, 312, 315, 319, 322, 325, 328, 331, 341, 359, 360, 361
Bundahishn 148, 220, 357
Bunjil 98

C

Campbell, Joseph 67, 68
Canaan 31, 78, 79, 237, 367
Canaanite 78
Canon 148, 360, 361
canonical 367, 377, 378
Carmel, Mount 150, 293, 294
Carrasco, David 82
Carthage 374
Catholic 379
Catholicism 96
Ce Acatl Topiltzin Quetzalcōātl 83, 84
Celtic 64
Chaldees 231
Charioteer 215, 218
Chariots of the Gods 106
Cheyenne 97
Chinigchinich 97
Chinigchinix 97
Christian 116
Christianity 117
Christian Mysticism 145
Christmas 26
Clark 35
Clarke, Arthur C. 141
Clark, Jerome L. 35
Code of Hammurabi 371
Codex 94, 379, 386
Codex Sinaiticus 379
Codex Vaticanus 379
Coffin Texts 254
Colorado 99
Colossians 375
Comforter 211, 275, 282

compassion 33, 37, 61, 115, 128, 152, 157, 168, 193, 199, 277, 311, 312, 313, 314, 315, 319, 325, 326, 361, 374
Confucius 128, 405
consciousness 8, 26, 31, 65, 66, 67, 70, 71, 118, 215, 216, 258, 296
Constantine 26
consultation 397, 401
Corinthians 375
Cortés, Hernán 87
cosmic 75, 120, 147, 148, 218, 220, 221, 241, 335, 348, 375
cosmology 57, 348, 349, 351
Cougnac Cave 72
Council of Nicaea 44, 150
covenant 31, 32, 121, 123, 157, 158, 176, 184, 187, 188, 225, 226, 235, 236, 237, 247, 249, 250, 252, 290, 292, 305, 334, 336
Creator 5, 7, 59, 141, 146, 148, 250
Cree 98
Crossan, John Dominic 243
Crusades 13, 276
cultural preservation 96

D

Dadistan-i-Dinik 324
Da'if 387
Dalai Lama 128, 152, 313
Dalá'il-i-Sab'ih 392
Daniel 193, 267, 268, 269, 270, 272, 297, 299, 300, 301, 302, 304, 305, 306, 369
Darius I 357
Darshan 115
DashAvatara 348
David 67, 82, 87, 110, 113, 115, 116, 150, 232, 233, 234, 251, 252, 253, 259, 271, 273, 291, 368, 369, 373, 396
Dawning Place 169
Dawood, Sunan Abu 385, 386
Deganawida 91, 97

Deism 144
Demon Mura 216
Denkard 357
dependent prophet 113, 114, 122, 123, 124, 126
detachment 168, 303, 326, 327, 328, 329, 330, 352
Deuteronomy 133, 188, 190, 249, 251, 253, 271, 272, 282, 309, 315, 318, 367
Devaki 256
Devarim 367
Devi 147, 346
Dhammapada 132, 316, 319, 322, 325, 328, 332, 360
Diacritics 9
Diakonis 46
Dilmun 60
Diné 98, 99, 100, 102
Dionysus 151
dispensation 32, 122, 123, 158, 195, 201, 236, 275, 295, 303, 305, 381, 391
diversity 27, 32, 92, 96, 97, 139, 143, 176, 293, 341, 346, 347, 361, 381
Divine v, 1, 2, 3, 5, 6, 7, 16, 17, 21, 23, 28, 41, 43, 44, 45, 46, 48, 49, 50, 52, 53, 58, 62, 64, 66, 67, 71, 73, 75, 76, 78, 79, 80, 81, 82, 86, 88, 90, 105, 108, 109, 111, 114, 129, 130, 134, 136, 146, 154, 155, 161, 165, 166, 172, 176, 178, 199, 211, 220, 221, 223, 228, 235, 239, 250, 264, 275, 283, 288, 321, 337, 339, 340, 346, 396, 398
Divine Educator v, 2, 5, 6, 7, 16, 17, 21, 23, 28, 41, 43, 45, 46, 48, 50, 52, 53, 58, 62, 64, 66, 67, 71, 73, 76, 78, 79, 80, 81, 82, 86, 88, 90, 105, 108, 109, 111, 114, 129, 130, 134, 161, 165, 172, 176, 178, 211, 223, 228, 235, 239, 250, 275, 283, 337, 340
divinity 57, 139, 217, 218, 245, 276, 317

Dogon people 107
dreams 56, 69, 243
Dualism 144
duality 147, 168
Dughdova 256
Durga 346

E

Eden 59, 60
Effendi 32, 47, 125, 126, 127, 176, 202, 203, 286, 288, 289, 342, 389, 390, 397, 398, 399, 405
Effendi. Shoghi 125
Egypt 13, 31, 32, 49, 58, 60, 75, 77, 78, 79, 80, 88, 90, 106, 110, 144, 150, 152, 187, 188, 189, 226, 237, 246, 247, 248, 249, 254, 295, 312, 367
Ehécatl-Quetzalcóatl 83
Elias 123
Elijah 123, 302
Emmanuel 116
Emmons, Henry 224
Enki 60, 119
enlightenment 115, 128, 138, 157, 194, 211, 213, 219, 220, 221, 256, 322, 359
Enoch 302
Ephesians 310, 375
Epistle of Barnabas 378
Epistles 373, 375, 376
Eschatology 383
Esselmont, John E. 22
Esther 369
ethical 28, 31, 32, 33, 37, 39, 40, 41, 89, 108, 128, 129, 143, 145, 221, 279, 312, 314, 324, 325, 378, 387, 389, 390, 392, 393, 394, 396, 400
Eucharist 277
Eve 51, 52, 59, 60, 271
evil 51, 52, 59, 60, 78, 148, 150, 168, 216, 219, 221, 239, 241, 246, 252, 299, 318
Exodus 26, 32, 51, 77, 78, 115, 116, 187,

188, 189, 190, 237, 247, 248, 249, 312, 367
Ezekiel 113, 207, 208, 209, 295, 297, 301
Ezra 268, 301, 369

F

Ferraby, John 241
Finkel, Irving 119
Flute 217
France 72, 75, 77
Franco-Cantabria 63
Fravashi 115
Fumane Cave 54, 55, 63

G

Gabriel 52, 257, 382
Galatians 185, 186, 375
Galilee 264
Ganesha 346
Ganges 46, 130, 285
Garutman 131
gate 158, 201, 203, 207, 209
Gathas 51, 219, 239, 355, 356, 357
Genesis 59, 60, 118, 184, 185, 186, 187, 231, 232, 236, 237, 252, 253, 285, 365, 367, 369
Gilgamesh 26, 60, 119
Gluskap 98
Gnostic 144, 174, 377, 378
Göbekli Tepe 49
Goliath 150
Gomorrah 150
Gospel 52, 137, 139, 191, 193, 194, 196, 199, 207, 232, 234, 242, 286, 361, 373, 374, 377, 378, 381
Gospel of Judas 377
Gospel of Mary 378
Gospel of Peter 378
Gospel of Thomas 377
Govardhana 218
Govinda 215
Gregorian calendar 303

Guardian 115, 126, 127, 176, 202, 390, 397, 399
Gucumatz 82
Gudakesha 308
Guna people 98
Guru Nanak 128

H

Habakkuk 206, 284, 368
Habib Allah 200
Hades 259
Hadith 34, 313, 320, 383, 385, 386, 387
hadiths 385, 386, 387
Hafiz 128
Hagar 187
Haggai 212, 368
Hague 396
Haifa 175, 176, 294, 398, 402
Hajj 336, 383
Halakha 272
hallucinations 69, 72
Hanif 121
Hanuman 347
Haram 121, 277
Haran 184
Hari 156, 214
Harun 122
Hasan 387
Hashim 235
Haudenosaunee 97
heathen 96, 295
heaven 6, 25, 44, 88, 93, 94, 133, 135, 136, 164, 192, 201, 205, 207, 224, 227, 228, 260, 263, 264, 265, 266, 275, 291, 298, 313, 314, 329, 377, 383
Hebrew 8, 78, 133, 149, 184, 185, 188, 190, 191, 192, 205, 236, 244, 247, 248, 251, 271, 272, 281, 284, 290, 302, 338, 365, 366, 368, 369, 370, 371, 373
Hebrews 77, 78, 80, 187, 188, 226, 236, 376
Hegirae 303

Heimdall 255
Heli 233
hell 25, 314, 383
Hellenistic 25, 174
Hellfire 383
Henotheism 347
Heraclitus 137
Herald 169, 203, 389
Herod 242, 243, 244, 245, 246
Herodotus 243
Hidatsa 98
Hifz 384
Hijra 384
Hijrah 241, 303
Hindu vi, 10, 18, 23, 24, 29, 38, 43, 44, 45, 51, 90, 96, 114, 117, 124, 130, 131, 144, 146, 147, 149, 151, 213, 215, 217, 221, 223, 225, 256, 281, 283, 285, 289, 304, 308, 311, 314, 317, 320, 324, 327, 330, 335, 341, 345, 346, 347, 348, 349, 350, 351, 352, 353, 359, 360, 405
Hiranyaksha 348
Holm, J. 46
Horus 75, 77, 152, 254
Huitzilopochtli 255
humility 303, 307, 320, 321, 322, 323, 339, 383

I

Ibeorgun 98
Ibn Majah 386
Ibrahim 121
ignorance 156
imagination 49, 56, 64, 106, 112, 141, 142, 145
Imam Bukhari 386
Immanuel 254
Inca 97
incarnation 86, 139, 152, 153, 154, 193, 213, 276
Incarnation 116
incarnations 46, 152, 153
Indian 34, 130, 146, 350

Indians 92, 96, 100
Indigenous 29, 95, 145
Indo-Aryan 29
Indo-European 26
Indo-Iranian 239, 355
Indra 131
interfaith 14, 36, 397
Iran 13, 100, 130, 200, 219, 239, 241, 355, 396
Iraq 119, 125, 204, 231, 278
Ireland 14
Iroquois 97
Isaac 134, 184, 185, 186, 232, 247, 252
Isaiah 113, 149, 184, 206, 208, 212, 252, 253, 254, 260, 261, 271, 272, 293, 331
Isha Upanishad 352
Ishmael / Ishmail 121, 124, 134, 184, 186, 187, 234, 235, 252, 285
Ishvara 114, 320
Islam 5, 10, 13, 14, 23, 24, 29, 31, 32, 34, 49, 78, 88, 117, 121, 123, 124, 130, 134, 144, 145, 146, 147, 149, 150, 153, 154, 155, 157, 183, 184, 185, 186, 187, 190, 192, 197, 201, 212, 221, 231, 232, 234, 236, 240, 241, 256, 257, 260, 276, 277, 278, 279, 281, 291, 299, 301, 302, 303, 304, 310, 313, 316, 319, 323, 326, 329, 332, 334, 335, 336, 338, 366, 381, 382, 405
Islamic v, vi, 13, 29, 34, 116, 121, 124, 158, 172, 198, 200, 202, 203, 234, 236, 241, 267, 276, 277, 278, 281, 282, 286, 303, 304, 306, 339, 356, 381, 382, 385, 386, 387, 393, 396
isnad 387
Israel 58, 79, 115, 116, 123, 133, 175, 184, 185, 199, 208, 225, 226, 227, 242, 244, 245, 247, 251, 252, 261, 271, 294, 309, 368, 370, 371, 372, 398, 402
Israelites 31, 32, 77, 78, 79, 80, 122,

123, 133, 150, 158, 167, 186, 188, 189, 190, 192, 225, 237, 247, 248, 249, 250, 252, 253, 366, 367, 371
Italy 54, 63
Itza 92, 93, 94
Iyatiku 98

J

Jacob 134, 184, 185, 232, 244, 247, 292
Jagannath 214
Jaguar 92
Jainism 128, 130, 405
Jamaican 26
James 7, 184, 322, 376
Japan 95, 153
Jeremiah 113, 226, 251, 252
Jericho 150
Jerusalem 133, 205, 224, 242, 244, 267, 268, 269, 270, 271, 284, 293, 298, 300, 301, 305, 368, 374
Jesus Christ 2, 3, 22, 26, 33, 44, 52, 58, 72, 73, 84, 88, 90, 91, 116, 117, 119, 121, 123, 125, 130, 133, 134, 137, 138, 139, 150, 153, 154, 155, 156, 158, 162, 163, 164, 168, 172, 189, 190, 191, 192, 193, 194, 195, 196, 197, 199, 200, 204, 205, 207, 216, 218, 219, 224, 227, 228, 232, 233, 234, 236, 241, 242, 243, 244, 245, 246, 252, 253, 254, 256, 257, 258, 259, 260, 261, 262, 263, 264, 265, 266, 267, 268, 269, 270, 271, 272, 273, 274, 275, 276, 281, 282, 283, 287, 291, 295, 296, 298, 299, 301, 304, 305, 306, 310, 313, 316, 319, 322, 325, 328, 334, 335, 338, 339, 341, 356, 361, 372, 374, 375, 376, 377, 378, 382
Jethro 189, 248
Jewish 29, 32, 47, 115, 116, 123, 185, 191, 192, 231, 233, 234, 243, 244, 245, 247, 253, 268, 269, 271, 272, 273, 301, 302, 305, 309, 331, 334, 367, 369, 371, 378
Jews 22, 34, 43, 77, 123, 133, 184, 242, 244, 246, 251, 252, 259, 271, 272, 273, 274, 305, 334, 369
Jibril 52
Jnana Yoga 330
Job 261, 262, 368
Jochebed 248
Joel 368
John viii, 14, 22, 116, 123, 134, 137, 138, 139, 158, 164, 189, 191, 193, 194, 195, 196, 200, 207, 211, 212, 227, 241, 243, 266, 274, 275, 281, 282, 283, 295, 301, 302, 303, 313, 374, 376, 377
Jonah 150, 261, 368
Joseph 67, 68, 191, 232, 233, 246, 254, 391
Joshua 122, 367, 368
Judah 226, 232, 242, 245, 251, 252, 291, 368, 370
Judaic v, vi, 183, 247, 365, 366, 369, 372, 373
Judaism 5, 23, 24, 25, 28, 29, 31, 77, 78, 116, 121, 122, 130, 133, 134, 144, 145, 146, 147, 149, 150, 153, 154, 155, 157, 183, 185, 187, 190, 212, 221, 231, 232, 236, 247, 251, 259, 260, 261, 262, 271, 272, 275, 291, 306, 309, 312, 315, 318, 321, 324, 328, 331, 334, 335, 336, 367, 369, 371, 373, 405
Judas 377
Jude 377
Judea 242, 271
Judges 368
Jung, Karl 70
Jupiter 151, 244
justice 3, 18, 19, 21, 31, 32, 34, 37, 76, 89, 127, 132, 134, 158, 162, 166, 169, 176, 180, 201, 202, 203, 221, 251, 277, 287, 293, 307, 312, 314, 315, 316, 317, 326, 334, 335, 339, 341, 368, 383, 384, 394, 395, 397

K

Kaaba 121, 234
Kabbalah 145
Kakusandha Buddha 360
Kali 18, 289, 347
Kalim Alláh 157
Kalki 225, 289
Kamsa 98
Karna 256
Kassapa 360
Katha Upanishad 330
kathavibhuva 357
Katun 93, 94
Kavod 115
Kena Upanishad 147
Keshava 217
Keshi 217
Keturah 236
Ketuvim 366, 368
Khalil Alláh 157
Khatam al-Nabiyyin 158
Khordeh Avesta 356
Khuddakapatha 312
K'iche' Maya 82
kindness 48, 167, 311, 312, 314, 316, 318, 319, 324, 325
Kitab al-Kafi 386
Kitáb-i-Aqdas 18, 91, 139, 235, 393
Klüver, Heinrich 70
Knox, John 302
Kohelet 369
Koine Greek, 374
Konagamana Buddha 360
Krishna 19, 21, 29, 51, 58, 114, 117, 130, 146, 151, 156, 167, 213, 214, 215, 216, 217, 218, 219, 221, 256, 347, 348, 350
Kshatriyas 349
Ku Klux Klan 279
Kukulkan 83
Kumeyaay 98
Kunti 256
Kurma 348
Kuru Kingdom 19
Kurukshetra War 215
Kuuchamaa 98

L

Lake Titicaca 98
Lakota 97
Lakshmi 346
Lalitavistara Sūtra 256
Lamb, Christopher 46
Lamentations 368
Laozi / Lao Tzu 128, 153, 255
Lawgiver 167, 189, 190
Leda 151
León-Portilla, Miguel 82
Levant 50
Leviticus 251, 325, 367
Light-bringer 98
l-Nasa'i 386
Logos 116, 117, 138, 194
Lone Man 98
Lotus Sutra 361
Luke 193, 232, 233, 234, 322, 374, 375, 377
Lumbini 359
Luminaries 114
Luther, Martin 14

M

Maani 94
Mábádi-i-Estediá 240
Machmad 284
Madhu Clan 216
Magdalene, Mary 378
Magi 242, 243, 244, 245, 246
Mahabharata 51, 124, 213, 256, 314, 324
Mahadev 285
Mahamad 285
Mahavakya 352
Mahavira 128
Mahayana 115, 152, 290, 360, 361
Mahdi 392

Maidhyoimah 124
Mainyu 144, 148, 219
Malach Yahweh 115
Mali 107
Mandan 98
Manichaeism 144
Man la yahduruhu al-Faqih 386
martyrdom 125, 270, 391
Mashiach 191, 251
Masjid al-Haram 121
Matarisvan 131
Matn 387
Matsya 348
Matthew 116, 192, 201, 227, 228, 232, 233, 234, 242, 243, 245, 246, 254, 261, 263, 265, 275, 304, 305, 313, 316, 319, 325, 329, 332, 374, 375
Mawdu 387
Maya 81, 82, 83, 92
Mazda 115, 144, 147, 148, 157, 219, 220, 221, 241, 243, 308, 315, 321, 357
Mecca 121, 234, 277, 285, 303, 382, 383, 384
Medes 243
Medina 79, 241, 303, 382, 384
Medusa 255
Meitreya 290
Menes 76
mercy 22, 117, 162, 168, 193, 198, 199, 257, 287, 312, 313, 321, 339
Merneptah 79, 80
Mesoamerica 81, 82, 88, 90
Mesoamerican 82, 83, 84, 88, 89
Messengers 23, 43, 44, 45, 47, 49, 50, 52, 57, 58, 75, 78, 94, 95, 97, 108, 114, 116, 117, 135, 170, 174, 188, 194, 197, 198, 199, 202, 211, 220, 264, 286, 290, 292, 302, 389, 393
Messiah 115, 116, 123, 191, 192, 223, 227, 232, 242, 243, 244, 251, 252, 253, 254, 258, 259, 271, 272, 273, 295, 374
Messianic 233, 251, 272, 291
Metteyya 290
Mexico 15, 50, 82, 86, 87, 99, 103
Micah 244, 245, 321, 368
Miccosukee 98
Midian 189, 248
Millerite Movement 297
Miller, Mary 82
Miller, William 82, 224, 296, 297, 298, 299
Minoan 64
Mirzá Buzurg 236
Mírzá Husayn-'Alí Núrí 173, 203, 204, 236
Mithra 26
Mitra 131
Moabite 370
Mobeds 357
monastic 360, 361
monotheism 28, 77, 78, 121, 153, 154, 157, 186, 187, 190, 192, 234, 236, 247, 276, 277, 281, 285, 287, 309, 365, 366
Montanism 224
Montezuma 87
morality 1, 3, 4, 7, 19, 21, 31, 32, 38, 39, 40, 61, 62, 76, 84, 89, 108, 118, 128, 143, 145, 179, 200, 211, 218, 219, 220, 221, 256, 288, 300, 314, 315, 316, 317, 331, 337, 340, 347, 349, 367, 372, 382, 383, 384, 394, 395, 398
Moses 2, 22, 31, 32, 51, 58, 77, 78, 79, 80, 113, 119, 121, 122, 130, 133, 134, 137, 157, 158, 167, 187, 188, 189, 190, 196, 218, 221, 236, 237, 243, 247, 248, 249, 250, 251, 253, 260, 282, 286, 287, 295, 302, 334, 338, 341, 366, 367, 369, 371, 373, 375, 382
Mother Corn 98
Mount Horeb 51, 189, 248
Muhammad 2, 13, 22, 34, 35, 52, 58,

91, 113, 117, 119, 121, 123, 125,
  130, 137, 158, 163, 168, 172, 189,
  190, 195, 197, 198, 199, 200, 201,
  219, 234, 235, 236, 241, 252, 257,
  273, 274, 275, 276, 277, 281, 282,
  283, 284, 285, 286, 287, 288,
  295, 302, 303, 305, 306, 334,
  338, 341, 382, 383, 384, 385,
  386, 387
Mullá Husayn 126
Mullá Muhammad 'Alí-i-Bárfurúshí 125
Muslim ibn al-Hajjaj 386
Muslims 22, 43, 96, 153, 172, 192, 235,
  274, 275, 276, 278, 279, 282,
  284, 285, 286, 302, 303, 305,
  313, 326, 382, 384, 385, 386, 387,
  392
Mystic 145
mysticism 26, 392

N

Naba'u'l-A'zam 213
Nabi 117, 198, 199
Nabiyyin 158
Nadhir 200
Nahuatl 82, 83
Nahum 368
Namibia 55, 63
Nanabush 98
Narasimha 348
Narmer, Pharaoh 75, 76, 77, 78, 110
Nathan 234
Natufian 49
Navajo 98, 99, 100, 101, 102, 103, 110
Nazareth 191
Nazca lines 106
Nazism 38
Nekhen 77
Nemterequeteba 98
Nepal 359
Nevi'im 366, 367
Nibiru 107
Nicaea 44, 150

Nicene Creed 44
Nicholson, Henry B. 86, 90
Nikaya 290, 309
Nile 89, 188, 248
Norse 144, 255
Nubuwwah 382
Numbers 244, 367

O

Obadiah 368
obedience 22, 121, 187, 319, 321, 383
Oceania 65
Ojibway 98
Olmecs 81
Omega 195
Osiris 88, 89, 152, 254
Ottoman 174

P

Pahlavi Rivayats 357
Paleolithic 55
Palestine 28
Pali Canon 148, 360, 361
Panchgavya 285
Panentheism 144
Pantheism 144
parable 150
Paran, Mount 284, 285
Parashurama 349
Parthasarathi 215, 218
Passover 237
Patmos 374, 377
patriarch 78, 121, 184, 185, 187
Paul 25, 123, 185, 259, 272, 374, 375, 376, 377
Payrignac 72
Pentateuch 236, 237, 253, 367, 373
Pepuza 224
Perseus 255
Persia 29, 94, 125, 130, 172, 200, 203, 208, 209, 219, 236, 243, 357, 369, 389, 393
Persian 8, 9, 25, 34, 125, 128, 172, 173,

201, 236, 240, 356, 391, 392, 395, 402
Peru 106
Peter 259, 266, 376, 378
Pharisees 288
Philemon 376
Philippians 375
Pilate, Pontius 44
Pilate. Pontius 44
pilgrimage 277, 336, 383
Pi-Ramesses 78
Plato 127, 174
Polytheism 144, 347
Pope 14
Post-Christian 256
Prajnaparamita 361
Prayers 65, 102, 277, 356, 383, 389, 392
prehistory 49
prejudice 15, 17, 96, 179, 341
prophecies 46, 65, 87, 94, 99, 100, 101, 102, 149, 158, 159, 174, 190, 191, 192, 193, 196, 200, 201, 203, 204, 205, 206, 207, 208, 211, 212, 213, 223, 224, 225, 226, 227, 228, 232, 233, 235, 236, 237, 239, 240, 241, 243, 252, 253, 254, 258, 259, 260, 261, 262, 263, 264, 265, 267, 268, 269, 270, 272, 273, 275, 276, 281, 282, 284, 285, 286, 289, 290, 291, 293, 295, 296, 297, 298, 299, 301, 302, 303, 304, 305, 306, 334, 338, 339, 341, 374
protector 196, 215, 216, 217, 218, 255
Protestants 14, 26
Proverbs 315, 322, 328, 368
Psalms 3, 189, 206, 209, 212, 259, 272, 318, 331, 368, 373
Pueblo 98
Purana 18, 51, 214, 215, 216, 217, 218, 285, 286, 289, 348
Pure Land Sutras 361
Pyramid 254

Q

Qa'im 172, 201, 202, 301
Qayyúmu'l-Asmá' 391
Quddús 125
Qur'an 29, 66, 117, 134, 154, 163, 172, 184, 186, 187, 188, 190, 191, 192, 194, 197, 198, 199, 201, 202, 213, 231, 234, 248, 259, 275, 276, 278, 282, 285, 294, 366, 381, 382, 383, 384, 385, 386, 391
Qur'anic 202, 278, 365, 383, 384, 385, 387
Quraysh 235

R

Ra 77, 152
Rainbow Serpent 98
Rama 114, 117, 349
Ramadan 277, 383
Ramayana 349
Ramses II, Pharaoh 78, 79
Ranchor 214
Rastafarianism 26
Rasul 116
Ravana 349
Redeemer 193, 262, 301
reflection 116, 164, 173, 193, 331, 332, 351
Reinterpretation 39
Remus 255
repentance 123, 234
resurrection 25, 88, 89, 93, 94, 95, 191, 227, 258, 259, 260, 261, 262, 265, 374, 375, 378, 383
revelation ii, iii, 5, 6, 7, 16, 21, 22, 26, 27, 28, 29, 30, 31, 45, 51, 52, 57, 66, 71, 76, 95, 96, 100, 102, 108, 109, 112, 114, 115, 117, 118, 119, 122, 124, 126, 129, 130, 135, 138, 139, 142, 145, 146, 149, 158, 162, 166, 169, 170, 171, 176, 185, 187, 188, 190, 194, 195, 196, 197, 198, 202, 203, 205, 210, 213, 219,

221, 223, 228, 229, 235, 236,
241, 246, 249, 250, 263, 266,
267, 271, 274, 275, 276, 282, 283,
284, 285, 287, 288, 291, 292,
295, 298, 300, 301, 303, 304,
307, 333, 334, 336, 337, 338, 339,
340, 341, 366, 372, 381, 390,
393, 394
revelations 6, 28, 108, 117, 120, 121,
122, 124, 126, 161, 221, 250, 265,
273, 274, 275, 282, 284, 304,
333, 336, 338, 381, 393
righteous 19, 132, 251, 259, 315, 317,
318, 324, 328
righteousness 18, 19, 132, 157, 166,
184, 185, 216, 219, 220, 225, 227,
239, 241, 252, 269, 289, 314, 315,
316, 321, 324, 327, 331, 375
Rigveda 350
Rig Veda 131
rishi 124
rituals 4, 18, 23, 27, 39, 50, 65, 66, 67,
89, 129, 138, 152, 243, 277, 300,
307, 335, 336, 339, 350, 351, 353,
356, 360, 367
Romulus 255
Rumi 128
Ruth 368

S

Sabbath 244, 336
Sa'di 128
Sages 124, 127, 128
Saguna Brahman 114
Sahabah 285
Sahífiy-i-Baynúbiyyih 392
Sahih 187, 188, 190, 192, 197, 198, 199,
200, 202, 313, 326, 385, 386, 387
Sahih al-Bukhari 313, 326
Sahih Bukhari 385, 386
Sahih Muslim 313, 326, 385, 386
Salat 336
Samaritan 237, 286
Samaveda 350, 352

Samuel 251, 252, 253, 368
Samyutta Nikaya 309
San Blas Islands 98
Sanskrit 28, 361
Saoshyant 132, 225, 239, 241, 243
Sarah 186
Saraswati 346
Sasaniyan 241, 356
Sat-Chit-Ananda 215, 219
Saturn 244
Saturnalia 26
Saul 251, 368, 375
Savior 116, 196, 227, 271
Seal of the Prophets 158, 169, 197, 198,
276
sectarianism 40, 300
sects 4, 5, 10, 13, 14, 38, 40, 49, 139,
150, 195, 378
Seminole 98
Serpent 82, 83, 84, 90, 91, 92, 98
Seth 88
Seventh-day Adventist Church 297
Shabbat 325
Shakya clan 359
shamans 49, 56, 65, 66, 67, 68, 69, 71,
73, 88, 152
Shatapatha Brahmana 351
Shayast-na-Shayast 324
Shekinah viii, 115
Shema prayer 309
shepherd 43, 134, 189, 196, 242, 248,
283, 284
Shepherd of Hermas 378
Shi'a 201, 287, 301, 302, 392
Shinto 144, 153
Shukla 350
Shyam 216, 217
Siberia 50, 152
Siddhartha Gautama 256
Sikhism 128, 144, 154
Sinai, Mount 32, 249, 367, 369
Sirius 107
Sistine Chapel 110
Sitchin, Zecharia 106

Siyyid 172, 235
Skeptics 299
Sodom 150
Solomon 113, 233, 234, 284, 368
Song of Songs 368
Sophia 174
Spenta Mainyu 219
Spinoza 144
Sramana 359
Stephen 207
Stoicism 144
St. Sebastian 72, 73
suffering 51, 73, 103, 245, 253, 261, 294, 303, 312, 319, 328, 359, 368, 374, 375, 376
Sufism 145
Sunan Abu Dawood 385, 386
Sunan al-Kubra 320
Sunan al-Nasa'i 386
Sunan al-Tirmidhi 313, 386
Sunan Ibn Majah 386
Súrih of Joseph 391
Sutta Pitaka 360
Swami Sivananda 147
Sweet Medicine 97
Syncretism v, 25, 26, 27, 30, 37, 39
Synod 374

T

Tabarsí, Fort Shaykh 125
tabernacle 6, 136
Tahdhib al-Ahkam 386
Taheb 286
Taittiriya Aranyaka 351
Taliban 277
Talking God 98
Talmud 325, 369
Tanakh 366, 369
Taoism 145, 153, 255, 405
Tarbuyotolami 50
Tarsus 375
Tathagatas 132
Tat Tvam Asi 352
Taube 82

Tawhid 153, 310, 382
Tehran 52, 173, 203
Teman 284
Temple, Robert K.G. 107
Ten Commandments 221
Terah 184
Terrorism 277
Tezcatlipoca 83, 86, 87
Theophany 116
Theravada 290, 360
therianthrope 54, 55, 57, 72, 75, 77
Thessalonians 265, 332, 376
Thomas 377
Tibetan 128, 152, 361
Timothy 310, 376
Tipitaka 360
Titus 305, 376
Tlahuizcalpantecuhtli 83
Tokyo 95
Tollan 84
Toltec 82, 83, 84, 86, 88, 90, 92, 94, 97
Tongva 97
Torah 66, 149, 158, 199, 247, 271, 272, 286, 325, 366, 367, 369, 371, 373, 381
transcendent 57, 95, 97, 149, 153, 155
Transcendental 145
Trinity 44, 84, 150, 151, 153, 154, 155, 276, 309
Tula 84
Tunupa 98
Turkey 49, 174, 224
Twlelve Disciples 123
Tymion 224

U

Udana 148, 325
Ulikron 97
Umar 303, 305
Ummah 334, 384
unity 9, 22, 27, 30, 32, 35, 36, 38, 41, 76, 92, 96, 97, 98, 100, 101, 127, 128, 133, 134, 135, 138, 139, 154, 158, 163, 165, 169, 175, 176, 179,

187, 190, 195, 198, 203, 209, 213, 214, 217, 221, 236, 250, 284, 292, 293, 307, 308, 309, 310, 311, 312, 317, 326, 334, 336, 337, 340, 341, 347, 352, 378, 381, 382, 394, 395, 397, 398, 400, 403
universal 1, 22, 35, 36, 67, 70, 89, 97, 113, 137, 169, 176, 180, 187, 196, 203, 206, 214, 218, 232, 235, 236, 264, 271, 281, 286, 293, 301, 307, 309, 314, 324, 334, 335, 339, 361, 372, 396, 401
Unknowable v, 141
Upanishads 3, 147, 308, 330, 351, 352
Ur 231, 365
Urbe Condita 255
Uruk 49
Utah 99, 110
Uthman ibn Affan 386

V

Vahid 172
Vaishnavism 347
Vamana 348, 349
Varaha 348
Varuna 131
Vasudeva 216
Vayikra 367
Vedas 18, 29, 124, 131, 289, 350, 351, 352, 360
Vendidad 318, 356
Venus 83, 88
Viracocha 97
virgin 233, 243, 254, 255, 256, 257, 258
Vishnu 18, 114, 147, 151, 213, 215, 216, 217, 256, 289, 346, 347, 348
Vishnu Sahasranama 217
Vishtaspa 124
Visperad 221, 356
von Däniken, Erich 106
Vrindavan 215
Vyasa 124

W

Wabanaki 98
Wangetsmuna 98
Wesakechak 98
West, Louis Jolyon 70
White Buffalo Calf Maiden 97
White Tezcatlipoca 83
Wilson, Wayne 99
woe 203, 294, 295, 296

X

Xian 153

Y

Yadava 216
Yadu Dynasty 216
Yahweh 31, 78, 115, 247, 248
Yajurveda 311, 350, 351
Yama 131
Ya'qub al-Kulayni 386
Yashts 356
Yasna 132, 219, 220, 308, 312, 315, 318, 321, 327, 331, 356
Yazatas 356
Yazdigird III 236
Yehoshua 190
Yeshua 190, 191
Yucatec Maya 83
Yusha 122
Yusuf Ali 194

Z

Zadspram 357
Zamyad Yasht 225
Zarathustra 24, 51, 124, 157, 219, 220, 221, 315, 356
Zechariah 271, 312, 368
Zephaniah 368
Zeus 151, 255
Zion 293
Zipporah 248
Zoroaster 28, 29, 47, 91, 124, 127, 130, 132, 157, 168, 219, 220, 221, 239, 240, 241, 246, 256, 355, 356

Zoroastrianism v, vi, 23, 24, 25, 28, 29,
    46, 115, 117, 124, 130, 132, 144,
    146, 147, 148, 150, 153, 154, 155,
    157, 219, 221, 225, 236, 239, 240,
    241, 242, 243, 256, 281, 304,
    308, 311, 315, 318, 321, 324, 327,
    331, 341, 355, 356, 357, 405

www.ingramcontent.com/pod-product-compliance
Lightning Source LLC
Chambersburg PA
CBHW030213170426
43201CB00006B/73